POVERTY AND PLANNING

POVERTY AND PLANNING

C. N. VAKIL

GREENWOOD PRESS, PUBLISHERS
WESTPORT, CONNECTICUT

Library of Congress Cataloging in Publication Data

Vakil, Chandulal Nagindas.
Poverty and planning.

Reprint of the ed. published by Allied Publishers, Bombay, New York.
Bibliography: p.
1. India--Economic conditions. 2. India--Economic policy. I. Title.
HC435.2.V33 1974 338.954 73-19310
ISBN 0-8371-7320-5

First published in 1963 by Allied Publishers Private Limited, Bombay

Reprinted with the permission of Allied Publishers, Private Ltd

Reprinted from an original copy in the collections of the University of Illinois

Reprinted in 1974 by Greenwood Press, a division of Williamhouse-Regency Inc.

Library of Congress Catalog Card Number 73-19310

ISBN 0-8371-7320-5

Printed in the United States of America

PREFACE

I AM INDEBTED to the various parties who have given their consent to reproduce papers first published by them or submitted to them. They are:

1. Mahatma Gandhi
2. The Indian Economic Association
3. The Osmania University
4. The United Nations
5. The Indian Society of Agricultural Economics
6. The International Economic Association
7. The Planning Commission
8. Kyklos—the International Review for Social Sciences
9. The Unesco
10. The International Social Science Council
11. The Indian Society of Labour Economics.

I must also thank Dr. P. R. Brahmananda for his consent to include the papers jointly done with him in this volume. It is a pleasure and a privilege for Teachers to come across young persons who have the making in them of leaders of thought in their field. Out of a number of such brilliant students whom I had opportunities to guide and who are happily placed in life, able to influence economic thinking and economic policy in different spheres, I would like to take this opportunity to refer to the unusual devotion to Economic Science which is characteristic of Dr. Brahmananda, and which has endeared him to his colleagues and students. His original outlook on economic problems, both theoretical and applied, as well as the sincerity with which he pursues his work compel admiration and respect. It is to be hoped that such persons will get that freedom of thought and environment, which may enable their work to flower into contributions, which may compare well with the best in any part of the world.

10th July 1963 C. N. VAKIL

PUBLISHERS' NOTE

THOUGH as explained by the author in the General Introduction, the selected papers included in this volume will, it is hoped, throw some light on the shaping of economic thinking during the period, from the point of view of an economist dealing with changing contemporary events, it would, we feel, help in a fuller understanding of the process, if a list of published and unpublished research work with which the author was associated was also made available. At our request, Prof. Vakil was good enough to give this information to us. It has been brought together in the form of a Bibliography of his works and is published at the end of this volume. This will show the pioneer work done by Prof. Vakil in research training for over a generation. He is specially known for the large number of distinguished economists that he has trained. A look at the Bibliography will convince any one of the vast amount of solid work that he was instrumental in producing, in almost all branches of Economics by inspiring a band of devoted workers to a new field of activity. Several of his works were the first research contributions in their respective fields, and have stimulated further work on the subject.

GENERAL INTRODUCTION

THE last generation has been a most remarkable period in the history of our country. It has witnessed rapid and fundamental changes in several spheres of life—political, economic, social and cultural. The future historian will have an exciting and challenging task to follow in its proper perspective the trend of events, which led to the emergence of Independence without blood-shed, from the most powerful Empire known to history, and which led to a strong urge for a better life for the average citizen in this vast country. The way in which since Independence the country has been making strenuous efforts to implement its desire for a better life, simultaneously in many directions, and has been facing diverse difficulties, affords no less exciting material for the future historian of human progress.

For this purpose among other things, the contemporary thinking of experts in different fields will provide an important source from which to construct a realistic picture of the complex Indian scene. From this point of view, it may be interesting to follow the thinking of a contemporary economist devoted to research and research training. Like many other important fields in the life of the country, research in economics was also comparatively a new field of activity and training in the methods of research in economics was also in its infancy, say about forty years ago. During the course of such work it was inevitable for the economist to look at contemporary events in a detached way and try to interpret current events to the best of his capacity. The observations of such persons made in such circumstances would throw some light on the shaping of economic thinking, which influenced current events in the country.[1] It

[1] Reference may be made to some occasions when efforts were made to educate the public on certain current economic events of importance e.g. (1) The Ottawa Trade Agreement by the publication of a pamphlet on the same in 1932 followed by various discussions, and (2) The War Time Inflation in 1943, by the publication of *The Falling Rupee* in January 1943, (second edition in February), and subsequent controversy on the subject. Among other things this took the form of a pamphlet on "Inflation or Scarcity" by Mr. G. D. Birla and its wide publicity in February 1943 in favour of inflation. During the Budget discussion in March, the Finance Member denied the existence of inflation. Threats of prosecution

is with this object that some of the papers written by me from 1928 to 1962 have been brought together in this volume, in the hope that this selection will enable the reader to follow the economic developments in the country during the period from the point of view of an economist dealing with changing contemporary events. Whereas for a fuller appreciation of such evolution one may have to look into various publications with which the author was associated throughout this eventful period, it is hoped that it would be possible to get some idea of the process with the help of the selected contributions made at different periods of time dealing with contemporary events.

For example, by 1928, when Gandhiji had already established his leadership and was expressing his views on vital current problems vigorously from week to week in *Young India*, he was anxious to utilise that medium for the discussion of the problem of poverty, its causes and remedies. A number of questions on the poverty problem of India were sent to several economists by Mr. Mahadeo Desai on behalf of Gandhiji on 9th February 1928. It appears that replies were not received from other economists. My replies were published in *Young India* in the form of five articles. Followng Gandhiji's suggestion to discuss the remedies of poverty, I contributed four more articles on that subject. Gandhiji wrote one article on each of the series expressing his views on the same. In reply to my request to publish these articles in book form, I received Gandhiji's consent in a letter dated 9th November 1928. In a subsequent letter dated 2nd December 1928, he also gave permission to include his articles in the same publication. I wrote an Introduction at the time for this proposed publication which was dated December 1928. Though it is not possible for me to explain now why the publication was not issued at

of the author of *The Falling Rupee* under the section of the Penal Code, which makes any one who takes away the confidence of the public from the currency, liable to two years' imprisonment were heard! An Economists' Manifesto signed by twenty leading economists of the country was issued on 12th April 1943 in which the need for combating inflation was stressed. The Government of India yielded in June by issuing Anti-inflationary Ordinances. Their annoyance however resulted in the prosecution of Dr. J. C. Kumarappa, Gandhiji's Economist, who wrote a series of articles on the subject in 'the Harijan' (later published in a pamphlet), quoting profusely from *The Falling Rupee*. He got two years in jail.

that time, I have thought it proper to retain the Introduction to these articles as written in December 1928; it is therefore that this is called the General Introduction. It is hoped that this will give some idea of the economic situation in the country at that time and the way in which the problems were discussed by those concerned. In any case, it gives an insight into the economic thought of Gandhiji. It would be of interest to compare the present trends in the economic policy of the country with the situation as seen a generation ago as well as with the views of Gandhiji. This forms the first part of this volume.

The second part includes five papers under the general heading 'the Formative Stage of Planning'. The difficulties for the formation of correct and effective economic opinion in the country under British rule and the way in which these difficulties were being gradually overcome as well as the way in which effective economic opinion could be formulated were examined in my Presidential address to the Eighteenth Indian Economic Conference held at the University of Patna on 26th December 1934 and the following days. It is well known that the economic policy of the British Government in India was dominated by *laissez faire*. After the First World War rapid changes took place in the world which resulted in a change in the conception of the State in relation to economic activities. Though this change affected British thought and policy in the U.K. it was not easy for the British administration in India to re-adjust its policy. A long process of education for the authorities in the form of a number of enquiries on different aspects of economic life were required to enable them to gradually change their outlook and accept the position that the State had some important part to play in the economic welfare of the people. The position of the State in relation to Economic Progress was the subject of a series of lectures delivered under the auspices of the Osmania University at Hyderabad in October 1937 dealing with this development.

The joys of Independence were accompanied by the sorrows of partition followed by mass massacres in the Punjab. It naturally took some time for the National Government to have a clear picture of the problems in the economic sphere. The economic situation at the early stage of our career as an Independent country and the struggles of those in authority to find a solution form the subject-matter of a series of four articles written in 1949. Those interested in the development of Planning in India have the publications of the Planning Commission available to them for study. The story of Planning in India before the creation of the Planning Commission has, however, its own interest. This story was presented in a paper submitted to the United Nations for discussion at a meeting of experts in Problems of Planning held at San Juan, Puerto Rico in 1950. It may be added that this paper was partly based on personal knowledge, as a Member of several sub-committees of the National Planning Committee appointed by the Indian National Congress before Independence, and as Economic Adviser (1945-56) to the Department of Planning and Development under Sir Ardeshir Dalal, which was created by Lord Wavell's Government a few years before Independence.

As President of the Thirteenth Indian Agricultural Economics Conference held at Trivandrum under the auspices of the University of Travancore on 26th December 1952 and the following days, I had the opportunity to review the position of the Agricultural Economist partly in continuation of what was said by me in 1934 in a similar capacity. The importance of agricultural development as the basis of our progress was emphasised.

Part III deals with technical papers on Planning and Development written jointly with my colleague Dr. P. R. Brahmananda, now Professor of Monetary Economics in the University of Bombay. Some of these deal with special topics indicated by the titles and were presented to different International Conferences, one of them being published in an International Review. Attention may also be drawn to the attempt made perhaps for the first time to estimate savings in the country in a paper submitted to an International Conference held in Japan in April 1960. Two of these papers were of a more general but fundamental importance and were submitted to the Planning Commission in 1955 in connection with the preparation for the Second Five Year Plan. Dealing with the question of the investment pattern for the Second Plan, one of the papers emphasised the need for having an adequate marketable surplus of food and other agricultural products to serve as the basis for economic progress in general and industrial progress in particular. The thesis was that unless the large agricultural population in the country had a marketable surplus of food, it would not be possible to develop industries as the growing number of industrial workers and related urban population would be dependent for their food supply on such surpluses. Besides, it was necessary to have an adequate local market for the products of the new industries which would be created; this would be possible, if the agricultural population had an adequate marketable surplus. If the new industries did not have such a market they would find it difficult to have economies of scale and their progress would suffer. In fact in the absence of such an effective demand within the country, they will be forced to work with reduced capacity allowing some of their equipments to remain idle. Some of these points were referred to in our publication 'Planning for a Shortage Economy' which examined the First Plan and was published in 1952. Unfortunately our view did not find favour with the Planning Commission. The Commission was apparently satisfied with the prosperous agricultural situation which existed at the end of the First Plan. They embarked upon schemes of capital-intensive industrial development not realising that such development would not be possible without adequate development in agriculture of the type suggested by us. The idea was further elaborated by us in "Planning for an Expanding Economy", published in 1956 soon after the Second Plan was brought into operation. Those who have followed the subsequent developments in the Planning effort must have realised the mistakes of the Planning Commission and the hasty adjustments that the Government had to make when food shortage became evident by the end of 1956. We are not yet out of the wood in this connection. It may be said that the difficulties caused by our continuing dependence on imports of food on the one hand, and our inability to achieve economies of scale for our industrise on the other, could have been considerably minimised. If not avoided. This point of view was emphasised in the publications referred to above and was officially submitted to the Planning Commission in the paper published here. Further work on these subjects has been done by Dr. P. R. Brahmananda.

Economic development is accompanied by social change as well as changes in other spheres of life. Sometimes there is a close inter-action between them. Unless we aim at balanced economic and social development, we shall find ourselves faced with awkward situations. In these days of specialisation, it is not always possible for an economist to specialise in and deal with related subjects; it is, however, desirable that the economist should be able to follow the inter-action of the movements in allied subjects with his own field. Some aspects of such allied development have been dealt with in Part IV of this volume, which though not strictly economic, has close relations to the problems of development. Out of the five papers included in this part, the first deals with the Economic Basis of the Communal Tension in India as seen in December 1930, in a lecture over which Mr. M. A. Jinnah presided. The Inter-dependence of different social sciences has been brought out in the paper entitled 'the Unity of Social Sciences'. The problem of business leadership in under-developed countries was examined in a paper submitted to the Panel for Management convened by the United Nations in 1957. 'The Social Implications of Technological Change' forms the subject of another paper. My work as Director of the UNESCO Research Centre for Southern Asia from 1957-60 was mainly concerned with this subject. I had the opportunity to deal with the Role of the Labour Economist under the rapidly changing industrial conditions in the country, as President of the Sixth Indian Labour Economics Conference held at Ahmedabad on 26th December 1962 and the following days, under the auspices of the University of Gujarat, a subject similar to the one dealt with by me in a similar capacity first in 1934 and later in 1952.

CONTENTS

GENERAL INTRODUCTION vii

PART I

THE POVERTY PROBLEM IN INDIA

Series of articles in response to an enquiry from Mahatma Gandhi in 1928, published by him in 'Young India' with comments ..

1. INTRODUCTION 3

2. THE POVERTY PROBLEM IN INDIA 7

3. OUR POVERTY BY MAHATMA GANDHI .. . 21

4. REMEDIES OF POVERTY 23

5. IN TEN YEARS BY MAHATMA GANDHI 40

PART II

THE FORMATIVE STAGE OF PLANNING

6. THE FORMATION OF ECONOMIC OPINION IN INDIA 45
Speech as President of Eighteenth Indian Economic Conference held at the University of Patna, 26-12-1934.

7. THE STATE IN RELATION TO ECONOMIC PROGRESS IN INDIA 69
Series of three lectures under the auspices of the Osmania University, Hyderabad on 11, 12 and 13 of October 1937.

8. WHAT IS WRONG WITH OUR ECONOMIC SITUATION?
Series of four articles published in a Bombay journal during 1949. 95

9. PLANNING IN INDIA 117
Paper submitted to the Meeting of Experts in Problems of Planning and Execution of programmes of Economic Development in Less Developed countries convened by the United Nations at San Juan, Puerto Rico in May 1950.

10. ROLE OF AGRICULTURAL ECONOMICS IN INDIAN ECONOMY 142
Speech as President of the Thirteenth Annual Conference of the Indian Society of Agricultural Economics held at the University of Travancore, Trivandrum, 26-12-1952

PART III

TECHNICAL PAPERS ON PLANNING AND DEVELOPMENT

(Jointly with Dr. P. R. Brahmananda)

11. TECHNICAL KNOWLEDGE AND MANAGERIAL CAPACITY AS LIMITING FACTORS ON INDUSTRIAL EXPANSION IN UNDERDEVELOPED COUNTRIES .. 167

Paper submitted to the Round Table Conference of the International Economic Association held at Santa Margharita, Italy from 28th August 1953 to 2nd September 1953 on Factors of Economic Progress.

12. INVESTMENT PATTERN IN THE SECOND FIVE YEAR PLAN 176

13. INSTITUTIONAL IMPLICATIONS OF A BOLDER PLAN 190

Working papers submitted to the Panel of Economists, Planning Commission in March 1955 in connection with the preparation for the Second Five Year Plan.

14. THE SIZE OF NATIONS AND DYNAMIC ADJUSTMENT: PROBLEMS OF DEVELOPING COUNTRIES 214

Paper submitted to the Round Table Conference of the International Economic Association held at Lisbon, Portugal in September 1957 on the Size of Nations.

15. PRICE STABILISATION VERSUS FISCAL STABILISATION 234

Article published by Kyklos (International Review for Social Sciences, Geneva) in its symposium II on Stabilisation and Development of Primary Producing countries in Vol. XII-1959.

16. CAPITAL SUPPLY AND GROWTH—SOURCE OF SAVINGS 246

Paper submitted to the Round Table Conference of the International Economic Association held at Gamagori, Japan in Economic Development with special reference to East Asia in April 1960.

PART IV

SOME ALLIED ASPECTS OF DEVELOPMENT

17. THE ECONOMIC BASIS OF THE COMMUNAL TENSION IN INDIA 283

Lecture delivered under the auspices of the Elphinstone College, Bombay with Mr, M. A. Jinnah in the Chair, December 1930.

18. THE UNITY OF THE SOCIAL SCIENCES 296

Paper submitted to the Seminar on Social Sciences convened by UNESCO at Delhi in January 1955.

19. BUSINESS LEADERSHIP IN UNDERDEVELOPED COUNTRIES 309

Paper submitted to the Panel on Management convened by the United Nations at New York in September 1957 ; later published in revised form in "Industrialisation and Productivity" Bulletin 2, United Nations, March 1959.

20. SOCIAL IMPLICATIONS OF TECHNOLOGICAL CHANGE 320

Paper submitted to the Round Table Conference on the subject held at Paris, 19-25 March 1959, under the sponsorship of the International Social Science Council with the support of UNESCO. Published by the Council in a Volume in 1962.

21. ROLE OF THE LABOUR ECONOMIST 333

Speech as President of the Sixth Indian Labour Economics Conference, held at Ahmedabad, under the auspices of the University of Gujarat on 26th December 1962 and the following days.

BIBLIOGRAPHY 349

INDEX 355

PART I

THE POVERTY PROBLEM IN INDIA

Series of articles in response to an enquiry from Mahatma Gandhi in 1928, published by him in *Young India,* with comments.

1. Introduction (10-12-1928)

2. The Poverty Problem in India (12-7-1928)
   (*i*) What are the Tests of Poverty ?
   (*ii*) Whether India Is Richer or Poorer Today than 25 Years Ago a Longer Period ? (19-7-1928)
   (*iii*) An Alternative Method (26-7-1928)
   (*iv*) Is Poverty General or Confined to Particular Groups ? (2-8-1928)
   (*v*) External Causes (9-8-1928)

3. Our Poverty *by Mahatma Gandhi* (8-9-1928)

4. Remedies of Poverty (27-9-1928)
   (*i*) Industry and Commerce (4-10-1928)
   (*ii*) Capital Resources (11-10-1928)
   (*iii*) Labour (18-10-1928)

5. In Ten Years *by Mahatma Gandhi* (1-11-1928)

Introduction*

INDIA is perhaps the most misrepresented and therefore misunderstood country in the world. Interested parties have employed all modern methods of propaganda to vilify Indian life and conditions without taking the trouble to understand and appreciate the deeper causes at work in the complex society of this continental country. In the social and political upheaval which is agitating this country at present, the economic aspect is sometimes ignored, more often not understood.

Those who generalise on the economic conditions of India, do not always seem to be conscious of the fundamental fact that they are referring to a heterogenous population aggregating to about one-fifth of the entire human race. Extreme varieties of climate from one end of the country to another, the existence of different races with differences in social and religious traditions and beliefs, and general illiteracy among the masses are among the chief causes which daily affect the productive activities of the people. The effects of western civilisation and methods of production seem to have been super-imposed on the indigenous base, but have not yet permeated in all their essentials. At a time when this process is going on on such a gigantic scale, we have a general awakening in the country which seeks for liberty and freedom in all directions. The desired progress in any aspect of human life is found more or less blocked by the absence of sufficient political power in the hands of the people of the country themselves. In consequence, we find that the cry for political independence is louder and more intense than for progress in other directions; but if any one cares to look deeper into the condition of Indian society, he will realise that the hopeless situation of the large masses of people who manage to eke out an existence somehow, is the real problem of India which will determine the future political structure of the country. Two alternatives may be imagined—(1) the masses may be crushed out of existence by sheer want in course of time or (2) they may grow desperate and become the powerful instrument

* Written by the author, 10-12-1928.

of revolution, the kind of which the world has not yet witnessed. He who desires a steady and substantial progress for the country, must necessarily be conscious of such possibilities, irrespective of the fact whether he is a leader of the people or a representative of the British government. History repeats itself; and it is not wise to presume that the huge population of India will not struggle for a better and freer existence even by means which may be condemned by social and moral thinkers, provided the existing consciousness for such progress is not directed in time in the right channel. When a man with an empty stomach either dies or tries to kill another, it is futile to argue or reason with him, and what is true of the individual is in general also true of the society at large as suggested above.

Volumes would be required to grasp fully the real situation regarding Indian economic conditions at present. Without going into all the intricate problems and all the details, an attempt has been made in the following pages to give as briefly as possible, an accurate picture of the position in general terms. Though there may be differences of opinion regarding the causes of Indian poverty or its present extent and intensity, the fact that the majority of the people live a miserable life is not denied by any one.

In view of the possibilities discussed above, it must be admitted that the remedies for the removal of general poverty from India should be such as would enable the people to reach the goal in the shortest possible period. But any remedy of this character, comes in the way of powerful vested interests, mainly British, and the application of the remedy therefore becomes difficult in practice. It is generally believed that the British government and the British commercial and industrial interests in India are not going to give up their hold on India in order to make room for the application of any possible remedy designed to improve the economic condition of the people of the country themselves.

It is therefore obvious that an analysis of the causes of poverty and a prescription of remedies for the same present great difficulties. The inherent difficulties of the problem are made more complex by the prevailing atmosphere in the country which demands loyalty either to the policy and opinion of the British Government on the one hand, or to the policy and opinion of certain leading persons like Mahatma Gandhi on the other. Those who cannot subscribe unreservedly to the views of either party are put in the unenviable position of being subject to undeserved criticism and attack on either side; but in the search for truth, the scientific investigator must be prepared to face difficulties of this nature and must have the courage of his convictions. If he allows himself to be prejudiced by pre-conceived notions on any problem, he would not be true to his duty, and he must therefore be prepared to express truth as he sees it.

In the following pages attention has been drawn, in the first place to various causes of poverty. For the sake of convenience, they have been divided into internal and external causes, and in analysing them, things had to be said, which are bound to be unpalatable to certain parties. For example, in discussing the external causes, an attempt has been made to describe the extent and manner in which the influence of the British connection has been responsible in bringing about the present state of affairs in India. It may be difficult for foreigners to realise it, but it is well known in India that a criticism of this character will not be made by certain people in India, particularly government servants. It is unfortunate that in summarising the causes of poverty as given by me, in his article entitled "Our Poverty", Mahatma Gandhi has over-looked the external causes and has therefore attributed to me some such delicacy in mentioning foreign exploitation as one of the causes. It is possible that if he had included the external causes of poverty as given by me in his summary, he would have referred to my attitude in other terms.

Referring to the remedies of poverty, it is well known that according to Mahatma Gandhi, the spinning wheel and the use of Khaddar are perhaps the only important remedies for the removal of poverty from India. One may admire the great tenacity and the overwhelming force with which the greatest of living Indians is preaching his gospel. But when we remember the great forces of International trade and modern methods of manufacture whose effects are increasing in spite of the movement led by Mahatma Gandhi, and when we realise that however much we desire, we are not likely to be cut off from the rest of the world, we begin to doubt the efficacy of the spinning wheel as the only remedy for the removal of general poverty. One does not deny the great potential good that can be done if the millions of farmers in India take to it during the off season when they have little or no work. But the charkha has not yet been able to remove general poverty from the country, though the movement of Mahatma Gandhi has been in existence for about 10 years, and if an attempt is to be made to think out remedies for the removal of the general poverty from the country in about 10 or 15 years as suggested by Mahatma Gandhi himself, it would not be wise for India to depend only on the charkha, which after all provides a subsidiary occupation, but to think of more fundamental causes and remedies affecting the productive activities of the people in all directions, primarily in agriculture, and also in industry, trade and finance. The attempt made in suggesting the remedies of poverty in the following pages, therefore has been in the hope that "it may prove a basis of discussion for evolving a well thought out scheme for a comprehensive economic policy for the solution of our poverty problem", and in such a discussion of the large and complex problems affecting Indian agriculture, industry and trade, the charkha has only a secondary place. In view of this, when Mahatma Gandhi observes that he claims for the spinning wheel "not a point in a circumstance, but the centre from which can radiate innumerable other things including many the learned writer has in view", the only answer then can be given is that with all respect to him, we must agree to differ. But when this difference of opinion is followed by remarks which pre-suppose that I had no first-hand knowledge of life in villages, it was to say the least both uncalled for and uncharitable. My personal enquiries in villages, of which Mahatma Gandhi has been informed, has led me to the conviction that though the charkha may do some good for some time and should certainly be welcome on that account, if we really desire that the general poverty in the country should be removed at an early date, we must be prepared for certain fundamental changes in our economic life and organization, the more important of which have been sketched in the following pages.

School of Economics and Sociology, C. N. VAKIL
University of Bombay

The Poverty Problem in India*

THE following four questions were recently sent to certain economists at the instance of Gandhiji, with a request to give their answers to the same. The questions were:

I. *What are the tests of poverty?*

II. *Whether India is richer or poorer today than 25 years ago or a longer period?*

III. *Is poverty in India general or confined to particular groups?*

IV. *Causes and remedies.*

I must admit that these are very difficult questions to answer. They involve a survey of Indian economic conditions in all their aspects, and would require volumes if satisfactory answers in detail were attempted. But as the answers were to be printed in *Young India* in the form of articles, I took it that they must be as brief as possible. The answers attempted by me do not therefore claim complete exactness, but I believe they will concentrate the attention of those interested in the main issues, and will thus be a basis for discussion.

WHAT ARE THE TESTS OF POVERTY?

Poverty and riches are relative terms. I may be richer than a beggar in the street, but poorer than a millionaire. The same is true of countries. England is richer than India, but is poorer than the United States of America at present. When we speak thus in terms of countries, what we really mean is that the average Englishman is richer than the average Indian, but is poorer than the average American. This distinction is important, because it is possible to prove that the total wealth of India is greater than that of England; we still however say that India is poorer because we know that the share of the average Indian in the annual production of the country is smaller than that of the average Englishman in his country.

The statement that the standard of living is low in India conveys the same idea as does the remark that India is poor. The difference

* by C. N. Vakil, 12-7-1928.

is that India is poor not because her standard of living is low, but the standard of living is low because the country is poor. This really means that the production of the country is so small that the share of each is not sufficient. This idea of sufficiency is also a relative term. A certain quantity of food is sufficient for me but it is not sufficient for another man who does more physical work. The same quantity of food will be more than sufficient for an apparently more comfortable man moving in a motor car, because he may be dyspeptic.

We have therefore to ascertain the point of view from which we consider the standard of living to be low in India. Because this will also enable us to determine the goal, namely, the point of view from which we should try to raise the standard of living in India under present circumstances. It is necessary to remember the present circumstances, because the next step has to be taken from the condition in which we are at present.

It is not difficult for even a casual observer to find that thousands of people in different parts of the country are ill-fed, ill-clothed and ill-housed. In the case of such people the standard of living is certainly low; it is lower than the bare minimum of subsistence. There are at the same time certain classes of people who are somewhat above the minimum subsistence level and are able to do their work efficiently. In other words these people have enough food and clothing and housing accommodation and a few other requirements to enable them to do the work that they may have undertaken in a satisfactory or efficient manner. Those who are able to enjoy more comforts or have more amenities of life are of course few in number. They will have more than necessary to keep them in an efficient condition; they are therefore called the richer class in society and are objects of envy by the less fortunate.

The people may therefore be divided into three classes: (1) those who are at or below the standard of minimum subsistence: (2) those who conform to the standard of efficiency and (3) those who are able to live in a standard of comfort. These must be the standards or tests of poverty or riches in any country. The quantity of requirements will vary from country to country and also with people having different outlooks on life. But the general tests remain the same. For example, when we say that the standard of living in India is low, we mean that the majority of people come under the first category, being at or below the standard of minimum subsistence. This being the case, it is impossible for us to raise the standard of living in the near future to such an extent as to bring the majority of people into the third category of "comfortable classes". It would be a sufficient revolution in the economic life of the country if we succeed in raising the standard to such an extent as to bring the majority of people into the second category of people who conform to the standard of efficiency.

WHETHER INDIA IS RICHER OR POORER TODAY THAN TWENTY-FIVE YEARS AGO OR A LONGER PERIOD?[1]

The answer to the question whether India is richer or poorer to-day than she was, say, 25 years or a longer period ago involves statistical investigations of an extremely complicated nature. The Indian Economic Enquiry Committee presided over by Sir M. Visveswaraya recently reported about the inadequacy of the material for an accurate conclusion on the subject even for recent years. They have suggested elaborate changes for overhauling the machinery of collecting statistical data which would be useful for such and other allied purposes. But these recommendations have been shelved.

In spite of this, estimates have been made from time to time of the average per head income of the people of India. These estimates must be taken with great caution, because in addition to the inadequacy of the statistical data on which they are based the method employed in each case is different. In the absence of better estimates, however, they may be taken for what they are worth as showing at least the general tendency.

The estimates[2] are as under:

Year	*Average income per head in British India*	*Author*
1871	Rs. 20	Dadabhoy Naoroji
1881	,, 27	Sir David Barbour
1901	,, 30	Lord Curzon
1911	,, 50	Mr. Findlay Shirras
1921	,, 74	Mr. K. J. Khambatta

1 19-7-1928.

2 For a summary of the methods employed in each case and other relevant details see C. N. Vakil, *Financial Developments in Modern India*, pp. 516-21.

The increase in the per head income as seen in this table is however not real. What we want is to ascertain the growth, if any, in the real wealth of the people, as measured in consumable commodities. In order to convert the nominal money income into real income, we must have resort to the index numbers of the general price-level in the country during these years, which will tell us the purchasing power of the rupee at each of these different dates and thus enable us to make a proper comparison of these figures.

The index numbers of prices in India are given in the following table[3] along with the average income.

Year	*Per head income (Rs.)*	*Index Nos. of prices*
1871	20	93
1881	27	100
1891	not known	110
1901	30	120
1911	50	140
1921	74	378(1920)

We know that prices have fallen in India since 1921 and the index number for a recent year, say 1927, would therefore be smaller. But the per head income would also be smaller in almost the same proportion because it measures the production of all goods in the country in terms of money by means of current prices. The only difference will be that due to a material increase or decrease in the volume of production in recent years as against that in 1921. But we can safely ignore the difference and say that the tendency shown in the above figures is generally true to-day.

The estimate for 1881 was the first made officially and if we therefore take it as the basis of comparison we shall be erring on the safe side. On this basis we find that the money income increases from Rs. 27 in 1881 to Rs. 74 in 1921 or in the proportion of 100 to 274. During the same period rupee prices have increased from 100 to 378. This means that in order to have the same real income in 1921 as in 1881 we must have Rs. 378

3 19-7-1928.

in 1921 as against Rs. 100 in 1881. We find however that we have only Rs. 274 in 1921 as against the required sum of Rs. 378, which shows that the average Indian is poorer today to the extent of 1—274/378 or nearly 2/7, or we are poorer to-day than 40 or 50 years ago.

AN ALTERNATIVE METHOD[4]

Because of the inherent difficulties of such calculations it would be better to test the results by an alternative method, if possible. The above conclusion that India is poorer to-day than 40 or 50 years ago means in other words that the struggle for existence is greater to-day with the great majority of the people than it was in the earlier period. This implies a state of over-population in the country with reference to the available means of subsistence at present.

Whether a country is over-populated is again a question which does not admit of exact statistical verification. If however we have sufficient indications taking all things into consideration, to point to this conclusion, we may be justified in laying down a general proposition. If we find that India is over-populated with reference to the available means of subsistence at present, the above conclusion based on average per head income will be strengthened.

The general law of Malthus that there is a tendency for population in any country to increase at a faster rate than the means of subsistence remains unchallenged. We are not concerned with the exact rates at which the increase takes place; what is evident however is that unless certain counteracting forces operate, the equilibrium between population and means of subsistence will be disturbed. The well-known method of preventing such a calamity are moral restraint and artificial birth-control on the one hand and steps to increase the means of subsistence at a faster rate on the other. In the absence of the effective operation of such conscious efforts on the part of the people, Nature intervenes to restore the equilibrium. Such natural intervention takes place when the problem is really serious, when large numbers of people live even below the minimum subsistence level.

4 Submitted on 26-7-1928.

Whatever the form of Nature's intervention in this way, neither the process nor the result is desirable.

The process is not desirable because it takes the form of, say, famines or epidemics with all their horrors. The result is not desirable because the root of the trouble does not go. The surplus population may be removed for the time being by famines or epidemics, but the remaining population still lives on the margin of subsistence and soon increases its numbers calling once again for Nature's remedy. This will mean a repetition of the horrors in one form or another at sporadic intervals, usually in an unexpected manner.

If we find the existence of such events, known as "positive checks to population" in economic language, in a country, the only conclusion will be that the majority of people in that country are in a state of low economic vitality or live at or below the margin of subsistence and that Nature intervenes from time to time to restore the equilibrium. If on a long view of things we find that the intensity of such events is increasing, we shall be further justified in concluding that the maladjustment between population and means of subsistence is increasing or that the country is becoming poorer and poorer. This problem has been studied with great care and ability by Mr. B. T. Ranadive (M.A.) who wrote a thesis on the subject for the M.A. Degree of the Bombay University. The following facts have been summarised from his work on the population problem of India which will soon be published.

Positive Checks in British India

The following figures of deaths from different important causes will be of interest:

Period	*Deaths due to*	*Number in lakhs*
1871-1921 (50 years)	famines	288
1896-1921 (25 years)	plague	100
1901-1921 (20 years)	malaria	183
1918-1919 (9 months)	influenza	133

The greater portion of the mortality due to famines took place in the period before 1900. The greater portion of the mortality due to plague took place in the period before 1911. The mortality due to malaria was greater in the decade 1911-1921 (97 lakhs) than in the former decade (86 lakhs).

We thus find that whereas famines and plague operated as important checks to population in a great measure in the latter part of the last century, the positive checks in this century have taken the form in a greater degree of plague, malaria and influenza in an ascending order. Not only is the mortality due to these causes in an ascending order, but it must also be noted that the more powerful causes belong to more recent times; the most potent cause of death in recent times—influenza—has beaten all records, having taken more than 133 lakhs of lives in the short space of nine months.

The effects of these positive checks are greater than those indicated by the above figures. On the one hand they increase the death-rate; on the other they reduce the birth-rate. Because in addition to those who die, there are large numbers who survive the attacks of these diseases. But those who survive have their vitality greatly impaired, which results in a reduced reproductive capacity. The existence of a low vitality among people open to frequent attacks of malaria is so common that it does not require any elaborate proof.

The following figures bear out the above remarks. They show that the tendency of population to increase is in operation in spite of the effect of the powerful checks mentioned above. There is a sort of sequence observable in these figures. If the increase in population in one decade is large, there follows a decade in which one or the other of the positive checks is in operation, thus reducing the rate of increase in that decade.

(population in millions)

Year	*British India*	*Indian States*	*Total*
1871	190	50	241
1881	199	55	254
1891	221	66	287
1901	231	63	294
1911	244	71	315
1921	247	72	319

In view of the increase in population indicated by these figures, the question is whether the resources of food supply and other necessaries of life have increased in proportion. In the absence of reliable statistics we have to be satisfied with the general aspects of the problem. If we take the acreage under the principal foodgrains, say, rice and wheat, we shall find some increase, but if we also take into consideration the estimates of yield we find that the increase is not in the same proportion. This shows that the extension of cultivation does not bring proportionate returns, or what is called the Law of Diminishing Returns is in operation.

The excessive sub-division and fragmentation of land throughout the country is another important sign of the same tendency, namely, that a larger population is trying to live on the land, which has not increased in the same proportion in area and yield.

The fact that people are willing to pay higher rents for these uneconomic holdings does not show the existence of prosperity, but shows the existence of great competition among a large number of people to have even a small piece of land for eking out a low subsistence at any cost in the absence of other types of work. This is borne out by the fact that the percentage of people dependent on agriculture is on the increase, as can be seen from the following figures:

Year	*Percentage of people dependent on agriculture*
1891	61.1
1901	66.5
1911	72.27
1921	72.98

The remaining people who are entered in the census as dependent on other sources of income, are also on detailed consideration found to be dependent partly and in varying proportions on the Land. In view of this, it is generally true to say that about 85 per cent of the population is dependent directly or indirectly on the Land.

The increasing intensity of positive checks on the growth of population and the salient facts regarding the principal industry, namely, agriculture—the increasing percentage of people who are dependent on the land, which is parcelled into pieces too small for profitable cultivation and which shows a tendency to Diminishing Returns—show that the conclusion based on the *per capita* income to the effect that the country is getting poorer is substantially true.

IS POVERTY GENERAL OR CONFINED TO PARTICULAR GROUPS ?[5]

In view of the situation already described this question need not detain us long. Though it is impossible to give even approximate figures, it is quite true to say that a large majority of the people are poor in the sense that they live at or below the margin of subsistence. Another way of replying to this question is to point out that only a few groups of people are in an efficient condition and may be called well-to-do compared with the rest. The small percentage of people who come within the taxable limit for the purposes of Income Tax,[6] and the small percentage of people who are able to pay land revenue of any magnitude, show that the total number of people who are in a comparatively efficient position is very small.

CAUSES AND REMEDIES

Poverty in a country may be due to defects either in the production of wealth or in its distribution. Both these problems are equally important, but it is obvious that if the production or the national dividend is small the question of distribution would be of comparatively lesser importance. We have already seen that in India the production falls short of the numbers or that there is a want of equilibrium between population and production. This means that though the question of distribution has its own importance, we in India have under present conditions to think much more of production . Unless we produce more there is little to distribute.

Let us consider briefly the causes of this state of affairs, namely, of the fact that there is a want of equilibrium between population and production in our country. We shall for the sake of convenience divide the causes into internal and external.

Internal Causes

1. The large majority of our population that is about 85 per cent are connected with agriculture directly or indirectly. In spite

5 Submitted on 2-8-1928.

6 The number of assessees to Income Tax was a little above 3 lakhs in 1926-27, out of a population of 25 crores or 0.12 per cent.

of the existence of cottage industries and other side occupations in different parts of the country it is generally well known that the majority of the agricultural population has not enough work during the off season which means for about five months in a year.

2. It is a notorious fact of our social life that the active workers in each family are few. Usually the earning member of a large family is only one, rarely more than one; whereas other members of the family, depend on this only source of income. Even if we make allowance for the household duties of the female members in the family it is generally true that the working member in a family shoulders the greatest burden and that there is a good number of dependants old and young in an average Indian family. This is more true of the urban population and the higher classes, though the agricultural population is not quite free from this characteristic. It would be interesting if the census gave relevant details in this connection but even in the absence of statistical proof this general fact cannot be denied.

3. Of a somewhat similar character are those large numbers of able-bodied beggars (*sadhus* or *fakirs*) who are dependants on society in general for their maintenance. We do not deny the right of those who are engaged in religious service to expect from society sufficient allowance for their maintenance. But with a few honourable exceptions the present state of religious mendicants in our country is far from satisfactory from the point of view of any kind of religious service in the true sense of the word either to themselves or to society.

4. The fourth cause may be ascribed to climatic disadvantages. Without going into details of differences in climate in the different parts of the country, it is true to say that on the whole the climate of the country comes in the way of continuous and sustained work either physical or mental.

5. A somewhat peculiar cause operating in our country against greater production is a kind of mental attitude which may be described as the want of the economic motive either due to the philosophic idea of renunciation of all desires, or to the continuous state of helplessness and poverty in which the people have been living, or to the want of education and consciousness about their own potentialities, or a combination of these. In con-

sequence, we find a large number of people resigning themselves to fate and not exerting themselves as much as they can for greater production.

6. The faulty or one-sided educational system, which creates large numbers of educated men who are not fit for work other than that of the liberal professions or clerks, has led to the present state of affairs in which we find great unemployment or underemployment among the educated young men of the country.

External Causes[7]

The chief external cause is the great change in the economic life and organisation of the people caused by the close connection of India with the rest of the world for the purposes of international trade and commerce facilitated by modern means of communication. It is not suggested that international commerce in itself is an evil from which India is to stand aside, nor is it suggested that the changes brought about by international commerce on us have been entirely to our disadvantage. What is meant is that the nature of our commercial relations with other countries has not been to our best advantage, and that the adjustment in the internal economy of the people required by this great change is not yet complete; in other words we are still passing through a transition period with all its disadvantages. Besides, this internal adjustment has its own peculiarities which are not in the best interests of the people of the country. In order to understand the full significance of these remarks we shall have to consider briefly the main features of our commercial and industrial relations with other countries and chiefly with the United Kingdom.

With the establishment of British rule and particularly after the mutiny we have had peace in the country. It has been a peace in the military sense inasmuch as we have not had any invasion of the country nor any internal disturbance of a widespread nature. But there has been an economic invasion of a more thoroughgoing and silent nature supported by the highly organized industrial system of England and other countries and patronised by the Indian administration. This economic invasion has been, as it were, both from within and from without. On the one hand

[7] Written on 9-8-1928.

we are having large quantities of manufactured articles of a variety of kinds, the introduction of which in the country has been systematically encouraged; on the other we have large numbers of foreign capitalists who have been allowed to settle in the country for the purposes of industrial and commercial exploitation. On the one hand we find therefore that we are not in a position to compete with most of the manufactured articles sent to us by other countries though for some of them we are well situated. On the other hand we find that some of the most advantageous avenues to trade and industry are in the hands of foreigners, in which therefore the people of the country have few chances.

What is meant by the above remarks is that because of centuries of misrule and unsettled conditions we were not prepared for the economic invasion in the form of the imports of manufactured articles from the West. Consequently our artisan class engaged in small industries had to give way gradually, which resulted in an increasing pressure on the land. This economic invasion could only be met by the development of modern industries in India. The people were not however equipped with all that knowledge which is required for starting and maintaining on a large scale industries of the modern type. Because of this ignorance and also because of the *laissez faire* policy of the Government, the people remained neutral spectators while this invasion was going on, and in fact they supported the same process by being gradually accustomed more and more to the use of the imported manufactured articles.

In spite of these difficulties when efforts were made by the people themselves to develop indigenous industries on modern lines they did not meet with favour because of the same policy. The history of the cotton duties and the excise duty on Indian mill production is a sufficient illustration of this attitude on the part of the authorities. As against this we find a great departure in the *laissez faire* policy in those cases in which British capital and enterprise could be encouraged to take to certain industries in India for which she had or was likely to have a monopoly position or which could supply some principal want of the United Kingdom, for example the jute and tea industries.

It is because of such reasons that we found ourselves in a helpless condition during the war and could not avail ourselves of the splendid opportunities created by the war to develop some of the industries. We had to look on when Japan and the United States of America gradually captured our markets with ease by displacing the United Kingdom to a certain extent. Thus we find that on the one hand we are suffering from keen foreign competition in certain industries, and on the other hand some of the successful industries in the country which have a monopoly position happen to be in the hands of non-Indians. It must be admitted that the advantages to the country in connection with those industries which are controlled by non-Indians are more apparent than real.

The war, however, taught a great lesson to the authorities themselves who realised for the first time that a stronger industrial India would be a greater military asset. This resulted in lengthy enquiries which were ultimately followed by the adoption of a policy of what is called Discriminating Protection. We do not propose to discuss the features of this policy. It would be sufficient to say that however halting in its nature it is a step in the right direction. Unfortunately the introduction of this policy was accompanied by a severe depression in trade and industry of a world-wide nature which affected India considerably, and also by the exchange policy of the Government which aggravated the effects of the depression. The combined effects of these causes made the very first Act of Protection of little value in its early stages. The magnitude of the problem which has to be solved with the help of this policy will be realised when we remember that only one per cent of the population has been absorbed by the existing manufacturing industries which have come into existence during the last 70 years. To develop Indian industries in the shortest time possible, in such a way as to absorb the maximum population required under our circumstances, is the great task for which perhaps a much bolder industrial policy will be required. It may be pointed out that if we take into account the smaller industries of a scattered nature the total population engaged in them is about 10 per cent inclusive of that engaged in the larger factories. But these smaller industries are by no means in a flourishing condition and a detailed investigation is necessary before remedies can be devised to put them on a sound footing.

Any one who studies our trade figures and agricultural statistics for the last 50 or 60 years will be led to believe at first sight that we have made great progress in agriculture. But these figures of growth in the agricultural industry have to be taken in relation to the increasing numbers that are subsisting on the land. Apart from some specially favoured tracts the agricultural industry is in a bad way chiefly because of the fact that too many people are trying to eke out an existence from the land for want of other suitable occupations. In consequence, we find that the land in most provinces is sub-divided and fragmented to a degree which is unprofitable for cultivation; we find in the case of several crops the tendency to Diminishing Returns in operation; we also find in spite of the development of irrigation the helpless dependence of a majority of the cultivators on the rains; and we find no substantial change in the methods of agriculture in spite of the work of the Agricultural Departments. Besides, the co-operative movement has touched only a fringe of the great and universal evil of indebtedness. When we take into consideration all these factors we realise the gravity of the problem in spite of the greater exports of the agricultural stuffs from the country which the trade figures show.

Our Poverty*

It is to be hoped that the reader has followed the carefully and ably written articles of Prof. C. N. Vakil which he recently contributed to this journal on the problem of India's poverty. Prof. Sam Higginbottom sent me a circular letter propounding the following four questions:

I. *What are the tests of poverty?*

II. *Whether India is richer or poorer today than 25 years ago or a longer period?*

III. *Is poverty in India general or confined to particular groups?*

IV. *Causes and remedies.*

As a layman I could but give my evidence on the questions without carrying conviction to a critic. I therefore had the important and pertinent questions circulated among economist friends with a request to answer them in some detail if they could make time for the purpose. Prof. Vakil promptly responded with the articles to which I have drawn attention. The series is really not concluded. When I came upon the last chapter dealing with the remedies, I observed that it admitted of re-writing with a view to fuller and more accurate treatment. I am now trying to induce Prof. Vakil to re-write the chapter if he can possibly find the time and has the inclination. If he does send me anything the reader may expect a further instalment. Meanwhile he may regard the series as concluded.

The articles show clearly and I venture to think conclusively that India is poorer today than 25 years or a longer period ago and that the poverty is general and not confined to groups. Prof. Vakil has applied two tests for proving his proposition. He has shown that though during the past 40 years our average income has increased in the ratio of 1 to 2.74 (and he has accepted top

* by M. K. Gandhi, 8-9-1928.

figures in every case) the cost of living has increased in the ratio of 1 to 3.78, in other words we are poorer today to the extent of 2/7 than we were 40 years ago. He then examines the population figures and arrives at the same conclusion by showing that whilst the population has increased the capacity for coping with the increases has not only not kept pace with the increase but has probably deteriorated.

Prof. Vakil has enumerated the following six causes for this growing poverty:

1. Not enough work for the vast mass of the agricultural population during the off season.
2. The social system which imposes the burden upon one person of supporting a large family.
3. The presence of a large number of able-bodied beggars miscalled *sadhus*.
4. Enervating climate.
5. Resignation to fate and consequent want of determination to fight against poverty.
6. Faulty educational system.

Whilst these are contributory causes of more or less value, with the exception of the first none seems to me to go to the root of the matter. There is no doubt enough in the chapters to show that foreign exploitation of India is a cause of poverty. But in collecting the causes the Professor has evidently felt some delicacy about mentioning what is obviously a primary cause. This exploitation is a hydra-headed monster taking a variety of shapes to suit given occasions. The marine, the military, the currency, the railway and the revenue policy of the foreign Government is directed deliberately to promote an exploitation such as the world has never before witnessed. Poverty of India will never be removed so long as the exploitation continues unabated. Even the spinning wheel or any other subsidiary occupation that may be provided for the millions of peasantry will bring only partial relief, if the terrible drain as Dadabhai Naoroji called it is not stopped. He, therefore, who would explore the remedies for removing poverty has to tackle first the question of stopping the continuous drain.

Remedies of Poverty*

Introduction

In the articles on "The Poverty Problem in India", the readers of *Young India* were given a brief statement of the nature and causes of poverty in the form of answers to certain questions, the genesis of which has been explained[2] by Gandhiji. In connection with the 'Remedies of Poverty', Gandhiji expressed a desire that I should attempt an outline of a scheme of economic reform from the point of view of one, who is placed at the head of a department which is charged with the work of removing the existing poverty in 10 or 15 years from now. The wishes of Gandhiji have a compelling force; and in spite of the difficulties involved in any such attempt, I have undertaken it, in the hope that it may prove a basis of discussion for evolving a well-thought out scheme for a comprehensive economic policy for the solution of our poverty problem.

In view of the large size of the country and the population, and the variety and complexity of the various causes that have led to the present state of affairs, it is difficult to suggest remedies which can solve the problem in a reasonably short period and which can be generally accepted. Because in any such suggestions, there are bound to be differences of opinion, both on grounds of general principles as well as in detail. In one sense, the task is impossible, because complete removal of poverty has not been achieved even by those modern countries which are recognised as prosperous and rich. But it is certainly true that given the will and the power, it is possible for a beneficent Government to devise remedies which may go far towards the solution of the problem even in a short period of 10 years. Any such scheme will pre-suppose certain political machinery, and the point of view here adopted is on the supposition that the necessary power to execute the proposed scheme will be there, in the form

* 27-9-1928.

1 These were published on 12, 19, 26 of July and 2, 9 of August 1928 in *Young India*.

2 *Young India*, 6 September, 1928, article on 'Our Poverty' by Gandhiji.

of a new Indian Government, similar to that outlined say in the Nehru Report. Another important thing which must be borne in mind in making such suggestions is that the progress in the immediate future must start from the conditions in which we are at present, and that, therefore, due attention must be paid to them in constructing any scheme of a practicable nature. It may be added that in order to concentrate attention on essentials, I propose to confine myself only to fundamentals. A detailed discussion of all issues will require volumes.

The Basis of the Scheme

It is obvious that if India is to grow richer, or in other words, if the average Indian is to get a larger share for himself from the total production of the country, then on the one hand the production itself should be increased, and on the other, it should be so arranged that the total production should be available for distribution within the country itself, that is, among the sons of the soil. Though the problem of an equitable distribution of the national production among the different classes of people in the country is quite important, it is comparatively less serious, till we have succeeded in securing a much larger production, the whole of which is available to the people themselves. The main policy should therefore be, as said above, produce more and secure all for the people of India, arranging affairs in such a manner that the internal distribution may be equitable.

Agricultural Production

It does not require any long argument to say that the problem of poverty in India is closely connected with the life of the rural population and with the question of making agricultural work profitable. It is not my purpose to summarise the recommendations of the Royal Commission on Agriculture, some of which are quite good, but I would prefer to emphasise the few outstanding things to which attention should be directed. We have seen in former articles that a much larger population tries to subsist on agriculture than is possible under present conditions, and that unless the surplus population is removed from agricultural work to other occupations, the acuteness of the problem will remain. The excessive pressure on the land is shown among other things by the increasing tendency to sub-division and fragmentation of holdings, with the result that the majority of agricultural holdings are so small and so scattered that even if the other requisites of cultivation are available, the farmer is sure to find his work difficult and unprofitable. It is not suggested that we should have very large holdings with a view to introduce large-scale agriculture, but what is required is the creation of a state of affairs in which an agricultural family shall have at least a sufficiently large plot of land to cultivate, all in one place, so that the family may have enough work and enough reward to be able to live in efficiency, if not in comfort. It is obvious that the exact size of the holding, whether it should be 5 acres or 15 acres, will be different for different areas, and will have to be determined with reference to local conditions, and therefore no uniform figure for all India can be laid down; but it must be admitted at once that any such measure, if properly carried out, will mean the displacement of a certain number of agricultural workers, who will have to be absorbed in other occupations. Once this is achieved, it will be possible to introduce with effect some of the well known remedies of agricultural improvement, namely, better seeds, better implements, better manure, sinking of wells, and the creation of other irrigation facilities, the spread of the co-operative movement, and suitable education.

The Small Holdings Bill before the Bombay Legislative Council does not attack the problem boldly and provides only for the prevention of further fragmentation in the future, and a re-distribution of existing plots of land, so that the cultivating units may be larger than now, without affecting the people in the way suggested above. From this point of view, the measure, though a very small step in the right direction, must be welcomed, and it is difficult to understand the opposition to it from certain quarters.

It may be pointed out that a large number of agricultural families at present are in debt, that therefore, they are not able to introduce better methods of work, which are costly, and that if this is so with the small holdings now in their possession, the problem will be still more difficult with somewhat larger holdings. In order to remove this difficulty, two suggestions must be made, one relating to agricultural finance, the other relating to land revenue policy. The experience of the co-operative movement has shown that the problem of indebtedness of the villagers cannot be solved, unless they are enabled to start with a clean slate, by the redemption of their existing debts to *sowcars*. In order to do this, there should be instituted what are known as Land Mortgage Banks, which will take over the existing debt of the farmers from the *sowcars* on easier conditions. In addition to this, if the provision of current finance is made easy by the spread of co-operative societies, the impetus provided by larger units of cultivation will do its work.

The facilities and impetus thus provided will not work, if the pressure of the land revenue burden is not relaxed, at least on those parties who are least able to bear it. If the land revenue policy is purged of the idea that the land revenue is rent, and if it is adjusted with due reference to the capacity of the farmers to bear taxation, the results of the impetus and facilities provided as suggested above will be much greater. The only remedy that will solve the difficulty is to bring the Land Tax in line with the Income Tax; and just as those whose income is below a certain minimum are exempted from the Income Tax, those whose income from the land is below a certain minimum to be fixed with reference to agricultural life and conditions should also be exempted from the Land Tax. It may be possible at the same time to allow Local Bodies to tax the agriculturists by some cesses on the land to a certain extent, the proceeds being utilised for the benefit of the people of the area concerned.

There are other problems connected with agriculture, like research in agricultural methods and crops, which though quite important in themselves are less fundamental and may not be touched here. But closely connected with any improvement, there is the other fundamental problem of education, which, however, we shall discuss by itself separately, after referring to the other aspects of economic life as such.

New Fields of Work

As we have seen above, a certain number of people will be displaced from the land, if the above suggestions are followed, but it is obvious that the remedy will be worse than the disease, if at the same time adequate steps are not taken to provide suitable employment to those people who may thus have to be removed from the land. This means that the scheme for the consolidation of holdings should be put into operation gradually, in such a manner that a gradual absorption of the displaced people in other occupations may become possible. In other words, the rate at which other, suitable employment can be found for such people will determine the rate at which the above reform can be introduced in the agricultural life of the country.

The question then is, what are the possible avenues of work which must be opened up for large numbers of people? In the first place, it is desirable to bring under the plough those lands in different parts of the country, which are now lying idle for one reason or other and which are classed as "Cultivable or Culturable Waste". This will certainly involve some scheme of agricultural colonisation, under which people from one part of the country may be required to migrate to another where new agricultural work is available. What has been done in the Punjab Canal Colonies, what is likely to be done in Sindh when the Sukkur Barrage Project is completed, and what is being done in certain large areas which are now lying waste in the Nizam's territory, may be done in other parts of the country with effect. The probable number of people that can be thus absorbed in useful agricultural work, which is bound to bring additional wealth to the country, cannot be easily estimated, till a detailed survey of such possibilities is made. Even the Agricultural Commission which had sufficient resources at its disposal to make such an attempt has not done so, but it is safe to assert that the possibility is large, so far as the published figures of what is known as "Cultivable Waste" areas indicate. In this connection, the following figures regarding the classification of area taken from the *Agricultural Statistics of India*, 1925-26, *Volume I*, published this year, along with the official interpretation of the same, will be of interest.

	Acres in thousands	*Per cent*
Forests	86,937	13.1
Not available for cultivation	1,50,194	22.6
Culturable waste other than fallow	1,51,872	22.9
Current fallows	49,306	7.4
Net area sown	2,25,849	34.0
TOTAL	6,64,158	100.0

"Of the total area, 86,937,000 acres, or 13 per cent are occupied by forests; and the area not available for cultivation, i.e., land absolutely barren or unculturable or covered by buildings, water, and roads, or otherwise appropriated to uses other than agriculture, amounts to 150,194,000 acres or 23 per cent. The balance 427,027,000 acres or 64 per cent represents the area available for cultivation. *Of this,* 151,872,000 *acres or* 23 *per cent of the total area represent culturable waste other than fallow, i.e., land available for cultivation but not taken up.*" (italics mine)

INDUSTRY AND COMMERCE[3]

Simultaneously with this, steps must be taken to develop other industries in the country. The industries to be developed may be classified into two: (1) cottage industries, (2) large-scale industries of the factory type. The development of cottage industries will provide work for those who are not willing to migrate to other areas and also for the ordinary farmer, who even under the proposed new conditions, may not have sufficient work during the off season. The exact nature of the different cottage industries which can be brought into existence in different parts of the country will be subject to local conditions, and will therefore require detailed investigation, but in the meanwhile, the immediate introduction and popularisation of the charkha is bound to be a great help in this direction.

The development of large scale industries will further afford great scope for the absorption of large numbers of workers, who if properly attached to the works need not think of going back to the land. In view of the backwardness of the country in this connection, and the great competition of cheap manufactured goods of highly organised foreign industries, it is impossible to make progress in this direction, unless a vigorous policy of Protection is adopted. The principle of Protection to Indian industries has been accepted by the Government of India to a limited extent and the policy is known as one of Discriminating Protection. But if we consider in detail the intensity of the problem in India, and the urgency of finding proper remedies, a slow process like this, when other countries are fast developing their industries, will not be of avail. In other words, a much bolder

3 By the author, 4-10-1928.

policy is needed which will help several industries, for which there is great scope in this country, for example, sugar, oils, hides and skins and so on. The Tariff Board has already considered the question of certain large industries, like cotton, steel, matches and paper, but a detailed consideration of the position of each of these industries shows that the steps taken by the Government are not adequate to meet the situation.

Foreign Capitalists

The question of industrial development as suggested above raises delicate and difficult problems, if we are going to see that the production of the country is made available to the people of the country themselves. It is well known that certain large industries like Jute and Tea are in the hands of foreigners, and it is possible that foreign companies may come and settle in the country with a view to taking advantage of the system of Protection that may be established. The problem of Indian poverty cannot be solved, unless steps are taken to prevent foreigners or non-Indians from enjoying the fruits of the industrial exploitation of the country. This difficulty applies not only to industrial concerns, but also to commercial companies, banking and insurance companies, railway and shipping companies and so on. In order to ensure this, so far as the future is concerned, it is easy to lay down that no new foreign company of any description shall be allowed to settle in the country for industrial exploitation and for certain kinds of business, which may be specified in detail. So far as the existing foreign companies are concerned, some of which have been working for many years, the problem will raise difficult political issues, but without looking far into the future, referring to the next 10 or 15 years only, the policy of gradual Indianisation of such companies should be adopted. A reasonable notice should be given to all such concerns to Indianise themselves, both in the matter of ownership and control, say at least to the extent of 60 per cent in a given period of time, say 5 or 10 years. It may be pointed out that the majority of shares of Jute mills in Bengal are now owned by Indians, though the control of the Jute mills is still in the hands of non-Indians. If the ownership is thus Indianised to the extent of 60 per cent the question of control being Indianised will not be difficult in practice, and what has already taken place in the case of the Jute industry, without any compulsion, can be brought about, if necessary by compulsion, in the case of all such other foreign concerns.

In the case of certain industries in which the national interest is vitally affected, the policy should be more thorough-going, for example, in order to develop an Indian Mercantile Marine and ultimately an Indian shipping industry, Indian coastal traffic should be reserved to Indian shipping companies, as is done even now by many advanced countries.

Nationalisation of Industries

The policy of nationalisation of industries will have both advocates and opponents, and the principle has not yet found general acceptance; and in fact, even if the principle be accepted for the sake of argument, the adoption of such a policy for all industries is not practicable for many years to come in this country. But there are certain industries for which the policy of nationalisation is both immediately practicable and in the interests of the country herself. So far as the railway industry is concerned, it is the property of the State, in some cases, if not now, after a certain period, and therefore at the earliest possible opportunity, the railways in India should be made both State-owned and State-managed. So far as the railway rates are concerned, it will then alone be possible to insist with success that they are so arranged as to help Indian industry and trade. Another important industry which may be nationalised is the coal industry. The coal mining companies are partly owned by some railways, partly by foreign companies and partly by Indian companies. The coal mines are situated chiefly in Bengal, and they must be considered to be an important factor in the development of industries and also in supplying fuel to the railways. With the nationalisation of railways, the nationalisation of coal mines, which supply the most important item of cost to the railways, will become essential, and some of the difficulties from which the coal industry is suffering at present will be removed by its concentration under one control.

The position of the oil industry is as important as that of coal because of the increasing use of mineral oil in modern times both in industry and transport. The extent to which the control of the oil industry and trade has raised international complications because of this is well known, and it would be in the true interests of the country to nationalise the Indian oil industry. The urgency of doing so has been forcibly brought to our notice by the disclosures of the Tariff Board in connection with its recent Oil Enquiry.

In the case of those existing foreign companies, which do not Indianise themselves in the manner suggested above, during the fixed period, a penalty should be provided and the State should be ready to enforce it, that the State will take over those industries after the expiry of the given period, if Indianisation as desired is not brought about. Certain utility services like the supply of electricity or gas, or tramway and bus services in Municipal areas, should be nationalised by arranging that the ownership and control of such concerns should be taken over by the Municipalities concerned.

CAPITAL RESOURCES[4]

The proposals made above both in connection with Agriculture on the one hand, and Industry and Commerce on the other, will require large amounts of capital before they can be carried out. For the establishment of Land Mortgage Banks, and the spread of Co-operative credit banks in rural areas, for the acquisition of at least a 60 per cent Indian ownership in the existing foreign concerns, and for the promotion of future industrial and commercial enterprises, as well as for the development of cottage industries, the amount of capital required will at first sight appear to be beyond our capacity. On proper consideration, it will appear that the question, though difficult, is not impossible of solution; it will require, in brief, a system of national banking and currency suited to our requirements, and working in order to fulfil the main object of a comprehensive economic development of the country.

So far as the capital resources of the country are concerned, an authority of the abilities and experience of Sir Basil Blackett himself has admitted that they are large enough not only to supply India's own requirements, but also for lending abroad. If this is true, and if we still hear of the scarcity of capital in India, it only indicates the want of an adequate machinery to mobilise

4 By the author, 11-10-1928.

these resources in a proper manner. The one reason why Indian capital is not forthcoming, though it is believed to be in existence, is the prevailing divorce between the modern banking system in cities like Bombay and the indigenous banking system in smaller towns, and in the villages. Some of the indigenous institutions which do banking work on old methods, stand despised, and their work is not properly linked up with the work of city banks. The extension of the work of the Imperial Bank of India by the creation of branches all over the country, though a good step in itself, cannot achieve success unless two important conditions are fulfilled. In the first place, the methods of Western banking system must be more and more adapted to Indian conditions and Indian methods, so that the practice of banking and the formalities thereof may be intelligently understood by all parties concerned. For example, uniformity of forms and technical processes, more in line with local customs, and the introduction of local languages in the transactions concerned, are essential before the local indigenous bankers begin to deal actively with the city banking system. Even more than this, is the necessity of creating and inspiring confidence among the people in the fact that their small savings, if invested in these institutions, are quite safe, and are available to them promptly and with ease, without unnecessary troubles and restrictions, and that they are likely to be used by the bank for the purposes of the economic development of the country, and not for the purpose, as they are likely to believe, of an anti-national government.

The problem will be further made easy if the currency system is definitely and permanently put on a gold basis, and is not subject to any manipulation by the Government. Events like those which occurred during the years following 1916 are bound to create a want of confidence and sometimes a positive distrust in the methods and even intentions of the Government, and such events, instead of helping the habit of investment, are great obstacles to that mobilisation of the potential capital resources of India, which we all desire.

So long as Indian capital is not forthcoming, for certain purposes of a desirable character, because of one reason or another, it is quite legitimate to import foreign capital under certain conditions. What we are suffering from to-day in India is not due to the importation of foreign capital, but to that of foreign capitalists. Other countries like the United States of America and Japan, which are considered economically very advanced in modern times, had also to borrow foreign capital in much larger quantities than we have done. But they were wise inasmuch as they arranged to pay the principal and the interest to the foreign creditor without giving him vested interests in their own country. On principle, a loan either internal or foreign will be justified in all those schemes for which there is a reasonable certainty of earning at least the interest charges in due course, and if this principle is properly followed, there is nothing to fear from the importation of foreign capital if necessary, because it will help in developing our resources earlier, with the help of which in course of time we shall certainly be able to shake off the foreign burden by liquidating both the existing foreign debt as well as other new debt which we may have to incur in future on the lines suggested above.

With these aims in view, an outline of the nature of banking institutions that we should have may be suggested.

1. A Reserve Bank of India, corresponding to the Central banks of modern countries, whose function shall be to control both credit and currency. It will be a Government bank in the sense that the balances of the Government shall be deposited with it and that monetary transactions of the State shall be managed by it as its agent. It will be a bankers' bank in the sense that all other banks shall look to it for help and support in emergency, shall in normal times be connected with it as member banks or depositors, and the whole credit policy of the country shall emanate from the Reserve Bank and be controlled by it. It will control currency in the sense that it will be the only institution which will be responsible for the expansion and contraction of the currency according to the requirements of the people as determined by themselves.

2. The activities of the Imperial Bank of India shall be curtailed in one sense so far as some of its present functions shall have to be transferred to the Reserve Bank, but in another sense, its activities should be considerably enlarged in the following manner. The Imperial Bank should be the pioneer bank to spread banking methods throughout the country and to help in all eco-

nomic activities. It should therefore have three main departments, agricultural, commercial and industrial. The agricultural department shall help the creation of Land Mortgage Banks and Cooperative credit banks in rural areas. The commercial department shall help the movement of trade both internal and external. The industrial department will make it its business to consider schemes of industrial enterprises with the help of experts and to finance them if they are approved. It should work through its branches throughout the country, but its work should not prevent the creation of other private banks dealing with one or the other aspect of its work; in other words, a proper coordination and even encouragement of private banking as suggested above should be brought about. And in order to inspire confidence among the people suitable legislation should be passed to regulate the work of private banking institutions. If the resources at the disposal of the Imperial Bank for any approved purpose are not adequate, it should be at liberty to raise loans both within India and from foreign sources. Though the initiative as to the requirement and the ultimate disposal of such loans should be left to the Imperial Bank, the intermediary in raising them should be the Reserve Bank, whose function of controlling credit will thus be safeguarded.

3. So far as the management of both the Reserve Bank and the Imperial Bank thus constituted is concerned, a statutory provision should be made in each case, which will provide for proper safeguards and checks in order to inspire public confidence. In order that such confidence may be assured, without which success will be impossible, and in order that the policy of the banks may be truly national in outlook and execution, the Boards of Directors should consist of highly trained Indians, representing different economic interests, with a reasonable proportion of Government nominees. Though it is possible to imagine that for certain kinds of specialised work, the requisite number of trained Indians is not available at the moment, it should not be a reason for postponing Indianisation, but it should be a reason to send the necessary number of qualified Indians for training abroad at the expense of the banks for the required work, and if in the meanwhile a non-Indian has to be employed, it should be on a contract basis for a given short period only.

LABOUR[5]

The scheme as a whole provides that the workers on the field will be smaller in number than now, and that those that are now in excess on the land will be provided elsewhere by the creation of new work of an industrial character. So far as such new work is confined to small cottage industries, it will not involve a great change in the social organisation, but to the extent to which such work takes the form of modern industries of the large-scale type, it will mean the creation of a large industrial population or of a body of industrial labourers who will have to be attached more to their work in the factory than to their tiny plots of land as hitherto. This means that the kind of problems which western countries have faced regarding the conflict between labour and capital may arise in the country and lead to undesirable results, if proper safeguards are not taken beforehand. Any scheme that provides for the economic development of the country must therefore take due note of such difficulties, and ensure that the industrial labourers shall have on the whole a better and more efficient means of livelihood than they now have in their unprofitable agricultural work. So far as hours of work per day or per week are concerned, and similar other conditions affecting women workers and children, the legislation in our country is already on the lines approved by international conventions. But though this is quite good so far as it goes, it does not mean that the environment in which the industrial labourers live at present, and the wages that they receive are in all cases the best from their point of view. The chief difficulty which will have to be overcome is the question of housing such labourers in urban areas in a manner consistent with their health and therefore efficiency. If this question is properly attended to, and in addition several beneficent schemes of welfare work are introduced along with large establishments, industrial work will be more attractive, and the attachment of the labourers to the factories greater.

The development of the trade union spirit on proper lines, the establishment of arbitration and conciliation boards for the settlement of disputes with the employers and, in course of time, the establishment of profit-sharing schemes would go far to pro-

[5] By the author, 18-10-1928.

vide that impetus to the labourers, which will be a necessary condition for the success of industrial enterprises in the country.

Social Changes

Without going into the details of this difficult problem, it must be mentioned in brief that a change in those social customs which are in themselves undesirable should be brought about at once, because of their effect on the economic life and organization of the people. No scheme for the economic progress of the country will be of any avail, if the increase in the production of wealth is accompanied by a greater increase in population. And in order that we may have an efficient standard of living, we should also take care that the race as such becomes more efficient physically, as well as in other respects. Though the question of artificial birth-control is neither practicable nor desirable under Indian social conditions, there are several other remedies which we can adopt, which may prevent the want of equilibrium between production and population. The prevention of early marriages and the removal of the ideas which lead to universality of marriage in India are things which will be of great help in this connection. Another great problem is that of adequate sanitation both in rural and urban areas, and of measures to prevent infant mortality, and the spread of disease. The removal of the purdah system and the employment of women in certain work suitable to them, such as domestic and educational or of the type of cottage industries, will also help. The abandonment of the idea of untouchability in connection with certain classes of people, and the prohibition of religious mendicants who do no religious work worth the name will contribute a large amount of useful energy in the work for greater national production, which is being wasted at present. Unnecessary expenditure on social and ceremonial occasions, usually much beyond the capacity of the parties themselves, is a fruitful source of indebtedness among all classes of people, and should be immediately curtailed.

Educational Reform

The carrying out of any such scheme of economic development and the necessary social changes presupposes both a better and a different kind of educational system than the one now in existence. It is most unfortunate that the educational system now prevalent has reference neither to the great agricultural industry of the country nor to the new manufacturing industries that await development. So far as the cultural value of Indian education is concerned, it teaches very little of Indian culture as such, and provides the young graduate with half-baked ideas of western culture. We find in consequence, that the educated young man on an average despises both agricultural and industrial work, and manual work in general, and has little or no understanding of the culture of his own country. It may be pointed out that the few brilliant men, who have shone in certain fields of knowledge, have done so not because of this educational system, but in spite of it. The misfits thus created swell the ranks of the unemployed instead of being able to utilize their energies and education both in their own interests as well as in the interests of the country.

In order to remove these defects, in the first place, we should have the establishment of rural universities each of them catering for a small area, say a linguistic province to start with. The aim of a such a university should be to create an interest in the better understanding and improvement of the problems that affect the life of the rural people under its jurisdiction. This means that the schools and colleges, from the primary institutions to the highest post-graduate institutions, should be worked with new spirit, in order that either elementary or advanced knowledge suitable to rural life may be made available to those who seek for it, and that facilities for the highest research work in the same branch may be made available to those few who may find it possible to undertake it.

In the same manner, the city universities, like those of Bombay and Calcutta, should be more alive to city life, to industrial and commercial work and technique, and to the complicated social and economic problems that arise from the growth of modern cities. It is not suggested that the existing courses of study should be entirely scrapped, but it is certainly suggested that a proper adaptation of these courses on such lines is immediately desirable in the interests of the country as a whole.

While emphasis is laid on the adaptation of the work of universities to rural or city life as the case may be, sufficient knowledge, both of Indian and Western culture, should be imparted to the students at the different stages of their work. The co-ordination of rural and city life, the solution of communal problems by the creation of feelings of tolerance and mutual good-will, the removal of provincial jealousies, and the creation of a sense of real patriotism for the country as a whole—these are some of the very desirable objects on the fulfilment of which the economic and political progress of the country depends. The kind of universities suggested above can play a most important part in this direction by arranging a system of interchange of students at certain stages of their career. For example, it should be a condition of graduation in any university, that the candidate has lived and worked in another university, of a different type, at least for a year, and so far as higher post-graduate work is concerned, the greatest possible freedom should be given to the student to find his own teacher in any of the universities in the country. If this is realized, it will no longer be necessary for our young men and women to go abroad for ordinary studies and to beg for admission in foreign universities where we may not be welcome. It will then be desirable to send students abroad only for understanding the international outlook on a footing of equality, or for those few specialised studies for which we do not possess adéquate facilities.

It is assumed in the above suggestion that the principle of free and compulsory primary education, which has been accepted, will be carried out in practice with vigour and thoroughness, but with the necessary changes suited to our requirements as pointed out above.

I am indebted for the general ideas in connection with the aims of our educational reform, as explained above, to my friend and colleague, Dr. N.A. Thoothi, whose lectures on the subject to the post-graduate students of the Bombay University School of Economics and Sociology have been of great value to me.

Government Finances

The kind of schemes suggested above must have close relation to the finances of the Government. They will have to be adjusted to the new environment. Whereas Government expenditure shall be much more than now on things like educational reform, it can be curtailed to a certain extent so far as the military service is concerned and the higher appointments in the various Civil

Services. From the point of view of revenue, if the land tax is brought in line with the Income Tax, there will certainly be a large decrease, but the natural growth in revenue from the increased resources of the people will more than make good such loss. We can then expect higher yields from Customs and Income Tax, as well as from the larger incomes of big land-owners. Besides the nationalization of railways, coal mines, and oil sources as suggested above will bring in additional revenue. If necessary an inheritance tax or a tobacco monopoly may be instituted to find fresh sources of revenue. And for certain large schemes, if capital expenditure is desirable, it will be easy to raise loans on the credit of such increased resources, either internally or externally, and the raising of such loans by the Government will be facilitated by the creation of the kind of banking system outlined above.

In Ten Years*

PROFESSOR C. N. Vakil's instructive articles published in these pages are supplementary to the series he recently wrote on poverty and should be read together. I coaxed him to give the reader something more definite on remedies of poverty than what he had done in the article which I ventured to withhold and which he expanded into the four articles above referred to. I do not think that the programme sketched by the learned Professor can be finished in ten years. Perhaps it is impossible to devise a ten years' programme of improvement to cover a vast and impoverished country like ours.

An Attractive Programme

Let us however glance at Professor Vakil's remedies for India's central disease. He rightly says that the problem is how to increase production of wealth and how to distribute it equitably among the people, principally therefore, I presume, among the starving millions. To this end the learned writer

1. would recast small uneconomic holdings,
2. would pay off the debts of the ryot through mortgage and co-operative banks,
3. would revise the revenue law and graduate the land tax so as to bring it in a line with the income tax leaving a minimum of income from land free of tax,
4. would re-employ the population displaced through the recasting of uneconomic holdings by bringing under the plough cultivable waste, *i.e.*, 23 per cent of the total area available and by nationalising and thus developing large industries, .
5. would draw small and large capital by putting the banking system on a basis more in keeping with the requirements of the country than it is now,
6. would improve labour conditions so as to avoid war between capital and labour,

* Written by M. K. Gandhi on 1-11-1928.

7. would deal with such social abuses as child marriages, etc., which give rise to over-population and unfit progeny,

8. would radically reform the educational system so as to spread education among the masses and have it answer the needs of the people,

9. and would cut down the military expenditure and stop the drain from the country by manning the services with indigenous talent.

Who Is to Bell the Cat?

This is not an unattractive programme. But as I was re-reading the articles, the question continued to force itself upon me, 'Who will bell the cat?' There is hardly an item here which can be tackled without Government aid. And a Government that is admittedly based on exploitation of the governed will not and cannot, even if it will, undertake the proposed changes with the despatch necessary to create an immediate impression. It can undertake irrigation schemes, costing crores, it will not undertake sinking wells costing lakhs. What therefore Professor Vakil wants first is a summary programme of Swaraj, and having been chiefly instrumental in getting it, he can command the appointment of commissioner of banishment of poverty department.

This however is a heroic remedy and Pandit Motilal Nehru and the co-signatories to his report are the men to tackle it. Our author's was but to place a scheme before any government that would deal with the most pressing problem before the country.

Wheel of Prosperity

But I had hoped that the learned Professor, especially when he wrote for "Young India," would have examined the one sovereign remedy that has in season and out of season been advocated through these pages and has, so far as it has gone, been tried with no inconsiderable success. True, the Professor has hidden the tiny wheel in a little unseen arc of his circle of suggestions. I claim for it not a point in a circumstance but the centre from which can radiate innumerable other things including many the learned writer has in view. But the fact is, whereas it was possible for him with patient research carried on in a wellstocked library to write convincing essays to prove India's deep and deepening poverty, it was impossible without a close study of a group of villages with an open and receptive mind to spot the seat of the disease and to know the capacity of the patient to bear the remedy. A Gregg took a year of reading and living among the villagers to know the remedy and prove its worth with a freshness of outlook all his own. The cardinal facts to realize are that there is already terrible, forced unemployment among the toiling millions in that they have no work for at least four months in the year. Once that is realised, surely it follows that not a moment should be lost in bringing work to these millions so as to utilise their idle hours. The other fact to realise is that if the average income of the inhabitant of this land is seven pice per day, *i.e.*, less than two English pennies per day, at the present rate of exchange, the average income of the toiling millions must '*ipso facto*' be much less. He, who adds two pice per day to their income and that without any great capital outlay, makes a princely addition to their income and in addition revives the dying hope within the breasts of these millions. The further merit of this programme is that it is now in operation without Government aid. But it needs much greater encouragement and admits of infinite expansion. P. has shown elsewhere in this issue of "Young India" what America wrought through the wheel during those times of her Revolution. I invite the economists of India to study the movement on the spot. They have nearly two thousand villages to select from for their study and let them then condemn the movement if they can, or give it not a niggardly place that prudence or patronage can grudgingly afford but the central place it deserves.

PART II

THE FORMATIVE STAGE OF PLANNING

1. The Formation of Economic Opinion in India

Speech as President of Eighteenth Indian Economic Conference held at the University of Patna (26-12-1934).

2. The State in Relation to Economic Progress in India

Series of three lectures under the auspices of the Osmania University, Hyderabad on 11, 12 *and* 13 *of October* 1937.

(*i*) The Conception of the State in Economic Life; and the Changing Structure of the State in India (11-10-1937)

(*ii*) The Consequences of the Conception prior to 1921; and Gradual Change in Ideas since 1921 (12-10-1937)

(*iii*) The Struggle of the Period, 1921-1937, and the Clash of Ideals and Methods at Present and in this Immediate Future (13-10-1937).

3. What is Wrong with Our Economic Situation?

Series of four articles published in a Bombay Journal during 1949.

(*i*) The Problem—Internal and External Environment

(*ii*) *Congress Ideology and Efforts*

(*iii*) Economic Unrest

(*iv*) Attitude of Capital and Labour

4. Planning in India

Paper submitted to the Meeting of Experts in Problems and Execution of Programmes of Economic Development in Less Developed countries convened by the United Nations at San Juan, Puerto Rico in May 1950.

5. Role of Agricultural Economics in Indian Economy

Speech as President of the Thirteenth Annual Conference of the Indian Society of Agricultural Economics held at the University of Travancore, Trivandrum (26-12-1952).

The Formation of Economic Opinion in India*

The Honourable Mr. S. Abdul Aziz, Mr. Vice-Chancellor, Ladies and Gentlemen,

I thank you for the great honour you have done me in asking me to preside over the deliberations of this Conference. I am deeply conscious of the heavy responsibility, particularly because it is put on comparatively young shoulders. Your appreciation and co-operation, will, I hope, enable me to discharge my duty with that confidence which is the privilege of a riper age.

The State and Economic Life

The world is at present in an economic ferment and we find that the existing economic structure as well as existing economic relations have been completely upset. Neither the economic experience of the past nor the teachings of economic theory have proved a complete guide either in the understanding of the complex phenomena that have developed or in the search for their solution. Instead of this, we find gigantic efforts being made to restore order out of the prevailing chaos in different parts of the world on new lines with the consequence that the whole basis of economic life is gradually undergoing fundamental changes. On the one hand, we have the Russian experiment which involves a thorough overhauling of the social and economic structure and which has in view the communistic ideal. In order to achieve their ideals, the Russians have adopted a new method of economic approach, which has become popularly known as 'Planning'. Though this was ridiculed at first, the rest of the world, differing in their aims and policy, have however, found something to imitate in the Russian method, with the consequence that various countries are now adopting some sort of 'Planning' as the method to remove the existing economic ills. The paradox

* Speech as President of Eighteenth Indian Economic Conference held at the University of Patna, 26-12-1934.

of capitalism manifested itself in its extreme forms in the United States of America. The Americans are trying to remove the anomalies of capitalism by 'Planning' without any idea of overthrowing the capitalistic order in the Russian sense. Italy and Germany, on the other hand, have developed a form of State Capitalism, which also has 'Planning' as its principal method. We are thus presented with a clash of ideals, and therefore of actions, and though 'Planning' seems to be the common feature, its place and significance varies considerably in the scheme of things in the different parts of the world where it has been adopted; in consequence, the word 'Planning' has acquired a variety of shades of meaning, which are rarely clear to the minds of those who use it, with inevitable confusion in the current discussions on the subject. While this confusion lasts, what is clear, however, is the fact that the principle of *laissez-faire* is dead, and that the functions of the State in the economic sphere are considerably enlarged. With the increase in the functions of the State, a suitable machinery to carry out the same must be established and such machinery should have some plan to work upon. Though differing in type in each case, 'Planning' as the method for discharging this new function of the State, has become not only popular but essential. Two broad categories of this method may be distinguished. In some countries, a pre-determined economic and social policy involving a change in the basic structure of society leads to 'Planning' which is intended to put that policy into operation, for example, in Russia. In other countries 'Planning' is being adopted as a method to reorganize the economic life to suit modern conditions without aiming at a fundamental change in the existing order, though it cannot be denied that this is bound to involve a gradual drift away from the existing basis, for example in the U.S.A. and the United Kingdom. We come to the conclusion, therefore, that though the meaning of 'Planning' differs, though it has different grades or degrees, though the motives or outlook with which it is practised happen to be widely apart, it has come to stay, in as much as the State is now acknowledged as the chief guide and controller of economic life with or without a definite purpose, and adopts 'Planning' as its principal method.

British and Empire Economic Policy

Such far-reaching changes are bound to affect every country; in as much as this new change is a change primarily in the function of the State, the effect on India is being felt through England, because of our political relations. In other words, British policy and method are being reflected in this country in the gradual adoption or otherwise of the economic changes referred to above. With wonderful adaptability, England realized the folly of sticking to *laissez-faire*, and while revolutionary or spectacular changes were being adopted in other countries, she deliberately changed her entire economic policy as if overnight. The execution of the new economic policy in other countries, has involved important repercussions in the political field. Such far-reaching changes, involving interference in the details of the economic life of the people, which had to be promptly put into operation, would not be possible under the slow moving machinery of modern democratic institutions. The rise of dictatorship in those countries where Economic Planning is the order of the day, may be thus explained. Without changing her political structure, however, England managed to have the requisite force and promptitude of a dictator in her National Government which eliminated party politics for the time being. At the same time, she realised that under the new conditions, with the growth of powerful nations, British supremacy could not be maintained unless Britain could weld the Empire together by new ties, chiefly economic. In consequence, we find that during the last few years, the National Government in England has succeeded in bringing about a complete transformation of the economic policy of Great Britain, both within and without. We have the spectacle of the most highly industrialized country in the world, trying to protect its agriculture and industry. The Gold Standard now stands discredited by being thrown overboard by its chief custodian. The home of Cobden is now a place where restrictions and controls in trade, industry and finance flourish in such abundance that Cobden himself would not recognize it. The economic policy of Great Britain is now characterised by tariff changes, commercial agreements, and quota restrictions on the one hand, and on the other by the development of a 'sterling area', and the starting of Reserve Banks in Empire countries to work the new financial system. The growth of an Empire shipping policy with a view to reserve Empire trade for Empire ships, seems to be under consideration. A plan of complementary production and trade within the Empire by which the more developed parts will concentrate on the higher forms of production, leaving the less specialised forms to the backward parts, and by which an exchange of such products will be facilitated between the Empire group of countries, is gradually taking shape.

Empire Economic Plan

The effort to bring the scattered parts of the Empire into a line with this new Empire policy, has resulted in important political developments. Systematic propaganda with a view to creating opinion and goodwill among the peoples of the different parts of the Empire has been carried on. This has been supplemented by other methods differing in each case with the political status of the Empire countries concerned. Persuasion and treatment on a footing of equality have been adopted with the Dominions; an artificial or forced consent is the rule in this country; and a policy of active coercion has been adopted in the case of Crown Colonies, for example, in Ceylon. Whereas in dependencies and colonies, a free and frank consideration from their own points of view of the new policy has not been possible, in the Dominions where such consideration is possible, practical difficulties and controversies in the application of the new policy, have been noticed. The need for the enforcement of such an Empire policy in future has involved the institution of a chain of Reserve Banks in Empire countries which are to work under the guidance of the Bank of England; and permanent machinery to watch the development of trade and to suggest ways and means for co-operation may grow. It may also in due course, involve a corresponding change in the political structure of the Empire, which, however, is a problem beyond my scope. My present purpose is to trace the existence of an Empire Economic Plan and see its influence on Indian Economic policy. We have literally to trace such a plan by putting together the various measures which have recently been adopted, for the Empire Economic Plan is essentially different from the Soviet Plan. Unlike the

Soviet method, the Empire Economic Plan is not outlined as such beforehand; nor is it meant to be worked out within any defined time limit as in Russia. Unlike the Soviet Plan therefore, the existence of the Empire Economic Plan must be traced from the deliberations of different Empire Conferences, the pronouncements of Empire Statesmen, the definite actions taken in different countries in important economic matters, and from the general trend of opinion in Great Britain. Unlike the Soviet Plan, there is in the new Empire scheme no intention to revolutionize society in the interests of workers and peasants. But there is every intention to make the Empire one large economic unit, working in co-operation apparently for the benefit of its component parts, but really presenting a strong organized front to those outside the Empire unit. Besides the strictly economic considerations underlying this scheme, it has thus obviously an important political significance, and how each of these factors will react on the other, is more than one can predict, but it is certainly a matter which cannot be ignored.

British Economic Policy in India

So far as the economic policy of this country under British rule is concerned, it is well known that in the matter of trade and industry, British policy with free trade as the method was in operation in this country till 1924. The second stage is marked by the adoption of the principle of discriminating protection in 1924, when a definite departure in the industrial and commercial policy of the country was made. While this system is still in its infancy, it has been super-imposed, as it were, by the new Empire policy of which we have already spoken. In the field of finance, it is equally well known that since 1899, the sterling standard has been in operation in this country though different names have been given to the system. The continued opposition to the adoption of the Gold Standard in India in the past, the ratio controversy and the linking of the rupee to sterling since September 1931, are instances of the way in which British financial policy has worked in this country. The constitution of the Reserve Bank shows that British or Empire Policy will be imposed in this matter in the future as in the past.

Subordination of National to Empire Interests

We have thus two important forces working in the country; on the one hand the growing desire of the people for a better and a higher standard of life, and on the other hand, the needs of the Empire, both resulting in the realization of the fact that the economic advancement of the country should be systematically fostered. Though the desire is thus common, the outlook is different, which results in a clash of ideas and methods in connection with the measures to be adopted. This is so, because, whereas Empire policy is the key to the methods of the Indian authorities, national policy is the key to the demand of educated India. Whereas the former requires the planning and arrangement of things to further the interests of the Empire, the latter naturally fears that in so doing, national interests will suffer. Because of differences in political status, there is a consciousness that in the United Kingdom and in the Dominions, national interests will be safeguarded first and Empire interests will be looked after next, and there is a natural fear in the dependent parts of the Empire that national interests will be subordinated to those of the Empire. In India, the acceptance of preference for British goods in schemes of protection under the threat of withdrawal of protection,[1] the acceptance of the Ottawa Trade Agreement in spite of general opposition to it in the country, the linking of the rupee to sterling, the control over the Reserve Bank, the commercial and fiancial safeguards in the Federal scheme and the proposed statutory Railway Board independent of the future Federal Legislature—these and similar measures are illustrations of the trend of events explained above; they can be understood and even appreciated from the point of view of the Empire in the light of recent developments; and at the same time the opposition to them in this country can also be equally easily understood and appreciated, due to fears justified by past experience and current knowledge.

Recent Economic Measures by the State

The imposition of the Empire Economic Policy on India is not without its counterpart in parallel measures for the development

[1] Arrangements have been made for a new Indo-British trade agreement which will lay down the principles to be followed in fixing Indian protective duties on United Kingdom goods, including textiles.

of the country within. What could not be dreamt of in the days of *laissez-faire* up to 1913, is now justified as a matter both of necessity and of policy. We have, in the first place, for the improvement of agriculture and rural conditions generally, the work of well organized bodies like the Imperial Council of Agricultural Research, and the Central Cotton Committee. Measures for the improvement of the economic conditions of the rural population were considered at a Conference of Ministers and officials of Central and Provincial Governments held in April last. An intensive programme for developing marketing facilities for agricultural products was considered to be the measure most likely to lead to substantial results. A scheme of marketing surveys as a preliminary to devising methods for the better marketing of agricultural produce has now been formulated, and it is expected that the work will be started soon. The position of the farmer is to be further improved by legislation for the relief of debt and by other measures. Some of this legislation[2] which is still under consideration has aroused acute controversy and will be discussed by this Conference. The C. P. Debt Conciliation Act passed in 1933, was amended this year; the C. P. Moneylenders' Bill has become law; and schemes to start Land Mortgage Banks have been formulated in Bombay and Bengal.

The question of the low price which the farmer has been receiving for his product has drawn the attention of the authorities. In this connection, the Crop Planning Conference held a few months ago considered ways and means for the co-ordination of agricultural production for the country as a whole. Suggestions were made to Provincial Governments for keeping up the cultivation of different crops at a remunerative level. More definite action has been taken in the case of sugar cane, and jute. Legislation has been passed with a view to seeing that the growers

[2] The following bills may be mentioned in this connection:

(*a*) The Punjab Relief of Indebtedness Bill.
(*b*) The U.P. Agriculturists' Relief Bill.
(*c*) The Encumbered Estates Bill, U.P.
(*d*) The Usurious Loans Act (U.P. Amendment) Bill.
(*e*) The U.P. Regulation of Sales Bill.
(*f*) The U.P. Temporary Regulation of Execution Bill.
(*g*) The C.P. Debtors' Relief Bill.
(*h*) The Bombay Money-lenders' Bill.
(*i*) The Madras Debt Conciliation Bill.

Some of these bills have been passed since this was written.

of sugar cane receive a fair price, and regulating the price at which sugar cane intended to be used for the manufacture of sugar is purchased. Part of the proceeds of the excise duty on sugar imposed this year is to be utilized for the purpose of helping the grower of sugar cane. In the case of jute a scheme of voluntary restriction of the area under jute cultivation helped by official propaganda has been put into operation by the Government of Bengal, and the idea of compulsory restriction is in favour in some quarters. The object in either case is to enable the farmer to realise a better price for jute.

In the matter of trade and industry, in spite of the fact that as in other parts of the world, they are passing through a period of severe depression, the new departure in State policy has resulted in the growth of new industries on the one hand and of possibilities of trade in certain directions on the other. Though the protective policy inaugurated in 1924 is still in its infancy and has revealed many defects in working, it must be admitted that large industries like those of steel and cotton would have suffered a severe setback in the absence of protection, and that new industries like those of sugar and matches would not have come into existence or flourished. The Ottawa Trade Agreement with the United Kingdom was followed by a Commercial Agreement with Japan; efforts are now being made for fresh agreements with other countries, and certain interests in Great Britain are arranging to get special privileges in trade. A trade treaty with Burma which is to be separated under the Federal scheme, is in contemplation. Trade Delegations have recently visited Africa and Afghanistan, and Indian Trade Commissioners have been appointed in London, Hamburg and Milan, and are likely to be appointed in a few other centres in the near future. Some Provincial Governments have passed legislation with a view to giving financial and other assistance to small industries. Progress in this connection has been slow chiefly owing to the limited resources available for the purpose. This work is to be supplemented by the Bureau of Industrial Intelligence and Research, which has been attached to the Indian Stores Department. The function of this Bureau is to collect and disseminate industrial information, to assist in industrial research and to help the Provincial Governments and industrialists in the matter of industrial growth.

In the financial sphere, apart from the controversial issues such as the control of the Reserve Bank or of the exchange rate of the rupee or of the exports of gold, we may say that the creation of the Reserve Bank of India may supply a long felt want for the co-ordination of the money market in this country with our currency policy, and generally give an impetus to the growth of a sound banking system.

Recent Economic Measures by the People

While these illustrations indicate the nature of the activities of the State in economic matters, it may be pointed out that the people on their own behalf have also taken an active interest in the economic development of the country. The creation of the Swadeshi spirit corresponds to the 'Buy British' slogan in Great Britain and is an essential complement to the policy of protection. The All India Spinners' Association has done useful work in connection with one important village industry, and its work is now to be supplemented by the creation of the All India Village Industries' Association which will look after other cottage industries. In the case of large industries, though all is not well, we find a movement in some cases towards a joint organisation for common purposes, particularly for marketing the product and eliminating unnecessary competition as in the case of cement and sugar. The Cement Marketing Company of India is a well organised pool, which has full control over the marketing of the cement manufactured in India because all cement factories have joined it. The Company also controls the quantity and quality of production. The work of the Indian Sugar Mills Association is more limited in scope. Chiefly with a view to meeting the competition of foreign sugar at the port towns, this Association has drawn up a scheme for the marketing of sugar, by which a certain percentage of the production of certain groups of factories in the U.P. and Bihar will be pooled, and sold in the port towns at rates which will meet the competition of foreign sugar in these towns. We may say that this is a development in the direction of cartellisation, a form of industrial growth which is becoming common in the West in the case of important industries.

The Formation of Economic Opinion

This rapid survey of changing events in the economic sphere in the world in general and in our country in particular, indicates that the trend of thought and of events is definitely towards a new economic order. Whether it is Capitalism or Socialism that ultimately succeeds; whether it is Imperialism or Nationalism that holds the field, the fact is obvious that no country is now allowing its econonmic life to drift, and that every country is anxiously planning economic measures with a view to its prosperity and progress. Though the degree and nature of planning differ according to the motives with which it is undertaken, the fact remains that we have now an undisputed expansion of the functions of the State in economic matters and the tendency towards this expansion may further increase in course of time. It is inevitable therefore that the economic policy and the economic growth of a country will in the future be shaped to an ever increasing degree by the State. In the case of a country, where the State is responsible to the people of the country or makes an effort to represent the national will, there will not be that clash between economic policy and opinion which may be noticed in a country like ours. At this juncture therefore, the formation of the right economic opinion for an economic policy in general as well as for the solution of various problems in detail, is a most urgent need. With the planning of economic measures, the planning and organization of economic opinion must precede and be concurrent. A critical and scientific study of plans and measures, public and private, helped by informed and free discussions by disinterested persons, with a view to forming the right economic opinion in the interests of the country, will be a national service of the greatest importance. It is in order to emphasise the need for the formation of such opinion that I have sketched at some length the recent movements in the economic sphere in this country and elsewhere. The formation of the right economic opinion should be of vital importance to any country, even in normal times. Its importance to our country at the present juncture is of much greater moment, because we are passing through a period of transition, and because economic policy once formed and adopted, may take such roots that it would be difficult to change it. It is therefore wiser to think of the policy beforehand and shape it in a manner calculated to serve the best interests of the country.

Agencies for the Formation of Economic Opinion

In this connection, let us make a brief survey of the more important parties and their methods that are responsible for the formation of economic opinion in this country. We shall then be in a position to see whether we, as academic economists, can play a useful part. We can say in a broad way that at present the economic opinion in the country is formed by (*a*) Government, (*b*) Commercial interests, British and Indian (*c*) Legislatures and Politicians outside the Legislatures, (*d*) Financial and Economic Journals and (*e*) Academic workers. So far as the Government is concerned, it influences economic opinion by a variety of annual and other reports, which it publishes; by the special studies of certain problems which it undertakes, by the reports of committees and commissions which it appoints from time to time, and by important speeches or pronouncements of members of the Government and high officials. The strong point in the opinion thus being formed is that it is supported by a systematic study of facts made by well-equipped departments and highly trained officials. At the same time, the publication of data and views is often made according to the convenience of the Government. The weak point is that it very often reflects the set notions of the Civil Service in the attempt to justify Government policy. Besides, there is an intolerance on the part of the Government of criticism of their policy in and out of the Legislatures, and such criticism is often branded either as politically minded or even as racial, in spite of the well known fact that the Government policy and measures themselves may have been dictated by political and imperial considerations.

So far as British Commercial interests are concerned, we find that they are better organized and have full time workers for the study of the various problems that concern them. Well equipped with data and material suitable for their purpose, they are able to influence Government opinion more effectively; this is so because on the one hand they are naturally willing to support Imperial Economic Policy and on the other, they have an easy access to authorities, both in England and India, socially or otherwise. So far as Indian Commercial interests are concerned, they are growing in importance in the formation of economic opinion, but compared with their stake in the country, their organization is far from adequate. So far as a systematic study of problems is concerned, with a few honourable exceptions, it may be said to be absent. So far as the staff of the Indian commercial bodies is concerned, it is mostly clerical and is not equipped for research and investigation of those manifold complex current problems which require knowledge and training, essentially different, and often superior to that possessed by the staff of these bodies. Indian commercial interests usually find themselves in opposition to the policy of Government, but they are not always able to support their opinion with that convincing proof, which can come out of a systematic study of a high order. For example, in connection with the Ottawa Trade Agreement, a detailed study of the trade with non-Empire countries and of the effect of the Agreement on small industries could have been organized by the Indian Commercial bodies; the Government of India having omitted these aspects from their review, we are now left with a one-sided view of the situation. So far as the politicians in and outside the Legislatures are concerned, without going into details, we may say that the position is roughly of the same nature as is true of British commercial interests on the one hand and Indian commercial interests on the other. The same general position is reflected in the case of Financial and Economic Journals; in this case, however, we have in recent times, a few exceptions of the type of weeklies like 'Indian Finance' and 'The Indian Economist,' issued from Calcutta. There is nothing in Bombay to compare with the valuable work done by these weeklies in Calcutta.

So far as agricultural opinion in the country is concerned, it is unorganized, and the position is such that it is often difficult to find what the true agricultural opinion is with reference to particular problems. The position is at the same time clouded by the fact that Government and British Commercial interests on the one hand and Indian Commercial interests on the other, are all fond of defending their policies in the name and interests of the farmer. Whereas this is so in the case of agriculture, the growing number of industrial labourers have some organisation varying in importance and usefulness in different parts of the country.

There is great room for improvement from the point of view of the industrial labourer in the existing state of things, so far as the formation of opinion in his interests is concerned.

The Academic Economist

This brief analysis of the way in which economic opinion is formed, shows that in proportion to the magnitude and importance of the problem, the existing arrangements for leading public opinion in regard to economic policy and problems, are wholly inadequate. In making this observation, I have not referred to the position of the academic workers, which I propose to discuss in greater detail. It may, however, be assumed that the general criticism regarding the inadequacy of the existing agencies for the formation of the right economic opinion is applicable also to academic workers. In the case of a backward country like ours with innumerable complex internal problems and with an unusually large population, the economic problem is already sufficiently acute to demand the concentration and efforts of a large army of scientific workers for its study and solution. To this problem is now added the urgent need in view of recent tendencies in the economic sphere for a more organised and prompt effort to study current problems, both in their local and international aspects. In other countries, Universities and other academic institutions are highly equipped both in the matter of library and other facilites as well as in the matter of trained staff in each branch of Economics, which makes specialisation possible. Compared with this equipment and compared with the magnitude of our problem, the existing equipment and resources of Universities and other academic institutions in the matter of economic studies in our country, may be characterised as poor. The amount of literature issued in connection with each important economic problem in important world centres on the one hand, and the amount of work required to be done in each problem with reference to this country on the other are so vast that it is absolutely necessary to have specialists in each branch. Whereas comparison is often made between the work of economists in this country and that of economists in the West, the important fact is often forgotten that whereas in the West specialisation in each branch is both facilitated and encouraged, two or three teachers are required to be masters of all branches of Economics in the Universities and Colleges in this country.

Moreover, in other countries, academic work is supplemented or encouraged by the organized work of other bodies; for example, political parties, commercial organizations or specially endowed research institutions engage highly trained workers for the study of current economic problems from their respective points of view. There is a natural process of action and reaction between the strictly academic workers and the non-academic workers in the matter of investigation and research in economic problems, which results in a constant criticism of one another's point of view, ultimately resulting in the establishment of truth. Besides educating public opinion by means of their publications, such bodies provide leaders of thought with useful material. Very often such work anticipates and creates a demand for public enquiry, or supplements the work done by Government; sometimes, it covers fields wholly ignored by Government and in any case, it affords an intelligent corrective to data and opinion made current by those in power. This kind of work also results in a constant flow of highly trained academic men into Commerce and Politics. In any case, such contact between academic experts and men of affairs results in a co-ordination of ideas and a scientific study of facts without which life in modern countries would be guided and controlled in a one-sided fashion.

Limitations of Academic Work

Unfortunately, even the limited resources that we possess in the academic sphere cannot be fully utilized for that larger purpose which I am contemplating in this discussion. To make my meaning clear let us for a moment analyse the existing talent and resources in the form of College and University teachers that are available. The other class of workers in the field of economic studies are so few that one need not consider them in this connection. In the first place, there is a class, perhaps accounting for a large percentage of the total of teachers who are poorly equipped, which is no fault of their own; the fault is of the institutions and the system. The point, however, is that we cannot hope for any useful or original work from this class of teachers. In the second place, there is a class of well equipped teachers, who, by their training and inclination are in a position to do useful work, but are poorly paid and often over-worked. Though a fortunate few of these may in course of time go up the ladder, on the whole, we can have few hopes from this class of teachers. The third class of teachers, chiefly those in Government service in the superior grade, are as a rule both well equipped and highly paid. From the point of view of their own personal ambition, once secure of tenure in the service, the impetus in their case to do original work is comparatively little. But the great factor which works against this class of teachers is the existence of a positive hindrance in the form of restrictions by the authorities on the free expression of opinion. A scientific worker ought to be allowed to express his opinions freely, irrespective of persons and parties. The government servant, however, in this country is required to worship government more than science, and if his work happens to uphold the views of the authorities, he may be patted on the back; on the other hand, if his views are likely to go against the policy or the opinions of the authorities, they may not be expressed; if he does express them, he will suffer. The fourth class of teachers working in Universities and private institutions, who are both well equipped and well paid are comparatively few in number. They have opportunities for independent thought and facilities for work, which though poor compared with those available in the West, must be characterized to be quite good under our conditions. The limited amount of original research work on different economic problems which has been published in recent years, is mainly due to these causes. It is obvious therefore that if academic workers are to play a better and more useful part in the formation of the right economic opinion in the country, we have to look to this fourth class of teachers and institutions employing them.[3] If the status of the academic economist in public esteem is raised on the one hand, and if public and private resources are spent freely in order to encourage and develop the work of this class of institutions and teachers, a desirable link in the formation of the right economic opinion will be supplied at this juncture of our country's history. It would be highly desir-

[3] This does not mean that the other classes should be ignored; there are good exceptions in each and ways and means for a general improvement of each class should be thought of.

able for those who are interested in this problem to think of ways and means for giving an impetus to scientific economic work of an independent nature. A few suggestions may, however, be made.

Suggestions for Improvement

(*a*) Endowment of Chairs and Fellowships for research work in economic problems; public funds should be spent to a much greater extent for this than hitherto; and it is an object towards which charity may be usefully directed. In addition, commercial bodies and magnates will do well to help in such endowments either for general or special studies. (*b*) The expansion of the Economics Departments of Universities and Colleges by the appointment of specialists in different branches of Economics who should be given facilities for such specialization and not burdened with other work. (*c*) Employment of a special research staff for the study of current problems by commercial and political bodies and organizations in the country. (*d*) Encouragement of research publications and their wider use and publicity. (*e*) Consultation with experts for advice on a footing of equality, either by Government, commercial bodies or political organizations, with adequate remuneration wherever necessary. (*f*) The removal of restrictions by government on their academic staff in the matter of expression of opinion on economic problems. At a time when the government are trying to be responsive, if not responsible, such a measure would be a statesmanlike gesture, removing public prejudice against government actions and enabling the formation of healthy economic opinion. One wonders how such restrictions could have continued with 'Education' as a transferred subject since 1921. (*g*) Government departments, semi-government bodies and commercial organizations should welcome independent research workers and give them willing help. The research worker is at present in many cases, considered a nuisance, causing disturbance in the existing routine of things in these departments and bodies.[4] He is often suspected as an agitator or as a spy who may misuse the information. Moreover,

[4] (*a*) In connection with a study of Railway Rates in 1931, the G.I.P. Railway refused permission to refer to published tariffs of former years, which were not on the market and which could not be had elsewhere; 1931.

with few exceptions, the attitude of highly placed persons, either officials or commercial magnates, with reference to a research worker, is neither pleasant nor encouraging. With the growth of democratic institutions in this country, government departments and other parties would do well to realize that the petty-mindedness, which usually characterises their attitude in this matter, is responsible for the accumulation or formation of prejudice which might well be removed and prevented by welcoming bona-fide research workers and giving them due recognition and facilities. (*h*) The encouragement by government and commercial bodies to societies and associations doing organized research work. (*i*) The improvement of existing government machinery in the matter of collection and publication of economic and statistical information and of expansion in those cases at least in which the magnitude of the work is such that private effort may not succeed.

Private Effort Towards Improvement

So far as private effort is concerned, the suggestions made above cannot be carried out unless those in possession of wealth, realise the full significance of this work in the interests of the country and are willing to spare funds for the purpose. Even if commercial bodies undertake to investigate their own problems by employing their own full time staff, the work done by them will usually be of immediate and passing moment of the short-view type. In order that a detached long view of current events may be taken, it is desirable that free scope should be given to academic workers by allowing them adequate opportunities. The opportunities may be of two types:—(1) facilities to study practical problems of commerce and industry and (2) financial help in the form of endowments of Research Chairs or Fellowships, or adequate grants for specific research problems by recognised workers. With a few honourable exceptions, it would not be untrue to say that in this country there is a divorce between the academic economist on the one hand and the practical businessman on the other. The former is considered too theoretical and therefore of little use by the latter; nor is the businessman will-

(*b*) In reply to a request for information regarding legislation to relieve the farmer from the load of debt in the Madras Presidency, the Registrar of Co-operative Societies, Madras asked me that the enquiry should be sent through the Vice-Chancellor of the University.

ing to recognise the status and position of the academic worker in practice. The academic person on the other hand is not always willing to make efforts to understand the point of view of the businessman, and apply his mind to practical problems.

Moreover, the want of agreement among economists on important problems often scares away the businessman; the latter must however realise that a difference of opinion either in any scientific work or in a practical problem is not an unhealthy sign; that such a state of affairs is true of many other walks of life; that the ever changing economic phenomena make it impossible for any two economists to look at them from the same angle; and that given sympathetic understanding and co-operation, ways and means could be found to reduce such differences to a minimum. To take an illustration, our medical advisers often differ both in their diagnosis and in their treatment. We complain of such differences, but still resort to the doctor. We do not prescribe for ourselves, nor try to improve upon given prescriptions, though each of us is more familiar with his body than the doctor. In the case of the economic doctor, we dispute his advice because he is not in agreement with his fellow worker; we do not allow him to diagnose the economic ills properly, but ask him for a sure remedy; we sit in judgment on his prescription, add to it or alter it as we like, apply it or not, but are ready to blame him for the consequences.

Coming back to the relation of the businessman and the economist, we may say that perhaps, the pride of wealth and power in the one case and the pride of learning in the other, are in conflict; but unless both parties realise that either has to give and take from the other, and that a co-ordination of the knowledge and experience of both on a footing of equality will alone result in the solution of current complex problems in the true interests of the country, the desired progress will not be possible. The businessman needs to give up his attitude of judging the academic person without giving him opportunities to study and understand practical problems; he must realize that that attitude is bound to offend academic pride and keep the true academic person at a distance from the practical man. The academic person on the other hand must realize that he has much to learn by way of information and experience from the practical man of business, which he can never hope to obtain from books. It is an understanding of some such nature and an appreciation by business magnates of the national importance of the work of the academic person, who is treated with the highest respect in spite of his comparative poverty that has enabled the creation of that class of scientific workers, who form the true backbone of current economic opinion in other advanced countries.

Government Effort towards Improvement

So far as the government effort for carrying out some of the suggestions made above is concerned, it may be admitted at once that the authorities in India are quite alive to the urgent need of improving and expanding their existing machinery and of giving facilities to private workers. The unfortunate part, however, is that their action is not in consonance with their ideas; financial and other considerations have come in the way of improvement and expansion, and the usual red-tape mentality comes in the way of giving facilities to private efforts. In fact, in some cases, this mentality acts as a positive hindrance as explained above. The hesitating attitude of the authorities, in the matter of economic investigation and research, compared with an obvious desire to do something, may be seen from the fact that three important reports on the subject have been issued in recent years without, however, any substantial result. The Indian Economic Enquiry Committee reported in 1925 in favour of a scheme for an Economic Survey of the country and for the institution of Central and Provincial Statistical Bureaux. It was unfortunately left to a statistician and an economist to strike the bottom out of the scheme from its very inception; for one is not in a position either to understand or appreciate the attitude of Mr. Burnett-Hurst in his minute of dissent to the scheme of Sir M. Visvesvaraya. Nothing came out of this; in the meanwhile, however, other countries were developing special economic organizations, both for expert advice and investigation to help the executive in their work. In order to advise the Government of India on the best method of doing similar work in this country, Sir Arthur Salter, Director of the Economic and Financial section of the League of Nations, was invited to this country. His report issued in 1931 outlined a scheme for an economic advisory organization which involved the creation of a Central Economic Advisory Council as well as Provincial Economic Advisory Councils, each assisted by an expert staff for the purpose of advising the respective governments on current economic problems. Nothing substantial came out of this report either. In January 1933, Sir George Schuster, the then Finance Member, was good enough to address the Sixteenth Indian Economic Conference at Delhi on the subject of an Economic Survey for India and the improvement of Economic Statistics. He invited the co-operation of the Conference and of the Indian Economic Association in that connection. In response to that suggestion, a special committee of the Association prepared and submitted a memorandum to Sir George Schuster and offered co-operation on behalf of the Association. This effort at co-operation on behalf of the Association was unfortunately treated with scant courtesy. By the end of the year, Dr. Bowley and Mr. Robertson[5] were invited to this country to report on the same problem. Mr. Robertson's presence at our last Conference at the Annamalai University, followed by a visit of one or both of these gentlemen to most University centres gave opportunities to Indian Economists among others, to explain to them the kind of work that was being done by them and what could be done given the necessary facilities and encouragement. In their report published in the beginning of this year, they advocated a scheme for an Economic Census of India with special reference to the Census of Production and reorganization of statistics. The scheme involves rural and urban surveys and contemplates close co-operation with Indian Economists through the Universities. For recognizing the status of the academic economist in general and of the Indian Economic Association in particular in the scheme advocated by them, we may well pay a tribute to these distinguished fellow workers in the same cause elsewhere. Though nothing, as usual, has yet come out of this report, if the Indian authorities and commercial magnates will take a lesson out of this report by recognising the status of the economist and the value of his work, and by helping and encouraging him, a great national service will have been rendered.

Though these reports have been shelved, a few minor efforts have been made, perhaps in the right direction. We have now

[5] Sir Denis Robertson.

Boards of Economic Enquiry or similar bodies in the Punjab, the U.P. and in Bengal, though the constitution and functions of these Boards vary in different provinces. Some expansion of the work of the Department of Commercial Intelligence and Statistics has recently taken place; in addition, a few more publications are now being issued by that Department. This is of such a limited nature compared with the magnitude of the task, which can be seen from the reports referred to above, that one may well despair of any substantial result. Besides the inherent limitations of Government work in this connection in any country, there are obvious limitations of a special nature of Government work in this country. Added to these limitations, when the Government is not in a mood to do more than the bare minimum compelled by necessity or circumstances, the need on the one hand of greater pressure on the Government to do more, and of private initiative and effort on the other, is all the greater. The necessary corrective to State effort which is provided by private effort in other countries, is a specially urgent necessity in our country, in view of our peculiar conditions, and it is to be expected therefore that those concerned will take a long view of this matter and make an organised effort in the right direction.

The Work of the Indian Economic Association

While criticising the existing agencies for the formation of economic opinion in the country and making suggestions for their improvement, I would be failing in my duty if I did not ask the members of the Indian Economic Association and of this Conference to think of ways and means by which they can play a more active and a more useful part in this national service. The two important ways in which the Association has been doing its work for the last 18 years are the publication of a Quarterly Journal and the holding of an Annual Conference in co-operation with the Universities. Without in any way disparaging the work of our Editorial Board or of the Managing Editor of the Journal at Allahabad, I think it would be easy to agree upon the proposition that there is great room for improvement in the quality of the material published in our Journal and also in the time of its publication. The Annual Conferences have provided meeting places for an exchange of views, chiefly for academic workers and those interested. Owing to great distances in our country and also owing to the want of encouragement or the absence of facilities, many persons who would otherwise take an active interest in the Conferences are prevented from attending them regularly. In consequence, though a few members regularly attend the Conferences, the composition of each Conference varies considerably from that of any other. Besides this difficulty, the quality of the papers submitted and the standard of discussion also needs to be raised. Some arrangements have been made in this connection as a result of discussions during the last two years, and it is hoped that things are somewhat better now than before, but we need not be ashamed of admitting the fact that here also, there is considerable room for improvement. I venture to make a few suggestions, which may form the basis of discussion, and if adopted, by general agreement will, I hope, enable us to improve both these features of our work.

In the first place, we may organize local centres, chiefly in University towns or other places wherever suitable arrangements are possible. The members of the Executive Committee who, as a rule, belong to different University centres, may undertake each in his own sphere to organize such a local centre. In other places, other organizers should be found. The object of the organizer in each centre should be to bring together the members of the Indian Economic Association resident in the local area and those few selected persons, who by their knowledge and experience or position, are likely to help in the formation of a study group. This group so formed, may arrange for weekly or fortnightly meetings for the frank discussion of problems. The discussion should be preceded by an original study or investigation of the problem by one or more members of the group. The subjects of such study should be in the first place those fixed for discussion at the ensuing Conference and secondly those of local interest. The ultimate result of such discussion may be a paper either jointly written by some members of the group or by an individual. So far as future conferences are concerned, the papers submitted will have thus been the result of systematic study and mature deliberation. At the same time, there may be other material resulting from such study and discussions, which may well find a place in the Journal. If in course of time we find that this system works successfully and that we have more material than we can afford to publish in the Journal, we may think of arranging for the issue of special bulletins on special topics. Arrangements will have to be made for some contact between the centres during the course of the year, so that each may be aware of the progress of work in the other. In some cases, one centre may be in a position to help another by the supply of information or advice. The Annual Report of the work of the Association would then contain information regarding the work in different centres, which means that the centres will have to keep the central office informed of the work done in each place. The work of the Secretary of the Association is bound to increase and he may have to be provided with suitable assistance for the purpose. This would result in live and continuous work throughout the year by the members of the Association in different groups, and when the result of such work is pooled at the end of the year at the time of the Conference, we shall certainly have something of which the Association and the Conference can be proud. This will also enable those who for one reason or another, are not able to attend the Conference to contribute indirectly to the success of the Conference and of the work of the Association, because they would at least be in a position to help the study group in the local centre by their co-operation. This work should as far as possible be done in co-operation with Economic Societies or similar organizations, if any are in existence at any centre. These study groups should also be able to obtain the help and co-operation of Government Departments and of Commercial bodies in their work. By some such arrangement, which is in no way revolutionary and which would enable us to develop gradually from the existing nucleus that we possess, we should be in a position to make our opinion both weighty and valuable, to raise our status high in public esteem, to make the membership of the Association a matter of pride and privilege, and to make its work in general a thing which those concerned cannot afford to neglect. In organizing on the lines I have suggested the financial aspect has been borne in mind; though there will be some additional office expenditure, it will be within our means and will be worth-while. It should not be difficult for us to be able to increase our membership if our work improves, in which case increased fees will more than meet the additional expenditure. The work of the local centres will automatically attract interested persons who will be willing to join the Association.

I realise that the success of our work may depend on the co-operation and in some cases, even the financial assistance of Universities, commercial bodies and persons and of the Government, but we cannot expect to get such assistance unless we have gone a step forward ourselves and created a demand for it. In spite of difficulties, I am optimistic that once the value of our work is appreciated on its merits, such assistance would be forthcoming. In doing so, however, we shall have on the one hand to give an assurance and on the other to ask for a privilege that our work shall be on scientific lines and in the true interests of the country; it shall therefore be free from pressure of outside parties or of those with pre-conceived notions. The task of a scientific investigator is difficult because he cannot please parties if he worships science and truth. His work should therefore be all the more valuable and deserving of encouragement by all those who realise that at this juncture in the history of our country, organized progress in this connection is both desirable and urgent.

Conclusion

Out of the darkness created by systematically fostered prejudices and organized selfishness, a ray of true economic light may yet penetrate. The force of that light for good will depend on the devotion of the disinterested economist to his science, helped in his difficult task by those in power and authority in private and public life. We can only pray that the foresight necessary to bring forth such devotion and such help will not be lacking, and that the privilege of an atmosphere of freedom in which alone creative thought may blossom will not be denied to the economist; otherwise the thinking that is done to order or in an atmosphere of fear and suspense will be like the incoherent mumbling of a man in dotage, the precursor of the approaching end.

The State in Relation to Economic Progress in India*

THE CONCEPTION OF THE STATE IN ECONOMIC LIFE AND THE CHANGING STRUCTURE OF THE STATE IN INDIA[1]

Introduction

I AM indebted to the authorities of the Osmania University for giving me an opportunity to visit this historical city, which is now the city of modern learning on the most up to date lines. You can be proud for having the finest University Buildings and the largest University Area in India, in which to pursue your studies, you can be prouder still in having set the difficult example of teaching modern subjects through an Indian language. Whereas other and older Indian Universities are still struggling to solve the problem of the medium of instruction, you have already solved it. In the history of Indian Education, this will be recorded not only as a most patriotic measure taken in an Indian State, but also as a unique example of how the State can help to bring about economic progress by spreading the light of knowledge to the many, which cannot be done by the foreign medium through which we have to teach elsewhere. And if I have to talk to you today in English, and not in Urdu or Hindi, the fault lies in our educational system, which I trust will be improved soon, following the example of your University.

The State in the Nineteenth Century

Before we consider the problem of the State in relation to economic progress as it affects us in this country, it would be better to be clear about the general conception regarding the economic functions of the state in modern times. During the last century

* Series of three lectures under the auspices of the Osmania University Hyderabad, on 11, 12 and 13 of October, 1937.

1 Lecture I, 11-10-1937.

there were broadly speaking, two distinct views regarding the economic functions of the state. In England it was believed that the state should not interfere in economic activities, and that it was best to leave the people alone in their efforts to increase production as well as to distribute the same among themselves. Partly because of her early start as an industrial nation, and partly because of her oversea possessions it was convenient for England to adopt this attitude. In other countries, chiefly in Germany, a different view prevailed to the effect that the state should in a variety of ways help the people to increase production. State assistance to industries was one of the chief methods by which this view was put into practice. So far as the removal of inequalities in the distribution of wealth was concerned, though socialistic ideas did not prevail fully, steps were taken in some countries, chiefly in Germany, to introduce social legislation with a view to improving the condition of the poorer sections of the people. To some extent these ideas influenced legislation even in conservative countries like England.

The chief reason why most of the countries other than England adopted a policy by which the state was required to take an active part in economic matters was the fact that they found themselves late in the field so far as industrial progress was concerned, and realized that they should organize themselves on national lines, if they were to develop their economic resources and increase their trade. This explains the existence of tariff systems prevailing in different parts of the world and other measures to develop industries and help trade, during the last century.

The State in Modern Times

Since the War the conception of the state in relation to its economic activities has been considerably expanded. In spite of the differences in outlook between the different states in the nineteenth century the people were on the whole left free; they received state assistance in some way in most countries unlike in England. But nowhere did the state take upon itself the functions of direct control of economic activities. We now find that these ideas have been thoroughly changed. Instead of leaving the people to carry on their economic activities in a free manner, the state prefers to control and guide the economic activities of the people in an organized manner. Whereas the State was concerned essentially with the problems of the security of its subjects in the nineteenth century, it is now concerned also with problems of the prosperity of its subjects. These tendencies have revolutionised the structure and machinery of modern states. There are differences in degree regarding the extent to which the state intervenes, either in organizing production or distribution of resources within its territory. There are differences also in the outlook or the ultimate aim with which such intervention takes place. In Russia the instruments of production are controlled by the State, industries have been nationalized and the national production is distributed among the people with a view to satisfying the needs of the largest possible number as far as possible. In Germany and Italy production is considerably controlled from the centre, though radical efforts at equitable distribution of resources are not made. As against the socialist economy in Russia we have, a kind of state capitalism in Germany and Italy. To carry out both these different types of economic organization, centralisation is required to such an extent that power has to be entrusted to dictators. In other countries like England and America, we have democratic institutions still surviving, but these have been adapted to new circumstances. The Roosevelt Regime in America has been characterised by the most gigantic state effort in a capialist economy to introduce measures for general recovery, in almost all spheres of economic activity. To carry out these measures Roosevelt was given extraordinary powers. The National Government in England in recent years has reduced the party system of Government to a formality, and has thereby assumed special powers, which has enabled it to introduce promptly thoroughgoing measures of state assistance not only in industries, but also in agriculture, trade and other spheres. The state has thus given up its former attitude of *laissez faire,* and is now regulating in a variety of ways economic activities in agriculture, industry, trade and transport, and is also trying to bring about better distribution by spending more on social services, from resources obtained by taxing the rich. Whatever the form of government, it is thus obvious that there is an increasing interference by the state in the economic sphere and this tendency has come to be known as planned economy.

Absence of one State in India

In order to be able to study the problem with reference to our country, we have to remember two broad facts, firstly, that we do not have one state in the counry, and secondly, that the structure and functions of the state or states existing in the country, are in the process of evolution, and have undergone fundamental changes particularly in this century. In view of this, any attempt to study economic progress in India, in relation to the state, will have to be an attempt to consider the changing economic outlook of the state with reference to its changing structure and functions. So far as the first point is concerned we have merely to remember that geographical India is different from political India. In the first place, there is the obvious division of geographical India into two broad political divisions, namely British India and Indian States. Though there are many things in common both between the governments of these respective divisions and their people, there are vital differences inherent in the organization of the political machinery prevalent in these divisions. The Indian States present among themselves a large variety, partly because of their size and status, and partly because of the resources at their disposal. The personal rule of the ruler has been in many cases tempered by Advisory Councils, consisting of men well known for their administrative experience or expert knowledge, and efforts are being made to introduce representative institutions, as in the territory of H.E.H. the Nizam. The ideas current in British India and the changes which occur from time to time in British India do influence the Indian States, but nevertheless, in considering the position of the states in relation to economic progress in India we must think of them separately from British India.

In British India also we do not have one governmental authority throughout the country. As we shall see immediately we shall have to remember the differences in the functions of the Central Government on the one hand and of the Provincial Governments on the other, to be able to have a clear view of the economic progress in the country in relation to the state. Though there are many things in common between these separate units, there are bound to be differences in their economic outlook particularly in the future. To appreciate this possible tendency in the future, it would be convenient to consider the position of the British Indian state in three stages, first up to 1920; second, during the period 1921 to 1937; and third at the present moment.

The Bureaucratic State

Up to 1920, in British India we did have one state; it may be described as the Bureaucratic State. Though we had the Central Government and the Provincial Governments then as now, the Provincial Governments up till 1920 were merely the agents of the Central Government, and the methods and policies adopted in the provinces were determined at the centre on uniform lines. So far as the economic outlook of the Bureaucratic State in British India up to 1920 was concerned it was chiefly borrowed from England. As in England it was believed by the authorities here that the function of the state was mainly the maintenance of security, that is of law and order. The state was not concerned with measures calculated to bring about the prosperity of the people, that is to increase their productive capacity. It was assumed that such capacity would be better increased, if the people were left to themselves and that therefore, state interference in the economic sphere was not desirable. The actual working of this idea in practice will be reviewed in some detail in the second lecture. We may however, anticipate some conclusions of that review, that the adoption of these ideas was unsuited to Indian conditions, and that it left us in an economically weak position. Though leaders of Indian opinion did point out the need for a change in the economic policy of the country, their voice was ineffective.

From another point of view, this state of affairs was inevitable. The Bureaucratic Government of India was only an agent of the British Government. The history of this Government is chiefly one of an organized effort to consolidate British Rule in India. For this purpose, the Government of India had to act mainly as the Police State; its strong arm maintained peace and order. An alien government trying to consolidate its power over a vast continent in this way naturally hesitated in taking bold steps for economic or social improvement, lest such steps came in the way of vested interests leading to discontent. Not having the sanction of public opinion behind its administration, the Government of India preferred merely to act as an efficient policeman.

Dyarchy and Bureaucracy

During the period 1921 to 1937 this position was changed due to the Montague Reforms. Whereas the Central Government still continued to have the form of the Bureaucratic State, the Provincial Governments got some autonomy. They were however, organized as Dyarchical States, in which bureaucracy still retained its power in substance, though it was tempered to some extent by public opinion as voiced in legislatures, and by the existence of Indian Ministers in charge of transferred departments. As we shall see later, this was a period in which a gradual change in ideas took place, and the need for the state to adopt measures for the economic improvement of the people was realised. Barring the change in the conception of the duty of the State towards the people, this difficult period did not result in any substantial improvement. In other words, at a time when the rest of the world including England, was radically changing in practice the functions of the state in the economic sphere; when the state in other countries was taking over more and more economic activities with a view to control and guide productive activities, we in this country needed a process of education for the authorities to change over from old ideas to modern views. In other words, during the period 1921-37, the conception of the state regarding the maintenance of security remained unaltered, with this difference that the state now began to accept in theory that the prosperity of the people was also the goal for which the state should strive.

Limited Democracy and Triarchy

Under the Government of India Act, 1935, we have a further change in the nature of the state in British India. Dyarchy has been abolished in the provinces; they are now considered as separate units of Federal India, and each is to be governed by democratic institutions limited in a variety of ways in the form of special responsibilities of the Governor; and in the form of the continuation of the vested interests of the Imperial Services. In view of these limitations, the state in the provinces may be described to have the form of Limited Democracy. The capacity of this kind of state in the provinces to bring about more prosperous conditions for the people is further limted by the financial resources at their disposal. Besides, we have to remember the fact that the Bureaucratic State continues at the centre, and is due to be transformed into the Federal Government of India at an early date. The nature of the Federal Government will be such that the future Central Government may be described as the Tri-archical State in as much as there will be three distinct groups struggling for power in that state, namely (1) the representatives of the people in British India; (2) the representatives of Indian States , and (3) the Viceroy. The prosperity of the people will depend on the actions both of the Provincial and the Central Governments, because though the Provincial Governments will be in closer contact with the people, the Central Government will have certain large economic policies under its control, the determination of which will affect economic life in the country. In view of the change in ideas referred to above, we may say though the maintenance of security still remains the chief function of the state in India, the desire to bring about prosperity is now likely to be translated into practice, but the effort will be within a limited sphere, with limited resources and limited power.

Scope of the Lectures

We have so far reviewed in brief in the first place the conception of state in economic life that dominates state action so far as economic progress is concerned, in order to study the same with reference to India, and other relevant problems. Having thus cleared the ground, we shall be able to discuss in the second lecture how the conception of the state in economic life that prevailed in India prior to 1921 worked in practice; we shall further trace briefly how this conception has gradually changed since 1921. In the third lecture, we shall consider how the new ideas could not be fully practised in the period, 1921-1937, leading to unrest and consequent troubles. This will bring us to the problems of the present and the immediate future, in which we shall point out how we are likely to have a clash of ideals and methods before we settle down to ordered progress.

THE CONSEQUENCES OF THE CONCEPTION PRIOR TO 1921 AND GRADUAL CHANGE IN IDEAS SINCE 1921*

Security Services

We have seen that up to 1920 the state in British India was organized as one unit, that its form was bureaucratic and that so far as its functions were concerned it was wholly guided by the 19th century idea of preserving law and order, and leaving the people alone to share their economic destines. This will be clear if we analyse the expenditure of the Government in the years prior to 1921. We find that as a rule the military expenditure of the Government of India dominates its budget; that it is invariably about 50 per cent of its total expenditure; and that if we add to it the other expenditure on maintenance of law and order within the country, that is the expenditure on police and part of the expenditure on Civil Services which were charged with magisterial duties, we find that the expenditure on Security Services was more than half of the total. Out of the remaining resources, the Government of India had to find certain fixed charges, such as interest on debt, sterling payments to England, and a costly Civil Service, all of which between them absorbed the greater portion of the remaining revenues. This left only a meagre amount for beneficial expenditure. This explains the comparatively slow progress even in education, leaving aside directly economic aspects of progress.

In pointing out that the Security Services absorbed the greater portion of the resources of the Indian Government, we must remember that it was not merely the security of the people of India on which these resources were spent. They were spent also for the security of British Rule in India; and part of the military expenditure of India has always been for Imperial purposes.

Agriculture

The way in which this conception of the state prevented economic advance may be further realized, if we analyse in brief, a few of the leading aspects of the economic life of the country during the period prior to 1921. Taking agriculture, the basic industry of the people first, we find that the entire land revenue

* Lecture II, 12-10-1937.

administration of the country was governed by the theory of rent. Imbued with Ricardo's classical theories of rent, taught in British Universities, the Indian Civil Servant assumed that the same was applicable in *toto* to Indian conditions. He believed that land revenue did not have an element of taxation, and that it could be increased without doing any harm to agricultural prosperity. The rigidity of the land revenue administration and the burden of land revenue which was increased at each settlement were carried to such an extent that they became a nightmare in the life of the agricultural population. Due to this and other causes, the agricultural occupation has become unprofitable in most parts of the country. Whether it is the existence of tiny and fragmented holdings or the state of indebtedness of the farmer or a combination of these and other factors, we cannot get away from the conclusion that the majority of the population who follow this occupation have to do so in spite of its unprofitable nature because of the want of an alternative.

Famine Policy

There were a few redeeming features in this situation. In the first place the Government of India adopted a famine policy to help the affected areas. The underlying idea was security of life by prevention of starvation in areas of acute distress. In normal times, protective works were constructed with a view to increase the powers of resistance of the people to face a famine. However laudable these humanitarian attempts may be, they can at best be described as indirect attempts to help the people, so far as economic progress was concerned. It was perhaps the same rigid adherance to the narrow conception of the state, whose function was security, that made the Government of India alive to the need of preventing people from starvation. We have some parallel to this effort in the modern practice of giving doles to the unemployed in highly industrialised countries. The unemployed are thus kept content, leaving the capitalist structure of the state undisturbed. The famine stricken people in India were given similar help and kept content by the Government of India, lest they became a source of unrest and trouble to the police functions of the Indian State. If the Government of India had a broader conception of the duty of the state to the people in normal times, they would have taken adequate steps to organize direct beneficial services to help the agriculturist to produce more, and to improve his condition to such an extent that he may not be faced with starvation, in times of famine. Besides the famine policy, the Government of India took some steps to help the agriculturist, by instituting the Departments of Agriculture and Co-operation. The Departments of Agriculture were however, charged merely with the duties of information, advice, demonstration and research. Their work and their methods were such that even to the present day the average farmer in the country is ignorant of their existence. The Co-operative Departments, started with the best of intentions, have not succeeded in creating a spirit of co-operation and self-help among the people; in most cases the Co-operative Society is only one additional organized *sowcar* in the rural areas. In spite of the persistent agitation of leaders of public opinion in the country regarding the evils of land revenue policy and the need for state action for agricultural improvement, the Government of India were slow in realising the realities of the situation.

Industries

If we look at other aspects of economic life we find that the smaller industries in rural areas gradually went out of existence due to the competition of imported manufactured goods. The people who were thus thrown out of employment could not find sufficient scope in larger industries and had to go back to the land. The large scale industries could not with a few exceptions make adequate progress because, the state, wedded to *laissez faire* principles, did not believe in giving them any assistance. In fact the way in which in the name of these principles, the Indian Cotton Industry was penalized by an excise duty in the interests of Lancashire, is one of the most miserable chapters in the economic history of Modern India. It was assumed in responsible quarters that India was an agricultural country only, in the sense that it could not be and need not be industrial. The talk of industrial development in those days was almost ridiculed or treated with faint praise. In consequence, the pressure of the growing population on the land was increasing without an adequate outlet in industries, either small or large. Rural life has been thus demoralized, and people seem to be eking out an existence without that interest in life which makes it noble and worth living.

Railways

So far as the development of transport facilities is concerned the different parts of India have been connected by a net-work of railways, which has made movement within the country both for passenger and goods traffic comparatively easy and cheap. Whereas this is true compared with the state of the country a hundred years ago, if we compare the transport facilities in this country with those in other countries at the present moment we shall realise the inadequacy of the facilities that we have. Considerable work remains to be done to link up the rural areas with the main railway lines. This may be done either by the development of motor traffic or by having feeder railways wherever possible. This presupposes however, the existence of suitable roads in the interior for which great efforts have yet to be made. Even with reference to the existing railways, it must be pointed out that they link up chiefly the urban centres and that they are partly organized for military purposes. In the actual management of the railways in this country, the freight policy has not been conducive to the interests of this country. It has encouraged more the foreign trade than the internal trade of the country, and has thus been instrumental in helping foreign industries often at the expense of Indian industries. It is not possible to go into the other details of railway management such as for example, the huge contrast between the facilities afforded to the insignificant minority of those who travel in the higher classes, and the vast majority of the passengers who travel in the third class. We must however point out that in one important aspect the railway policy was a definite departure from the traditional policy of *laissez faire*. Though the railways in this country were instituted with the help of Companies, the initiative came from the state, which gave the inducement of a guaranteed interest to the Companies and maintained a general control over railway administration. Whatever the defects in the early history of the railways in this country, the contracts with the Companies provided for the ultimate ownership of the state in due course. In view of this, the state is now the owner of most of the railways in the country, and is likely to be the owner of the remaining railways in due course. We have thus a rather anomalous but desirable position in as much as we have, or rather are soon likely to have, nationalization of railways, under a Government which is not socialistic in its outlook and methods.

Currency and Banking

In the sphere of currency and exchange, it has been wellknown that Indian interests and the Indian point of view have been often subordinated to the requirements of the City of London. The manipulations of the Indian currency and the exchange ratio of the Rupee to the Sterling have been the subjects of the most acute controversy. The desire to continue this control which involves the subordination of Indian interests, is reflected in the Government of India Act of 1935, by which it is not possible for the Indian Legislature to consider questions affecting the currency system of the country without the previous consent of the Viceroy. In the sphere of the money market and the banking system no steps were taken for long to develop the indigenous system; the modern banking system has been confined chiefly to the cities and is not sufficiently co-ordinated with the indigenous system. We have thus a wide gap between the urban and rural areas so far as the movement of money within the country is concerned. The comprehensive survey of the situation made by the Banking Committees which reported a few years ago has revealed the weaknesses in the situation. But with the exception of a few pious wishes definite steps towards the improvement of the banking system to suit our requirements still remains a matter of the future. The problem has now been taken up by the Reserve Bank.

Security and Population

It is thus obvious that the Government of India concentrated its energies and resources more on security than on prosperity. With the security thus granted to the people of India the population of the country increased enormously. But in proportion to this increase the avenues of employment did not increase, with the consequence that we began to have an increasing pressure on the land. Agricultural life which had already become difficult because of reasons mentioned above now become precarious in the extreme.

Want of Equilibrium

This rapid survey of the situation in different aspects of economic life shows that though some progress has been achieved in some directions, there are many more acts of commission or omission which have not been conducive to real economic progress. In consequence, we are presented with a serious want of equilibarium in the economic organization of the country at the moment. We have a vast and increasing population living on the verge of existence, an almost desperate life. Having lived for generations on an occupation which involves continuous loss and a perpetual state of indebtedness, they have come to believe that the environment in which they are placed is almost natural, from which there can be no escape. The desire to improve their lot or the economic motive has died out because of the conviction that the fruits of such additional improvements are not likely to be their own. This miserable state of affairs affecting the large majority of the people is reflected in other branches of economic life, in as much as industries large and small cannot flourish when the purchasing power of the majority of the people is so low. In other words, a comprehensive approach to bring about a balanced economic life in the country has not been made and the situation has been allowed to drift from bad to worse.

State Apathy

While this was happening the state was looking on; it was beyond its scope to interfere; the people of this country were suddenly brought under the full impact of western trade and industry; but they were not fully equipped to meet the same with advantage; the apathy of the state in the matter of direct help to organize the people into a strong nation must to a large degree be held responsible for the increasing helplessness in which they found themselves. This helplessness was revealed during the War period, when we could not avail ourselves of the new opportunities to develop our industries; it was further revealed during the recent depression when we found ourselves unable to resist the effects; and it is now revealing itself in our inability to move with the world in its march towards economic recovery.

Unlimited Powers with a Limited Outlook

The state in India, before 1921, partly because it was a bureaucratic state with unlimited powers to carry out things promptly, and with a highly organized machinery at its disposal to execute its decrees, was in a strong position to undertake a system of planed economy in the interests of the country. But such an outlook was at the time alien to the spirit of the Government in the country. It was wholly guided by the nineteenth century idea of preserving law and order, and leaving the people alone to shape their economic destinies. There were a few attempts calculated to remove misery or to increase the material welfare of the people, for example, the famine policy of the Government of India was intended to relieve distress and to prevent the occurrence of famines as far as possible. Under pressure of public opinion a few steps were taken to help rural areas by means of the institution of the Departments of Agriculture and Cooperation. But these departments have had a subordinate place both from the point of view of their status and resources, and in spite of honest intentions have been able only to touch the fringe of the problem.

Slow Change in Outlook

This limited outlook had to be changed by the force of circumstances during the period 1921 to 1937. This was partly due to the effect of rapid changes regarding the functions of the state in economic life in the west, which were revolutionzing the attitude of the people in England in these matters. *Laissez faire* was dead even in England and state intervention in economic activities had come to stay. No longer could the British authorities stop the extension of the conception of the state in economic life in India which was hitherto desired by leaders of public opinion, and which could now be expressed to a greater degree than before under the Montague scheme of constitutional changes. In spite of this, it must be pointed out that the rigidity of the old conception in Indian administration was so strong, that the desired change required a process of education of the authorities in India, at a time when the western world was witnessing rapid changes in their economic life and organization.

Process of Education

(a) Industrial Progress

During the War the British authorities realised for the first time that a stronger industrial India was a greater military asset to the Empire. This led to the appointment of the Industrial Commission under the guidance of the man who controlled the Department of Munitions in India during the War, Sir Thomas Holland.

The possibilities of industrial development in the country were fully surveyed by this Commission. But the change in policy was not possible until what is known as the Fiscal Autonomy Convention was suggested by the Parliamentary Committee which considered the Government of India Act, 1919. In view of this, the Indian Fiscal Commission was appointed in 1921, with the result that the policy of Discriminating Protection recommended by them was adopted by the Government of India and the Indian Legislative Assembly in 1923, and we had the first Protection Act with reference to the steel industry in 1924. Since then we have had the developmnt of several other industries by this policy, some of which would not have come into existence but for such assistance.

(b) Railways

The Acworth Committee on Railways which reported in 1921 recommended among other things state management of railways, owned by the state. They also suggested several ways by which railway extension and improvement could be carried out and industries dependent on railways could be developed.

(c) Roads

A few years later the Committee in Road Development reported as a result of which we have now a special fund started for the purpose, out of which the development and improvement of roads are being financed.

(d) Agriculture

The Royal Commission on Agriculture surveyed the whole field of agricultural life in the country and issued a report which will remain a classic document for students of Indian Agriculture for many years to come. This gave an impetus to the Departments of Agriculture to work more actively and thoroughly for the development of agriculture. The Imperial Council of Agricultural Research came into existence as a result of the Commission's recommendations and is trying to co-ordinate research in agriculture, animal husbandry and marketing.

(e) Banking

The Banking Enquiry Committee brought to light the serious want of co-ordination between indigenous banking and modern banking, and also emphasized the need for the development of rural banking which had also received attention at the hands of the Agricultural Commission.

Partly due to the reform in banking emphasised by these bodies and partly due to the need for a Reserve Bank of India pointed out by the Royal Commission on Currency and Exchange it was decided to bring into existence such a bank. The first attempt to create such a bank met with a failure on account of constitutional difficulties. The Reserve Bank of India which has now been brought into existence, is charged among other things with the duty of findings ways and means, in due course, to develop rural banking on the one hand and to link up indigenous bankers with modern banks in the cities. Some steps in this direction are under consideration.

(f) Rural Debt

Whereas these efforts may prove of some benefit in the future the difficulties of the farmers regarding their debt became serious due to the depression and consequent fall in the prices of agricultural produce. In view of this steps were taken by several Provincial Governments by legislation to relieve the farmer of his debt to some extent. At the same time Land Mortgage Banks have been brought into existence under state auspices to give long term loans to farmers under certain conditions.

(g) Labour

With the development of industries in the country which was contemplated by some of the measures mentioned above, problems of labour were likely to be created. The Royal Commission on Labour went into these problems and as a result of their recommendations labour legislation has been revised in recent years.

Theoretical Change in the Conception of the State

Some of the steps mentioned above indicate the general tendency towards a broader conception of the functions of the state in economic life rather than an achievement in direct benefit to the people. Some of them have been too recent for us to be able to trace their effects; some of them on the other hand are very narrow in their scope so far as the solution of the problem which they are attacking is concerned. In any case the mass of voluminous literature which these Commissions and Commtttees have produced during these years have at least resulted in the awakening of ideas, both among the public and the authorities which may be summed up by the statement that by this long drawn out process of education, the conception of the state in economic life has been made broader, and the state in India now accepts its duty to take positive steps for the prosperity of the people in addition to the maintenance of security.

THE STRUGGLES OF THE PERIOD, 1921-1937, AND THE CLASH OF IDEALS AND METHODS AT PRESENT AND IN THE IMMEDIATE FUTURE*

New Ideas in Practice

During the period 1921-1937 the state in India as we saw before was altered to some extent in its structure. Those functions which if properly carried out were likely to result in economic progress like agriculture, industries, education, sanitation and so on were in the hands of the Provinces, who it was expected would be in a better position to manage these affairs by being in direct contact with the people. In spite of the gradual change in the

* Lecture III, 13-10-1937.

conception of the duty of the state towards the people which we have seen, the good intentions of the framers of the Government of India Act, 1919, were defeated in practice, by the financial provisions of that Act which left rigid and limited sources of revenue to the Provinces and the elastic sources of revenues to the Central Government. This resulted in widespread discontent. The discontent among the Provincial Governments themselves was partly allayed by the suspension of the provincial contributions which they were expected to pay under the financial arrangements then made.

Discontent among the Public

The discontent among the different legislatures in the country and among the public at their inability to achieve anything substantial under the New Constitutional scheme took another form. They realized more than ever that economic progress was bound up in may respects with political liberty, and that in the absence of the latter the former could not be achieved. They realized in other words that progressive realization of self-government in India was in substance a hollow formula, making it difficult for them to achieve reasonable progress in any direction. The progressive element in Indian politics as represented by the Swaraj party which joined the legislatures in 1924, retired in disgust from these bodies, and concentrated their energies in the organization of a politico-economic movement, in the hope of ultimately changing the existing order of things. The Swadeshi movement which was started as early as 1907, now became one of the chief planks of this political organization. It took the form of an intense propaganda for hand-spinning and hand-weaving of cotton, so much so, that the *charkha* came to be considered as the symbol of political freedom. The movement can be construed in one sense as calculated to give useful employment to the idle energies of innumerable cultivators in the country during the off season. The movement could also be construed as a method by which the people may be taught to develop and encourage local industries even at some sacrifice. It could also have a political lever in as much as, if it succeeded in reducing British imports to this country, it was also likely to succeed in impressing upon the British authorities the need for loosening their political control over this country. In order to make the movement popular, the use of khaddar by all classes of people rich and poor, was preached with a fair amount of success; in as much as, khaddar became a fashion, and in course of time the khaddar uniform came to be considered in the words of Pandit Jawaharlal Nehru 'the livery of our freedom.'

The Civil Disobedience Movement

This movement later took the form of the boycott of British goods which was organized on a large scale and for some time affected our foreign trade considerably. When these methods did not succeed they were ultimately supplemented by the Civil Disobedience Movement which was an organized protest on a mass scale against the existing regime. In the early stages the movement took the form of breaking the salt laws, thus showing that the system of taxation in the country was unsuited to the condition of the masses. This politico-economic movement called forth an organisation involving sacrifice on the part of large numbers of people of various ranks in the country, which can be compared only to the sacrifice which nations demand of their subjects in time of war, with the exception that the movement was carried on, on the principle of non-violence. Whatever the drawbacks of the movement, it succeeded in creating a mass awakening among the people of the country for a more decent economic existence, to achieve which a determined effort in the political sphere was considered necessary.

The Economic Basis of the Movement

We are not concerned with the political aspects of this struggle. The economic basis of it however, needs to be explained. In the history of most countries revolutionary movements have had usually an economic background. We need not refer for example, in detail to the misery of the French peasants in the Bourbons regime which led to the French Revolution; nor need we refer to the exploitation of the masses in Czarist Russia which ultimately resulted in the sudden destruction of that regime. It has rightly or wrongly been felt among large classes of people in this country that under British rule during the last 150 years, though life and property have been more secure than ever, it has been to a large extent a life without interest. The peace and security guaranteed to the average Indian by the British sword has resulted in a large increase of population, without a proportionate increase in the resources of the people. With the vast potential resources of the country comparatively undeveloped; with the increasing man power of the country in a state of comparative idleness, we were bound to witness a situation in which life should either decay because of want of interest, or rebel because of a desire for a better existence. It is possible by a large array of statistics to indicate progress here and progress there, in the production of the country. The progress must however be in relative terms. First, in relation to the increasing numbers of the people, second in relation to the new types of wants and requirements which came into vogue in this country due to Western contact. Third, in relation to the technological advances in other parts of the world. If we did not keep pace with such progress in the rest of the world, we were bound to be relatively backward. The apathy of the state led to a situation in which such progress could not be achieved.

The Act of 1935

While the national consciousness was thus being roused with leaders of public opinion in jail, the British authorities evolved the Government of India Act of 1935. This ingenious piece of legislation which is full of contradictions, which compromises principles, and which pleases nobody in this country, has created more problems for the country than it solved. The Provinces are now supposed to be independent units in charge of certain defined functions. To all obvious appearances they have unlimited capacity to develop the resources of the people. But the Act restricts them in a variety of ways in any forward action. One of the main difficulties is financial. The resources left at the disposal of the provinces are too meagre for any bold scheme of reforms. The share of income tax which has been theoretically assigned to them is not likely to be received by them for at least five years to come, and the period may be longer still. This relief is dependent mainly on the improvement in railway finance which however, is far from showing any substantial improvement. These somewhat cumbrous arrangements are mainly due to the conception of the state regarding security. The defence services have to be maintained by the Government of India and that Government should have therefore, sufficiently large and secure sources of revenue to maintain its military establishments. It is only after satisfying its need, that the Government of India can think of releasing surplus resources, if any, for the use of the provinces. In other words, provincal prosperity is thus subordinated to central security.

Financial Difficulties under the New Regime

It was the realization of this fact that the Act of 1935 so restricts the freedom of the elected ministers in the Provinces and that it is not possible for them to satisfy the growing demand in the country for economic improvements, that led to the hesitation among the majority party in the country to accept office under the New Constitution. We thus had a most unparalleled situation in the history of democratic institutions, in as much as, power was refused by those who alone could exercise it; the tension was eased by tact on both sides. Apart from the political significance of recent events in the country, the fact remains that in almost all provinces, the first budgets under the New Act have proved the urgent need of severe retrenchment on the one hand and of additional taxation on the other. If the responsible ministers that are now charged with the carrying out of governmental functions under certain restrictions are going to achieve direct or indirect economic progress by means of schemes such as (1) free and compulsory primary education; (2) extension of sanitary and medical facilities; (3) relief to the agriculturists from the pressure of land revenue and debt; (4) encouragement to the agriculturists in a variety of ways to do their best on the farm; (5) the development of small industries chiefly in the rural areas and so on—if these and such other items of progress are to be carried out, drastic steps for retrenchment as well as new avenues of taxation will become necessary. This is so all the more because by the provisions of the 1935 Act, it is not possible for the ministers to reduce expenditure in certain cases, say with reference to the salaries of the Imperial Services.

The Congress Ideals of Service

In spite of such severe handicaps, the determination to achieve as much good as is possible under the present circumstances is reflected in ideas which are novel in their conception, and still more novel in their practical application. Not only in the history of Indian Administration but also in the history of other countries, the desire to infuse a spirit of service in place of the current practice of large pecuniary gains, among the persons who are called upon to run the administration, is unique, and owes its existence chiefly to the anomalies created by the Act of 1935. This is reflected not only in the voluntary acceptance of small salaries by Congress Ministers, but also in suggestions for making education self-supporting. This determination to do best against odds may succeed in tapping unknown and undeveloped resources or energies in the process. While wishing the best of success to those who have undertaken these difficult tasks, the question nevertheless remains whether such a spirit of service can be maintained for a period long enough to reach the desired goal. The question would not arise if those who are trying to infuse this spirit held undisputed power throughout the country. The question does arise because of the absence of such power and the consequent fact that tendencies in other parts of the country where Congress Ministers are not in power may not be in the same direction. Though it is possible to imagine that the forces which the Congress policy is likely to let loose, are bound to overtake in due course the other Provinces where Congress is not in power at the moment, yet it is also possible to imagine that the existence of different policies in the other Provinces may prove obstructive to the realization of the new spirit of service with the help of which Congress hopes to achieve its purposes.

The Central Government

Besides, though it is possible to influence to some extent the non-Congress Provinces by these ideas, the difficulty of doing so, so far as the Central Government is concerned are almost insuperable. The Central Government controls economic policy in essential matters such as the protection of large industries, the making of commercial treaties, the control of currency, exchange and banking, and the control of the railway system. It is possible to imagine that difficulties may arise in carrying out the economic policy of a Province, if the policy of the Central Government in other related aspects is not in the same direction. As we have seen before, the Central Government is going to be constituted as a triarchical state, in which it will be impossible for any single party to have a distinct majority. The Federal Ministers of tomorrow will therefore, be members of a coalition government, and like all coalitions will compromise principles, will not be able to devise thoroughgoing measures and will also be faced with instability of power. Assuming that the Federation will be an established fact, we must also assume as a corollary that members of the Congress party will not be members of a coalition at the Centre as in the Provinces, and will therefore be in opposition. It must also be pointed out that the so-called elected Ministers of the Federal Government will be considerably handicapped in achieving progress, as in many spheres of economic activity their actions will be subject to the consent of the Viceroy, which may in other words mean either the consent of the Central Bureaucracy or of the India Office.

Can the Spirit of Service be maintained for long?

Another difficulty in the way of the Congress ideals of service is likely to be felt in course of time. So far as we can see, the Congress does not aim at a thorough overhaulting of the economic structure of society in the country. So long as life in other walks of life continues to be organized on the principle of pecuniary gains, there is bound to be a strong impetus to the best brains in the country to go in for those occupations which assure them such pecuniary gains. In the long run therefore, it will be difficult to maintain an equilibrium in the quality of the persons who wield political or administrative power, with the impetus of pecuniary gains reduced or removed from the field. No Government can subsist long with the deterioration in the quality of its personnel, and the Congress is bound to be faced with the dilemma, in view of the peculiar paradoxes of our situation.

Clash of Ideals and Methods

This brief analysis of the nature of the state in the country, that we are about to have, and this attempt at some anticipation of its possible working reveals the unfortunate fact, that we are about to pass through a period of transition, which will be characterised by a clash of ideals and methods, and therefore, by divergent results in different parts of the country. We are bound to have the creation of new desires and aspirations on the one hand, but in view of the clash referred to above, we are also likely to have the creation of new inequalities and new economic problems, which will tax the ingenuity of the future statesmen of the country to solve. From the point of view of the economic progress of the country as of progress in other directions, the future historian of India may have to record a chapter of fierce struggles and even of confusion and chaos, if this transition period for any reason becomes long. With the rapid march of events in the country in recent years and the spirit of nationalism which now pervades the younger generation, which is likely to be intensified by the ideals of the Congress which will be in practice in some parts of the country, the citizen of the future will be impatient, if this transition is prolonged making the realization of national aspirations difficult. If the future state in India, is to achieve economic progress, even though divided into several parts for the purpose of convenience, it should be guided by one common spirit, instead of being cut up in compartments which move in different directions. The structure of the future state of India may therefore, have to be radically changed if it is to fulfill the desire for economic advance. One of two alternatives are possible; we may have in course of time the domination of Congress ideals by force of numbers and organization as well as by the spirit of service in practice. The second alternative is a reconciliation of different points of view existing in the country, evolving a new state in which all may have a place for the common good.

The Indian States

In this discussion we have so far mainly confined ourselves to the state or states in British India in their relation to economic life and progress in the country. We observed at an earlier stage that the Indian States though constituted on different lines are influenced in their policy to some extent by changes that occur in British India. In fact, some of the larger aspects of economic policy, such as the currency and banking policy or the tariff policy of the country have been all along determined by the Government of India, and have affected the economic life of the Indian States as much as in British India. In the matter of railways, though some of the railways are owned and controlled by the states, in other cases, the bigger railways pass through states' territories, and all of these are coordinated by the Railway Board. It was the existence of these factors among other things, which perhaps made it possible to embody the conception of a Federal India in the Act of 1935. These All-India functions will hereafter be under the control of the Central Government, where the representatives of the states will have a substantial share, along with those of British India. Internally, however, the states will have full jurisdiction in other matters with reference to their subjects. In other words, whereas the economic policy of the Provinces will hereafter be shaped by elected ministers, that of the States will continue to be shaped by the rulers themselves. This contrast in the Indian political and economic situation is obviously due mainly to historical reasons. In view of progressive movements in British India however, it is likely that gradual changes towards the adoption of representative institutions by the states is likely to follow. The people of the Indian states cannot long be kept away from the fulfilment of their natural desire to fall in line with the people of British India, and to be able to determine their own economic future. This process need not be revolutionary; because already the states have in some cases instituted Advisory Councils which can be gradually replaced by representative bodies. In other words, the absolute rule now prevalent in Indian states may have to be gradually replaced by and take the form of limited monarchy, of which we have a model in the King-Emperor. Whereas considerable progress has been achieved in the economic sphere in recent times in larger states like Hyderabad and Mysore in the shape of large schemes of educational, agricultural, and industrial development, we are likely to find that the production and distribution of economic resources in the states may be in course of time determined, more according to the wishes of the people themselves than those of the rulers, however benevolent their intentions.

The Future Outlook

It is obvious from this analysis of the present economical and political tendencies in the country that things are at present in a flux; and that therefore, it is not possible to give even an approximately correct estimate of the way in which economic progress will be shaped in the near future. The only thing that can be asserted with confidence is that national forces have become sufficiently strong to assert themselves, and that we are passing through a process of transition in the political sphere, which will have far-reaching effects on our economic life and policy. When we have gone through that period of transition, let us hope that India shall be one, both geographically and politically, able to determine and execute her economic policy as one united unit. Social and economic planning will not then be on paper but will also be in practice. In the process of achieving that unity, India will certainly be a stronger and healthier nation devoid of its present weaknesses. And let us hope that the free atmosphere of our political life will be accompanied by a higher economic level in production and a better economic arrangement in distribution.

What is Wrong with Our Economic Situation?*

THE PROBLEM—INTERNAL AND EXTERNAL ENVIRONMENT

The Scope of the Series

THE object of this series of articles is to review the leading tendencies affecting economic life and problems in recent times, so that it may be possible for the layman to understand broadly the nature of the economic problem before the country and the efforts made to solve it. The layman is naturally bewildered and confused as to the many direct and indirect forces which are now creating new problems for all of us; he is merely feeling the pinch of these difficulties and is not able to see a ray of hope out of the same.

In this article we shall concentrate on some of the extra economic forces which have created a new environment in which our economic life has to be shaped. This environment is partly internal and partly external. It is with this background that we shall review in the second article the ideologies of the Indian National Congress in the economic sphere and the efforts of Congress Governments to implement the same. An effort will be made in the third article to analyse the nature of the prevailing unrest in the country and to examine the fundamental causes of the same, so that it may be possible to judge a given remedy in its true perspective. This analysis will be supplemented by a discussion of the attitude of Capital and Labour towards our economic problem and towards the efforts to solve it. This will enable the reader to appreciate some of the frictions and tensions through which we are passing, the early removal of which is obviously in the national interests.

Effects of War

It would suffice to say that the British regime in this country for over 200 years was characterised by a policy of economic

* Series of four articles published in a Bombay Journal during 1949.

neglect and consequent arrested development for the country as a whole. The comparative poverty of the country made it difficult for us to bear the effect of the process of systematic squeezing which was effectively carried out by the British Administration, in order to divert our limited resources to the war effort. In other words the war left us poorer in many respects than before. The advent of political independence made us forget to some extent the economic misery in which we were involved because of the effects of the war. To the layman the obvious effects of the war in his day-to-day life are felt in the form of scarcity of his daily requirements on the one hand and of rising prices on the other hand.

In the Wake of Independence

The joy of independence was however marred by the effects of partition followed by mass murders in the Punjab. This added to the prevailing economic insecurity and reduced the productive effort in consequence. At the same time it increased the pressure on the limited economic resources of the New Government in order to help the refugees from danger and rehabilitate them to useful walks of life. The long-drawn-out conflict in Kashmir now happily ended, and the equally long-drawn-out tension in Hyderabad also now set at rest, added substantially to the difficulties of the situation inasmuch as the strained resources of the National Government as well as its energies had to be diverted to these urgent problems and adequate attention could not be paid to the fundamental economic problems of the country.

Feudalism

The loyalty of the Indian Princes to the British Rulers was recognised by them even while quitting power inasmuch as by emphasising the Theory of Paramountcy which was supposed to lapse with the lapse of British Power, the Princes technically became independent. The Dominion of India was thus presented at its very birth with a problem which if not solved without delay, would have created many ulcers in the body politic, with obvious repercussions in the economic life of the country. Thanks to the sagacity, initiative and drive of Sardar Patel, the Princes are going out of the picture like a pack of cards, making way for the introduction of democratic institutions and the levelling up of the administration of these areas to the standards of Provinces, either by merger or by the formation of Unions and so on. The change in the political map of the country thus brought about has its obvious effects on the economic map of the country. We shall now be economically united as never before and in due course it should be possible to mobilise and develop the economic resources of United India in the interests of the people of the country. For the present, however, these revolutionary changes have added to the complexity of the economic problem.

External Forces

So far as the external forces are concerned they have taken a shape which was entirely unexpected by most people in this country. The recovery of the war-torn world, particularly in Europe has been rather slow. The destruction of industrial equipment and the consequent dislocation of trade has created immense problems for European countries some of which are involved in serious economic difficulties. The problem of scarcity and inflation from which we suffer is common to them though there are bound to be differences in degree. Heroic efforts are being made for their recovery both by the peoples of the U.K. and of Western European countries with the powerful support of the U.S.A. which has freely placed huge resources at their disposal in the form of Marshall Aid. The possibilities of having a settled economic life are however marred by the fears of atomic war and the race for armaments, which are characteristic of the policies of some of the leading powers in spite of the efforts of the UNO. The meetings of several bodies of the UNO have brought into greater relief the prevailing bitterness between the leading powers, and the world is left to guess the time when the spark may apply to start a conflagration. This situation is not conducive to greater production for peaceful enjoyment. At the same time nearer home we find a turbulent situation with recent events in China, in Indonesia and in Burma. The repercussions of these forces on the economic life of this country are not easy to determine. But it is clear that we cannot escape from them and have to be prepared to face them. The existence of the communist menace in the form of organised efforts to create economic dislocation by violence is a symptom of these external forces which must be taken note of in any consideration of the economic problems of the country.

Apart from this, the existence of these forces in other countries has led to certain immediate difficulties for us. For example, the problem of sterling balances and the way in which we can realise the same have disillusioned those who once thought that the accumulation of these balances was a great boon to us. Similarly, the difficulties of getting capital goods or machinery for industrial and other development have upset the plans both of Government and private enterprise and brought home to us our dependence on foreign help in this matter. The new dependence on foreign sources for large supplies of food has introduced an unusual feature in our balance of payments. Some of these difficulties have compelled us to borrow large amounts from the International Monetary Fund and the World Bank and to utilise some of the available sterling balances for consumers' goods instead of capital goods.

Relations with Pakistan

So far as our relations with Pakistan are concerned we started almost in a state of undeclared war on 15 August 1947. There was complete lack of mutual understanding and there was a plethora of mutual suspicions. The circumstances under which partition came into existence and those which followed the partition in the Punjab were likely to result in a tension of this nature. Fortunately, better counsels seem to be prevailing and the recent improvement in the political relations between the two Dominions seem to be having a more healthy effect on their economic relations. Though there is a lot to do yet before normal economic progress between the two Dominions could be restored, it is to be hoped that the new tendency will work in the right direction. In any case, it must be admitted that the tearing off of a large portion of the country by the formation of a separate Dominion at short notice, created serious dislocation in our economic life and relations.

The New Environment

These internal and external forces which together have created a new environment in which we have to live and work, are responsible for creating an economic problem for the country which is unparalleled in its complexity as well as in its magnitude. We are passing through all the difficulties of a transition from war to peace; of a transition from dependence to independence with the effects of partition added to it; of a transition from feudalism to democracy in about one-third the area of the country. In other words, we are passing through a great political peaceful revolution, which will provide absorbing material for the future historian. The pangs of this transition superimposed on the sub-normal economic situation in which we were left at the end of the war are difficult to bear. To chalk out and carry out an economic policy with a view to develop our resources and help the masses of the people in their economic misery under such complex conditions is a super-human task with which the National Government is faced.

Social and Economic Revolution

Before the people of the country were able to reconcile themselves to these tremendous forces which came almost simultaneously with bewildering rapidity, the Congress Governments thought of putting into practice their ideologies, and their election manifestos with a view to bringing about a new social and economic order, for which they had dreamt so long and for realising which they had developed an attitude of impatience due to the life of continued frustration in which they had to live under the British regime. Whether all those good things which the Congress had promised while in Opposition should be immediately implemented while in Power, and that too in the midst of the New Environment which they inherited is a question which has not been seriously raised among those now at the helm of affairs. It is not inappropriate to inquire whether while the people were not yet adjusted to the unusual uncertainties of the New Environment, it was wise to introduce a series of social and economic changes by legislation or otherwise in a short time amounting to another revolution. Without questioning the excellent motives of the authors of the social and economic revolution on which the Congress Governments have set their heart, one may still inquire whether the timing and speed of these changes are such as could be assimilated by the people, or whether they are likely to add to the existing dislocation and uncertainty caused by the New Environment referred to above. For an answer to these queries, we must wait for the next article.

CONGRESS IDEOLOGY AND EFFORTS

Formative Stage

It is difficult to summarise in brief the ideology of the Congress in the Economic sphere, partly becauce it may be said to be still in the process of formation. Though several resolutions have been passed by the Congress on its economic programme and reports on the same have also been issued, it is true to say that a clear conception of its ideology is slowly emerging from the actions which the Congress Governments are taking. We may however say in brief that the Congress aims at raising the standard of life of the people by using that the masses are able to have the essentials of life without difficulty, that they are anxious to remove gross inequalities among different classes of society and make available to all equal opportunities for economic gains, without accepting the Socialist ideals. In order to achieve this the Congress has in view comparative self-sufficiency in economic affairs particularly in the production of essential goods such as food and cloth. In this as in other spheres, the Congress ideology is dominated by Gandhian ideals, though in practice it has not been found possible to implement the Gandhian ideals in full. What is likely is that an economic ideology suited to our conditions is being gradually developed. It will be a mixture of Western influence on the one hand and of Gandhian ideals on the other, both working on the indigenous economic and social structure.

In order to assess this new tendency fully one may have to analyse in detail the report of the Economic Programme Committee of the A.I.C.C. on the one hand and the Policy Statements issued from time to time by the Ministers of the Government of India on the other. Whereas it is not possible to undertake this task in this article, it would be enough to say that whereas the former lays greater emphasis on Gandhian ideals, the latter take due note of the realities of the situation. It is well known however that in the various statements made by Ministers and other spokesmen of the Government of India during recent times, there has been some divergence of emphasis on the economic policy of the National Government. Some of these statements seem to have had unfortunate repercussions on different classes of people. For example, the capitalist class is known to have become nervous at certain pronouncements of certain Ministers. This is supposed to have created an adverse psychological effect on production at a time when more production is needed for the country. Some of these psychological factors have been taken into account more recently, particularly during the budget discussions, and efforts have been made by the Ministers of the Government of India to remove suspicions and to assure those concerned that the policy of the Government would be to encourage production and not be gudied by any abstract ideology. The very fact that these developments have taken place, within the short period which has elapsed since the National Government came into power confirms the general proposition laid down that the conception of the economic ideology of Congress is yet emerging and has to be understood in the light of actions that are being taken.

Whereas it would therefore require some time before a competent observer can generalise with confidence and interpret with understanding the economic ideology of the Congress, we shall briefly enumerate some of the more important measures of economic and social reform which the Congress is attempting or is about to attempt in the near future. This will enable us to have a rough picture of the Congress effort to bring about a new economic and social structure in the country.

Agriculture

So far as the principal industry of the country is concerned, viz., agriculture, measures have been introduced for the protection of the rights of tenants and for relief of indebtedness. Steps have been taken to develop the Cooperative Movement as an adjunct to help the agriculturists in their work. Legislation has been passed for the abolition of Zamindari in several Provinces, though the implementation of the schemes is taking some time because of obvious difficulties in carrying them out. The "Grow More Food" campaigns have been designed to help the agriculturist in a variety of ways to grow more food. Some useful work has been done in connection with the improvement of cattle and particularly for the dairy industry. The hope of helping agriculturists with artificial fertilizers is also likely to be realised. The new fertilizer factory at Sindri is due to function soon and its products will be made available to the agriculturist. A large number of river valley projects and hydro-electric schemes have been planned and some of them have been put in operation. As and when these schemes materialise they are likely to make large areas cultivable with the help of irrigation which these schemes will make possible. The river valley projects will also develop other industries and the electricity schemes will help considerably both in small-scale and large-scale industries as well as in supplying electrical energy for domestic use even in rural areas areas. At the same time large areas of land are being reclaimed with a view to making them cultivable. It is hoped that by a combination of all these efforts our dependence on imports of food will disappear by 1951, after which it is proposed that food will not be imported except under very serious circumstances.

Industry

In the field of industry Government has announced its intention of undertaking certain key industries and of helping others. This raised the problem of nationalisation of industries, about which diverse views exist in different quarters. The exact connotation of nationalisation of industries, i.e. the extent of State participation in the form of ownership and management of industries has not been made clear. Again vague ideas exist among the public about this move. More recently attempts have been made to remove the existing doubts by saying that for want of adequate personnel Government is not likely to nationalise industries in the immediate future. Apart from the uncertainties associated with this problem, it is true that Government has been planning to start new steel factories, that it has taken the major share in encouraging overseas shipping and aviation companies, and is undertaking large schemes of river valley projects and hydro-electricity concerns to which reference has been made above.

Labour

Simultaneously, considerable effort has been made to improve the condition of industrial workers partly by legislation and partly by executive action. The introduction of minimum wages, the settlement of disputes re. wages and dearness allowances and the working of Industrial and Labour Courts have all tended towards the gradual improvement of the position of industrial workers. Committees have been working with a view to devising schemes of profit sharing between capital and labour and also with a view to determining fair wages. Similar efforts for agricultural labour are under contemplation. All these efforts are giving the labourer his due place in the scheme of production and has introduced a new element in the economic structure of the country. Efforts are also being made to provide housing to industrial workers. Housing schemes for refugees have also been made on a large-scale.

Educational and Social Reform

Side by side with these measures fundamental changes in the field of education have been attempted. The introduction of basic education, adult literacy campaigns, the reform and control of secondary education by the State and the creation of Regional Linguistic Universities are instances of the attempt in this direction. So far as science and technology are concerned, special efforts have been made to develop the existing technical institutions by giving liberal grants, to encourage research in these subjects and to start a chain of national laboratories in each scientific subject in different parts of the country. Special arrangements have also been made for military, naval and air training such as the creation of the National War Academy near Poona. In order to systematise University education with reference to our new requirements a Universities Commission under the Chairmanship of Dr. Radhakrishnan is now working and its recommendations may be the beginning of a change in this field of education.

Equally important efforts have been made in the field of social reform. For example, the Harijan problem has now ceased to attract attention inasmuch as problems such as temple entry and removal of untouchability or encouragement of backward classes in other directions seem to have been taken up systematically. Changes in marriage and divorce laws have been attempted and a big effort to codify Hindu Law is being made. The introduction of health schemes on the one hand and social welfare schemes such as the Prohibition Policy on the other are intended to bring about the necessary social reform in different directions.

Economic and Social Revolution

This rough catalogue of measures in different aspects of life is obviously not exhaustive. To attempt an exhaustive list of measures undertaken or about to be undertaken would require elaborate research. It is sufficiently illustrative however to show that the National Governments have in a very short time embarked on a multiplicity of schemes affecting the very structure of society, aiming thereby to bring about a social and economic revolution in the shortest possible time. Without in any way questioning the validity or utility of any given scheme, one may say that these schemes present to the layman a bewildering maze inasmuch as he is not able to follow the significance of these attempts nor to appreciate the need for some of these radical changes. It is obvious that existing relations between different parties both in agriculture and industry have been seriously affected creating new problems and also creating doubts as to the efficacy of some of these measures, in any case regarding their speed. This new transition from the old social and economic order to which people were accustomed to the new system to be created has its own inevitable pangs in the form of tensions between different groups who must take time to adjust to these changes. On top of the existing transition from war to peace, from dependence to independence, from undivided to divided India, to which we have not yet adjusted ourselves, the creation of this new transition in the social and economic life of the country has led to a situation which requires both fuller information, clearer interpretation and easy understanding before the people can be expected to reconcile themselves to such fundamental changes. It must be said that people have inadequate information about these efforts and their effects, that their interpretation is either vague or incorrect; in any case, not as clear as it ought to be.

Social and Economic Research

These changes provide absorbing material to the research worker in economic and social fields. The research worker is however not always able to cope with the speed of these events, partly because he has not the necessary resources to carry out the research and also because he is often neglected in so far as the new scheme of things are concerned. If we take into account the attention paid for training and research in science and technology and the large amounts of expenditure incurred by Governments, it will be obvious that they have not realised the parallel need for a continuous examination in a scientific spirit by detached persons of changing economic and social phenomena. Whereas due to the various steps referred to above, we have an unparalleled laboratory of economic and social phenomena, for a proper investigation of which an army of trained workers could be usefully employed in the national interest, we have at present only a handful of such workers most of whom do not receive that encouragement and support in their work which is desirable. If the National Governments realise that just as in the technical field, in the economic field also expert investigation has its place and the lay politician should be humble enough to be guided by scientific advice instead of assuming for himself all the wisdom and knowledge in all branches of knowledge, then we shall have the true beginnings of a proper understanding of the economic and social changes which are brought about by measures of this kind. Failure to provide for this understanding would involve considerable difficulties for the Governments themselves, inasmuch as the uniformed voter of tomorrow will be called upon to decide these complicated and vital issues at the elections with half baked ideas and will be liable to be misled by political passions or interested slogans.

ECONOMIC UNREST

In the preceding articles we have surveyed the various external and internal forces which together have created what we have described the new environment involving a lot of friction in the existing relations in the economic sphere because of transitions of different kinds. We have also reviewed in brief the ideology and efforts of Congress Governments intended to solve the Economic Problem and have come to the conclusion that in their laudable efforts to bring about a social and economic revolution in a short time, they have added one more transition problem on top of the existing ones. Though the ultimate effects of the measures of the Congress may be good, so far as the present is concerned the question is raised whether the people were prepared for the speed with which a multiplicity of measures affecting the economic and social structure of society could be effectively carried out, at a time when people's minds were not prepared due to the continued suffering through which they were passing because of the events of the preceding few years. In order to appreciate this point we shall attempt in this article to analyse briefly the nature of the economic unrest which has developed among different classes of people and to try to assess the effects of the new measures as a solution of this unrest.

Effects of War

The general poverty of the masses of the people of this country is so proverbial that it does not require any elaborate statistical proof. The undue attention on urban areas and systematic neglect of rural areas which was a feature of the British Administration intensified the poverty problem of the country. During the war the British Administration found itself in the urgent necessity of utilising the resources of the country irrespective either of the wishes of the people or their capacity. In spite of the opposition of the Indian National Congress, they succeeded in organising the resources of the country in such a manner that they could be put to the maximum advantage for the prosecution of the war. The way in which the formal accounting of this process was done has deceived many inasmuch as an impression has been created, particularly by British propaganda, that Great Britain paid large amounts towards the prosecution of the war for India and in the defence of India. Whatever the formal method of accounting, the fact remains that so far as the materials and services of war were concerned they were taken out of the existing deficit economy of the country. In the first instance the share of Great Britain was treated as a loan to be repaid after the war. So far as the immediate effects are concerned the deduction from Indian resources of the materials required for the war effort both on Indian and on British account resulted in a process of systematic squeezing which left the country in a state of economic stagnation, the like of which was not known before. The common man felt the effects of this situation in the form of increasing scarcity of essential articles of life such as food and cloth and even shelter, and an equally increasing rise in the money price of his daily requirements. In a country which is accustomed to mass sufferings without organised revolt, these sufferings did not bring out that vocal reaction which would be characteristic of any other country. But the effects of the situation were bound to be far reaching and sure to reflect on the economic life of the country sooner or later. Whereas the masses of the people in rural areas did not protest except when roused to activity by Kisan Sabhas or similar organisations on occasions, the industrial workers in urban areas who were already organised in the form of trade unions, asserted themselves and demanded better conditions of life. At each stage of their fight for better conditions they got more conscious of their strength and utilised it for further struggles for still better conditions. The middle classes on the other hand found themselves gradually forced to reduce their standard of life because their income did not rise in any proportion to the rise in prices.

Effect on Producing Capacity

The effects on the manpower of the country from the point of view of efficiency as producers can well be imagined when this process developed from bad to worse over a series of years beginning from 1939. The worsening of the food situation as illustrated by the Bengal famine which led to deaths by starvation of large number, but which was also characterised by low nutritional level of many more whose cases have not been recorded, must have had adverse effects on the vitality and therefore the working capacity of millions of people. Similar defects regarding the scarcity of cloth have added to the inevitable unrest which must result from the absence of the necessaries of life for prolonged periods.

Effects of Partition

The reference to the scarcity of food and cloth is illustrative of similar scarcity of many other commodities which need not be discussed in detail; this is reflected in the prevailing high prices of most commodities. This unfortunate situation in which the country was involved as a consequence of the war was aggravated after the war was over by unexpected developments in the country. The widespread prevalence of riots in different parts of the country during 1946-47 created considerable tension making peaceful life difficult and rendering productive activity both in agriculture and industry somewhat shaken. The political discussions which were then going on regarding the future of the country created an element of uncertainty in the minds of the people. As an escape out of this difficult situation, when at least the partition of the country was agreed upon, for a time people thought that they will have independence with peace. Unfortunately for us, however, independence and partition were accompanied by the Punjab tragedy involving mass massacres and migration of millions of people from one Dominion to the other. The reactions of these events were far reaching and affected all parts of the country. Production suffered substantially at a time when greater production was the vital need of the country. Transport was strained at a time when it was needed as the principal adjunct to greater production and movement of commodities. The energies of the National Government were diverted to the huge problem of resettlement of refugees, and therefore they could not pay that undivided attention to the problem of economic regeneration of the masses of the people which they must have desired. The undeclared war in Kashmir and the prolonged tension in Hyderabad added to the same tendency, viz. of diversion of resources, energy and time away from the economic misery of the people.

Economic and Social Changes

However the Congress Governments both at the Centre and in the Provinces embarked upon a series of measures with a view to bringing about a social and economic revolution in the country. These measures have been briefly enumerated in the previous article. What is intended here is to consider briefly their immediate effects on the type of economic situation on which they were to operate. At a time when we had scarcely emerged from the evil effects of the war and still suffering from the evil effects of the partition and people's minds were not at rest due to the continuation and aggravation of economic misery, they were not prepared for sudden changes in their existing relations between different classes of people. What was wanted was more food and cloth and things of that nature along with peace and order before anything else could be considered. The new measures however created disturbances and shocks among the existing relations between creditors and debtors, between employers and employees, between landlords and tenants as well as between buyers and sellers. These shocks were not relieved by the uncertain economic policy in the field of controls. The working of controls had its own defects. The policy of decontrol was adopted in the hope that it would improve matters. It was however found to be worse than the evil which it was sought to remove. The reimposition of controls had naturally to be done at a much higher level of prices. The scarcity of food and cloth and other articles still continues and people are tired of red tape methods which inevitably accompany controls. They complain of difficulties in the distributive machinery. Serious efforts have been made to improve the control machinery. But these have not yet made adequate impression on the public mind. The prevalence of famines in certain large parts of the country have added to the existing difficulties. The mass of the people who are anxious to have a better state of affairs as speedily as the most ardent Congressman, fail to realise the effect of these measures in practice, because what they feel immediately are the sudden disturbances caused by these measures in the existing state of affairs. A sort of churning of the economic and social life of the people which has resulted on top of the existing unrest has led to serious questions in the minds of those who are able to think as to the direction in which we are moving.

Ray of Hope

This prevailing unrest has naturally been exploited by political and other groups in their own interests. This is reflected in the sharp division among organised labour. We have now three different organisations among labourers each trying to assert its claims over the others. One organisation is influenced by Socialist ideology, another by Communist ideology. The new labour organisation, I.N.T.U.C. is influenced by Congress ideology, and is naturally supported by Congress leaders. The recent failure of the Communist threat to paralyse the transport system of the country showed the strength of the Congress and Socialist groups in combination. The withdrawal of a Bill sponsored by the Central Government to make strikes in essential services illegal also shows the strength of the Government in its capacity to handle such situations. But nevertheless it indicates the latent forces in the country which are ready to take advantage of the economic misery of the people on which they naturally thrive. Recent utterances of Congress leaders show awareness of the fact that it is essential to remedy the economic ills without delay in order to preserve independence. And it is hoped that the available talents in the country will be utilised in this fight against economic evils irrespective of political leanings. The ray of hope is that though the efforts of the Congress so far have not yet made a significant effect on the prevailing economic unrest, they are determined to mobilise their resources with a view to removing economic evils as soon as possible. And if they are able to enlist both the sympathy and understanding and therefore the willing cooperation of the people as well as the services of all available people who can help, we may yet get out of the stagnation and build up a strong and united India, in spite of the unusual circumstances in which we find ourselves.

ATTITUDE OF CAPITAL AND LABOUR

We have so far briefly reviewed the nature of the economic unrest in the country as well as the type of solutions which the Congress Governments have been trying and the difficulties that have arisen in the process. We have reserved for a fuller treatment the attitude of capital and labour towards the new situation. Under democratic conditions, the consideration of this attitude is obviously important for problems which require the cooperation of all classes of people for appropriate remedies or measures which affect everybody.

Capitalist Attitude

The capitalist in this country as in other countries is working mainly on the basis of the profit motive. In this category we may include not only the industrialist but also the business man both large and small. During the war the capitalists got used to an unusually high rate of profits. In spite of the efforts of the Government to mop up excess profits due to the war by the Excess Profits Tax, it is well known that substantially large gains remained in the hands of the capitalists, partly because of the adoption of systematic black-marketing methods and also because of the widespread adoption of evasion of taxes. The Managing Agency System which is peculiar to this country gave unusual opportunities during this period to the unscrupulous Agent to make phenomenal gains. With the advantages thus obtained, the capitalist was anxious to utilise the new opportunities that he saw of industrial and other development when India became independent. He believed that it was his right to reap further benefits by exploiting the new opportunities for he naturally asked the question whether the Congress Governments should not reward him for the active or passive support he gave to Congress against its fight with the British.

The Disappointment of the Capitalist

The disappointment of the capitalist has been as great as were the hopes raised under the above circumstances. In the first place, along with others he did not realise that further industrial production in the country or even the continuation of the existing production after the war would not be easy because of the difficulties of obtaining machinery from foreign sources. Some of them who had great hopes of converting sterling balances into machinery were equaly disappointed, because they had not realised that these balances would be frozen and would be available in small instalments and would be used partly for consumers' goods. Besides these external forces, there were other powerful internal forces contributing to the disappointment of the capitalist. During the war the British Administration and the Indian Capitalist joined hands to keep industrial labour contented in order that the production required for the war was maintained at the desired level.

Dearness Allowances to offset rising cost of living, bonuses and other benefits were given liberally. The capitalist did not mind this. In fact, in some cases, he was encouraged in this, because if he did not use his war gains in this, they were likely to be taken up by the Government by way of E.P.T. The emoluments which labour thus obtained during the war developed a strong sense of solidarity among them and a consciousness of their importance and power. Labour was therefore not likely to give up these advantages after the war was over. In fact as was natural, labour organised itself to put a stiff resistance against the efforts of capitalists to reduce its rewards. Besides this natural desire to improve its own condition, the advent of the National Government gave the labour movement a further impetus, because the new Government was anxious to see that labour got reasonable conditions of life such as minimum wages, reduced working hours, better housing and sanitary facilities and other social benefits. The wage bill of the capitalist-employer direct or indirect went on increasing under these conditions after the war, at a time when he found that production could not be kept at a high level. The situation became somewhat uncomfortable for the capitalist, for schemes of profit-sharing and fair wages had to be considered on a footing of equality with representatives of labour. These tendencies made the capitalist realise the gradual weakening of his hold on the economic life of the country and the ultimate disappearance of opportunities to make large gains. These tendencies pre-suppose that the capitalist should be willing to work on minimum profits with maximum efficiency in the national interests more than for his own selfish requirements. Adjustment to this situation has naturally been difficult and has perhaps met with stout resistance from capitalists in general.

Relief in Taxation

The capitalists immediately began asking for relief in another direction, that is, from the prevailing high taxes. General complaints to the effect that taxes were so high that they took away all incentive for further production began to be heard from all quarters. The gradual tightening up of the administrative machinery for the collection of taxes and the public odium created against the evasion of taxes by the exposure of a few cases, led to an intensification of the campaign against high taxes. Falling production and the prevailing stagnation in the Investment Market helped the capitalist in this attitude, and they have at last succeeded in convincing Government that taxes must be reduced in order to help capital formation and give an impetus to the Investment Market. In spite of the gesture by the Finance Minister made in his Budget for 1949-50, the capitalist has realised that reduction in taxes cannot be substantial so as to restore his strength in his losing fight against labour. In fact, measures such as the limitation of dividends are intended to see that his gains do not go beyond limits.

Nationalisation

While the struggle of the capitalist against both labour and taxes continued, he found himself faced with the threat of nationalisation, thus depriving him of all potential opportunities for gains on which he counted. We find him therefore crying hoarse against the speeches of Ministers of the Government of India in which the capitalist methods are painted as undesirable in one way or another. The mistakes or inexperience of the present Government machinery in carrying out some of the existing nationalised services have been effectively utilised by the capitalist to sing the praise of private enterprise as the only efficient method of production. The continued stagnation in the Investment Market combined with falling production and the acknowledged inability of the Government to nationalise industries under present conditions mainly due to want of adequate personnel, have led to a situation, in which some soothing doses had to be given to the capitalist class, in order to persuade them to continue to function as producers and not to be afraid of nationalisation which should be treated only as a distant goal.

Reform of Capitalism

The above rapid survey of the attitude of the capitalist in recent times leads to the conclusion that capitalism in India is already on the defensive. Capitalists employ all the resources at their command to do public or private propaganda in their interests. This is indicated by the increasing control of the daily and weekly press by certain well-known capitalist groups, and the frequent contacts which are established by them with those in power at every available opportunity. It is possible that the capitalist class may succeed in its game for some time by these methods. But it has got to realise that if it wants to continue its existence as a socially useful class in future, the best line of defence for it is a re-adjustment of its attitude and methods of work to the new environment in which it finds itself. What is meant is that there should be a complete voluntary internal reform such as the abandonment of the monopolistic principle in the management of business concerns, due recognition of merit alone in such management by encouraging educated persons of ability, avoidance of waste and secret commissions, adoption of modern methods of efficiency and complete identification of the interests of capitalists with the interests of the country in its industrial and economic programme. This means that the present anomalous situation by which industry suffers but the capitalist still flourishes must end; and the capitalist should be satisfied with moderate returns and be willing to give their due both to the middle classes and labourers. The capitalist does show some awareness of the fact that he can no longer browbeat and exploit the middle classes or the labourers. He should realise that he would be swamped by the new forces to destruction, if he did not take care to reform himself in time. The capitalist is naturally afraid of the communist. If this fear is sincere, then the only alternative for the capitalist is to embrace the Socialist and make terms with him in time.

Capitalist Hesitancy

Whatever the future of the capitalist class in the country, it is obvious from the above that the capitalist has not yet readjusted himself to the new conditions and is still hesitating to perform effectively his role as a producer because, he is not able to locate his profits to which he looks first. Among the more important difficulties of the economic problem in the country we must assign its due place to this hesitancy of the capitalist; the earlier he is able to adopt a straight and clear attitude towards the new environment, the better for him and the country.

Responsibility of Labour

So far as labour is concerned, it must also share its responsibility in the difficulties that are now before the country mainly of falling production. In other countries such as England, labour had to fight its way to freedom and equal opportunities over generations. In the interval, it built up not only solidarity among its own ranks, but a national consciousness refusing to adopt methods which are likely to be against national interests. In consequence, the efficiency of the British worker remains high. It has increased in proportion to the advantages which it has obtained, justifying the theory that higher wages, reduced hours and better conditions in general tend to greater efficiency and therefore larger and better production.

The circumstances under which labour in India has been able to obtain certain advantages during recent years are such that it has not been possible for it either to develop that solidarity among its ranks or that national consciousness for efficiency which may be expected. There is a general complaint that whereas labour asks and gets more rewards it has not in all cases deserved them. The situation in which privileges are obtained without the discharge of corresponding responsibilities is obviously undesirable. It should be the duty of labour leaders while fighting for more opportunities for labour not to forget the other side of the picture, that the labourers for whom they work should have the conscious understanding of their responsibility and the necessary training for developing a tradition and an outlook for efficient work, which seems to be lacking in most places. This tendency has been noticed both among industrial workers as well as among other classes of workers such as domestic and office workers or other forms of private and public employment. Any sane person would agree that the worker in any walk of life should be assured of reasonable existence and adequate rewards for his work, and that his human personality should be respected. But if the worker does not rise to the occasion and is likely to believe that he can continue to ask for more gains without giving in return efficient work, he is in the long run committing suicide, because this tendency will result in an economic collapse leading to unemployment and its evil consequences for the labourer himself. Not only that but the general sympathy which exists in most quarters towards labour will also disappear, if labour is not able to deliver the goods in time. The existence of strikes in recent times, the complaints of absenteeism and go-slow methods in factories, the well known tendency of impudence continued with neglect of duty among certain classes of workers, must be held responsible for the prevailing fall in production or difficulties in increasing the same.

Conclusion

Just as the capitalist must readjust himself to the new environment, the labourer must deserve his reward and his new importance in the New Society that we are trying to build. We have got to achieve a balance in the new order; the continuation of the prevailing ill-balance is not likely to help anyone. To the extent to which the National Government succeeds in reconciling the conflicting claims of capital and labour and in persuading them to cooperate in the common effort, their efforts in the economic sphere will succeed.

Planning in India

EVOLUTION OF PLANNING

Early History

ECONOMIC Planning in India was advocated by Sir M. Visveswaraya, about 20 years ago. The Indian National Congress appointed a National Planning Committee on the eve of the war to frame an All-India Plan. The Bombay Plan (also known as the Tata-Birla Plan) made the people planning conscious. Other private parties also issued plans e.g. the People's Plan; the Gandhian Plan and so on. In June 1941 the Government of India set up an Inter-Departmental Committee for the investigation of reconstruction problems. In March 1943, this was replaced by a Committee of the Viceroy's Council with a separate Secretariat. This was known as Reconstruction Committee of Council (RCC). This Committee was assisted by a General Policy Committee and other Policy Committees formed to deal with specific subjects, consisting of representatives of the Governments of Provinces and States and some non-officials. Official Committees with Secretaries of various departments as Chairmen were set up to carry out preparatory technical work as well as a preliminary examination of the proposals. The Consultative Committee of Economists formed in 1941 was also continued. The Department of Planning and Development was created in 1944 under Sir Ardeshir Dalal, one of the authors of the Bombay Plan. The work of the RCC was thus given an impetus.

In 1944, the RCC published two reports on the progress made in drawing up plans. The first indicated the problems that were examined, and the second gave a summary of the views of the Departments of the Government of India on various proposals.

* Paper submitted to the Meeting of Experts in Problems of Planning and Execution of Programmes of Economic Development in less developed countries convened by the United Nations at San Juan, Puerto Rico in May 1950.

Objectives

At this stage of the Government plans, definite economic targets were out of question. General objectives were laid down in vague terms, e.g., (1) to raise the standard of living of the people as a whole and to ensure employment for all; (2) to increase the purchasing power of the people by an improvement in the efficiency of labour on the one hand and by a simultaneous development and reorganization of agriculture, industries and services on the other; (3) to stabilize agricultural prices at an economic level; (4) to intensively develop industries; (5) to remove the existing glaring anomaly of immense wealth side by side with abject poverty; (6) to raise the backward classes to the level of their more fortunate fellow citizens, and so on. The objectives included the development of electric power in order to facilitate industrial development and to a lesser extent agricultural development, pump irrigation and rural industry; industrial development with due emphasis on production of capital goods and necessaries as well as small scale and cottage industries; the development of roads, communications, and other transport services on a comprehensive scale, especially in rural areas; and agricultural improvement including the development of irrigation and the institution of anti-erosion and land reclamation projects. Development of public health, public instruction and housing and social services was also emphasized.

Central and Provincial Plans

The different departments of the Government of India, the Provincial and State Governments were asked to make detailed plans on the basis of the policy laid down in the RCC Reports with the above broad objectives in view. Each Province prepared its own plan; this consisted of a collection of schemes prepared by its departments. These schemes were in terms of money to be spent mostly on additional staff. The schemes did not have a clear economic outlook; there was no resources budget; nor a scale of priorities. The Central departments also made similar schemes pertaining to their respective spheres.

More definite efforts were made in connection with Industries. An Industrial Adviser was appointed in the Department of Planning and Development to evolve an Industrial Plan. A large number of deputies were appointed under him, each in charge of an industry or a group of industries. Twenty-nine Industrial Panels, each consisting of persons familiar with the industry in question or experts were appointed; a Deputy Industrial Adviser was associated with each Panel as Secretary and full-time officer to help in the work of the Panel. The reports of these Panels contain useful information on different industries, possibilities of development, nature of difficulties and some attempts at targets to be achieved including an idea of regional distribution of industries in future.

Anti-Depression Psychology

Before the Central and Provincial schemes could be integrated into a well-knit plan with proper priorities and due regard to the capacity of the country to put them into operation, the possibilities of a post-war depression and the need for maintaining expenditure after the war to prevent it were uppermost in the mind of the Government of India. Some time in 1945, the Government of India asked the Provincial Governments to be ready to implement those of their schemes which were likely to create immediate employment; the Centre promised financial assistance for this. The Finance Department estimated that during the first year after the war, a revenue surplus of Rs. 5,000 million was likely to accrue to the Central Government. Besides, it was also assumed that the Centre and the Provinces together could borrow from the market an equal amount, that is, Rs. 5,000 million without encroaching on the needs of private industry. The Central Government indicated that it would be possible for it to spare 50 to 66-2/3 per cent of its revenue surplus for the needs of the Provinces. No principles for the distribution of these sums among the Provincial Governments were, however, laid down.

In addition to the help that the Provinces could get from the Centre by way of loans and grants as above, the Provincial Governments had their wartime revenue surpluses which they could draw upon for post-war reconstruction programmes. If the Provinces succeeded in having surpluses on revenue account during the post-war period, these could also be utilized for post-war reconstruction; the Provinces estimated these at Rs. 2,000 million. On the basis of these estimates the Provincial Governments prepared their post-war plans to fight post-war depression. Some of these plans did not mention the goal very clearly and others did not give any indication of the time during which they were expected to bear fruit. Further, the time during which they expected their plans to be executed varied with different units. It is therefore not possible to give any definite indication of the physical results that were expected to be achieved as a result of the combined plans of the Central and Provincial Governments, which were more in the nature of an effort to prevent depression, than to have a co-ordinated system of economic planning.

Summary of Plans

The following table, however, attempts to give a picture of the targets so far as available up to December 1946:

Field	*Pre-planning position*	*Target*	*Period for fulfilment of the target*	*Remarks*
Food Production	60 million tons of cereals produced annually	4 million tons increase	1951-52	Plan the work of Agricultural Department of Govt. of India; but the target was not broken up into provincial targets.
Irrigation	91/4 million acres between 1919-1944	23½ million acres increase	10—12 years	The Government of India had set up two specialised agencies —A Central Water ways Irrigation and Navigation Commission and Central Technical Power Board, but lack of good field engineers and to some extent the inter-regional character of the schemes were holding up work.
Electric Power	Total installed capacity in Bri. India 1,176 thousand kws., in States 146 thousand	(*a*) An increase of 980 thousand kws.—420 thousand by Govts., 336 thousand by companies and 224 thousand by States. (*b*) An increase of more than 1500 kws.	1950 to 1955	

Field	*Pre-Planning position*	*Target*	*Period for fulfilment of the target*	*Remarks*
Roads	in 1943, 226 thousand miles of roads of which less than 68 thousands metalled.	(*a*) National Highways (Central Government) 5421 miles to be improved and 787 miles of new roads.	5 Years	
		(*b*) Provincial Highways. Major district roads and minor district roads—33,313 miles of improvement and 17,509 new mileage.		
		(*c*) Village roads new construction and improvement of 22,990 miles.		
Industries		(*a*) Central Government to start two important new projects, viz. the Sindhri Fertilizer and the Hindustan Aircraft.		
		(*b*) Most of the Provinces confining to technical training and cottage and small scale industries.		
		(*c*) Industrial targets of major industries set up by Panels given separately.		

Financial Aspects

The financial position of the combined plans of the Central and Provincial Governments is summarized below.

	Expenditure in millions of rupees in first five years			*Expenditure as percentage of total*
	Central	*Provincial*	*Total*	
Electrical Development	500	670	2600	20
Irrigation	—	1430	—	—
Posts and Telegraph	560	—	560	4
Railways	2300	—	2300	18
Industrial Development	150	210	360	3
Agricultural	220	1230	1450	11
Roads	390	1470	1860	14
Medical and Public Health ..	120	990	1110	9
Education	210	930	1140	9
Meteorology	50	—	50	—
Civil Aviation	250	—	250	2
Broadcasting	40	—	40	—
Miscellaneous (Labour, other public works, propaganda, mining, resettlement etc.) ..	400	830	1230	10
	5190	7760	12950	100

From this brief summary it seems that the Governments intended to devote quite a significant portion of the proposed expenditure to development of power, communications and agriculture. This was but natural in view of the strategic position of these fields. Only a small proportion of the total resources, less than 3 per cent, was to be devoted to industrial development. This was so partly because industrial development was largely to be left to private enterprise and was to be assisted mainly by tariffs, and suitable financial institutions such as the Industrial Finance Corporations.

The province-wise distribution of the expenditure was as under:

Province	*Total Develop-ment expenditure (Rs. in millions)*	*Revenue in 1938-39 (Rs. in millions)*	*Develop-ment expenditure as multiple of (2)*	*Expenditure per capita (in Rs.)*	*Expenditure per 1000 sq. miles (in Rs.)*
	(1)	(2)	(3)	(4)	(5)
Assam ..	265	25.8	10	26	5
Bengal ..	1595	127.7	12	26	20
Bihar ..	760	52.4	5	21	11
Bombay ..	528	124.5	4	25	7
C.P. ..	306	42.7	7	18	3
Madras ..	1294	161.3	8	26	10
Orissa ..	339	18.2	19	39	11
Punjab ..	1163	113.6	10	41	12
Sind ..	440	37.0	12	91	9
U.P. ..	1080	128.0	8	20	10

A glance at the above table makes it clear that the proposed expenditure was not based on the potential capacity for development of each area; for in that case backward areas like Assam and C.P. should have spent the most. C.P. was to spend the least per capita and per square mile; Assam's planned expenditure per square mile was very low. Because no principles for distribution of grants and loans by the Centre had yet been announced, this was not even in keeping with financial resources. In some cases as that of Bengal, the Province had to be politely asked to bear its resources in mind; in the case of N.W.F.P. the plan was so ambitious that it had not been included for analysis at all. We do not intend at this stage to go into a detailed province-wise distribution of each item of expenditure, but it is obvious that lack of a proper all-India perspective would also be reflected in these figures.

The Provincial Governments expected to raise their finances in the following manner:

Grants from the Centre	Rs.	2,700	million
Provincial funds including budget surplus ..	„	1,930	„
Loans	„	3,130	„
	„	7,760	„

EXECUTION OF PLANS

These plans came into force from the financial year 1946-47. It is four years since these plans have been in operation, and it would be appropriate to ask what the results have been. It should be noted that since these plans were framed, India passed through a major calamity—partition of the country in August 1947. The partition upset many calculations; because of the unhappy circumstances in which it took place, it led to a heavy influx of refugees on both sides. It also disturbed many of the previous calculations which pertained to undivided India. In spite of this, the plans have not yet been reviewed or revised as a whole.

The following table gives the Provincial expenditure upto 1949-50 (including readjustments on account of reduction in Central loans and grants.)

EXPENDITURE ON PLANS—PROVINCE-WISE

	Expenditure up to 1949–50 (Rs. in millions)	*Planned expenditure during first five years (Rs. in millions)*	*(1) as per cent of (2)*	*Expenditure as per cent of total*
	(1)	(2)	(3)	(4)
Assam ..	58	265	22	2.5
Bengal (West) ..	152	2595*	10	6.7
Bihar	150	760	20	6.5
Bombay ..	477	528	90	20.9
C. P.	236	306	77	10.3
East Punjab ..	149	11.63*	—	6.5
Madras	438	1294	34	19.2
Orissa	158	339	47	6.9
U. P.	470	1080	44	20.5
	2,288			100.00

*These figures are for undivided Punjab and undivided Bengal.

Leaving aside East Punjab and West Bengal for which we have no comparable figures, it seems that very few Provinces were able to spend according to their plans. From column (4) it seems that some of the Provinces accounted for quite a large portion of expenditure on planning. Bombay, U.P. and Madras, among themselves spent nearly three-fifths of the entire development expenditure. These are the provinces with better resources; but it also seems that throughout this period it was not lack of requisite finance that was holding up progress. The difficulties were more fundamental. The following table showing expenditure by years brings out this point:

EXPENDITURE ON PLANS—ANNUAL

	(*Rs. in millions*)	*Per cent of expenditure to total during the period*
1946—47	160	6
1947—48	270	11
1948—49 (revised)	790	31
1949—50 (Budget, before announcement of reduction in Central Grants) ..	1290	52
	2510	100

In the earlier years because of the need for preliminary preparations as well as scarcity of personnel and raw materials the expenditure incurred by the Provincial Governments fell short of the estimates. It was only in the year 1948-49 that expenditure on post-war development plans began to assume some importance. During the next year (1949-50), however, because of financial difficulties, the Central Government had to considerably restrict the expenditure on development programmes. Provinces like Assam, Bihar and Orissa which relied to a very large extent on the Centre for their development programmes had to radically revise their programmes downwards. The distribution of provincial development expenditure according to subjects during 1946-47 to 1949-50 is as under:

EXPENDITURE ON DEVELOPMENT—ITEM-WISE

Item of expenditure	*(Rs. in millions)*	*Per cent*
Civil Works	563	24.6
Irrigation	370	16.2
Electricity	335	14.6
Agriculture and Grow More Food.	281	12.3
General Administration and Miscellaneous	250	10.9
Education	183	8.0
Medical and Public Health ..	157	6.8
Industries	84	3.7
Forests	26	1.1
Co-operation	22	1.0
Veterinary	18	0.6
	..	100.0

It is very difficult to draw any conclusions from these figures of expenditure. It is obvious, however, that the actual importance given to industries as compared with that in the plans does not show any welcome change. In spite of the great importance of industries, the expenditure on industries by all except a few provinces has been negligible. The Province-wise distribution of item-wise expenditure brings out the ill-coordinated character of the plans. For instance, take the expenditure of Rs. 563 million on civil works. Of this, more than half was spent on buildings and only Rs. 260 million on roads. Nearly 50 per cent of this expenditure is accounted for by U.P. which is fairly well developed in road communications. Backward Provinces like Assam, C.P., Orissa and Bihar, which are badly served with roads spent less.

EXPENDITURE ON CIVIL WORKS

Province	*Rs. in millions*	*Percentage to total Provincial expenditure*	*Mileage of existing surfaced roads per 100 sq. miles*
Assam	21	4	2.0
Bengal	19	3	7.1
Bihar	26	5	5.7
Bombay	70	12	11.1
C. P.	52	9	4.6
Madras	73	13	18.0
Orissa	29	5	5.0
Punjab	15	3	5.4
U. P.	259	46	7.5
	563	100	

In irrigation the same mal-distribution is discernible:

Province	*Expenditure on irrigation (in million Rs.)*	*Net irrigated areas as percentages to net sown area*	*Per cent of cultivable waste in each province to total cultivable waste*
Assam	1	22.6	25.5
Bengal	8	20.5	2.7
Bihar	31	30.5	9.5
Bombay	19	5.0	1.2
C. P.	2	6.5	20.3
Madras	78	30.2	17.5
Orissa	4	25.9	4.6
Punjab	60	43.8	3.8
U. P.	58	31.3	14.7*
	261	..	..

* Excluding expenditure on multi-purpose projects which has been included in expenditure on irrigation.

C.P., in spite of having a very high percentage of cultivable waste and low proportion of irrigation, has spent very little on irrigation—one per cent of its development expenditure.

Lack of Co-ordination

In a recent report prepared by the Economic and Statistical Co-ordination Section of the Cabinet Secretariat it is observed that "These changes (revisions of targets, etc.) have not in any way altered the basic fact that the programme in its conception, preparation and execution has been and is unco-ordinated and lacks internal coherence and consistency with reference to any objective criteria" (*Provincial Development Programme*, p. 2).

Results Achieved

The more important question however, is not how far Government expenditure has kept up or fallen below the anticipated expenditure on planning, but as to how far the physical results have been anywhere near those that were expected. Unfortunately the information available on this point is scanty. But from our knowledge regarding the relation of actual expenditure to estimated ones, the course of prices and the general tendency of actual expenditure on projects to exceed estimated expenditure, it is obvious that the physical achievements fell far short of those desired. In spite of this both from the financial and physical view points the results taken in a proper perspective were by no means disappointing. An expenditure of Rs. 2,300 million on provincial development in the first four years of planning is an impressive effort. For the first time big projects had begun to be seriously thought of and implemented in India; things were on the move.

In terms of ultimate results achieved, however, the picture is disappointing. In the absence of detailed statistics, one must rest content with a rough idea of the results achieved in the two most important fields—agriculture and large-scale industries.

(a) *Agriculture.* The programme to which the Government of India seem to have attached the greatest urgency and importance was the Grow More Food Campaign or the idea of making India self-sufficient in the realm of foodgrains. In order to achieve this goal they were even prepared to make what seemed uneconomic diversions. For example, some of the Provincial Governments had compelled their farmers to switch over from the production of remunerative commercial crops to foodgrains. The campaign had a very early start. In spite of that even in this field production does not seem to have appreciably increased. Indian food production statistics are not very reliable, but the following table sums up the situation:

Year†	*Production of cereals*‡	*Increase over pre-war period*
	(in 000 tons)	*Acreage (in 000 acres)*
1939	50	19
1945	59	22
1946	53	21
1947 (*a*)	41	18
1948 (*a*)	43	17
1949 (*a*)	40	17

†Refers to the agricultural year ending in June.
‡Includes rice, wheat, grains, jawar, bajra, maize and barley.
(*a*) These figures pertain to the Republic of India only; the earlier figures are for undivided India.

The figures show no increase in food production. Even if they are an underestimate as they are likely to be because of their being linked up with procurement targets, it is certain that the increase in food production has not been sufficient to make possible a reduction in the amount of imported foodgrains[1] much less to ease the food position in the country or reduce the prices of foodgrains. The foodgrain rations which were usually at 1 lb. a week per adult during the war and were reduced to 12 oz. after the war continue to be at this reduced level.

[1] The imports of foodgrains increased from 1,000 million rupees in 1946 to 1,300 million in 1947 and 1,500 million in 1948.

(b) *Industries.* In the case of industries the situation has been better. Immediately after Independence industrial production was showing a dangerous decline. At one time (December 1947) the situation seemed so frightening that the Government of India had to devote all possible efforts just to maintain intact the volume of industrial production. This effort has succeeded on the whole; in respect of the two biggest industries—Cotton and Jute however, production shows a decline. Steel is in acute shortage. While miscellaneous industries show an increase in production, this has not been sufficient to replace the imports and meet increased demand. In quite a few important commodities industrial production has not reached its wartime peak. The situation may be seen at a glance from the Indices of Industrial Production given below.

INDEX OF INDUSTRIAL PRODUCTION

Year	*General Index*	*Cotton textiles*	*Jute*	*Steel*	*Chemicals*	*Paper*	*Cement*	*Matches*
1938	105.4	109.0	98.3	108.0	84.4	121.6	124.8	85.1
Peak production bet. 1939–45	120.0 (45)	122.9 (44)	99.5 (42)	142.9 (45)	153.2 (41)	196.5 (45)	196.5 (45)	90.2 (45)
1946	109.0	11.9	84.6	130.0	134.1	193.4	181.1	90.5
1947	102.4	95.8	79.5	121.8	11.12	143.7	158.5	77.6
1948	114.0	113.2	79.4	136.1	84.5	164.7	149.2	69.0
1947*	101.0	96.2	96.6	97.1	—	87.8	93.9	11.30
1948	11.20	110.5	100.2	97.1	—	92.4	100.7	129.4
1949	109.3	100.1	86.9	104.6	—	97.4	136.3	127.1

* While the earlier indices have been based on 1937=100, this row and those further downwards take 1946 as the base, and include some changes in the group composition.

It is obvious from these figures that in some important respects the situation is slowly but definitely turning for the better. Other available information seems to support the same view. Coal production is higher than at any time during the war—31,500 thousand tons per month for the Union of India in 1949 compared to 29,280 thousand in 1946 for the whole of Undivided India; so are its despatches (28,068 thousand tons cf. with 25,608 thousand in 1946). Installed plant capacity of electricity had increased from 1,376 thousand kwts. in 1946 to 1,411 thousand in 1948, electricity generated (monthly) from 4,032 million kwh. in 1946 to 4,920 million kwh. in 1949, and electricity sold from 3,348 million kwh. in 1946 to 3,984 million kwh. in 1949. The transport position has considerably eased. In spite of strained situation in foreign exchange because of the high priority given to imports of capital goods as well as their availability, imports of machinery and mill work have increased from 387 and 594 million rupees in 1946-47 and 1947-48 respectively, and to 767 million in 1949. There has thus been an all round welcome increase in industrial activity (see table below).

EXPANSION IN INDUSTRIAL CAPACITY

(Figures in Thousands)

Industry	*Unit*	*1946*	*1947*	*1948*	*1949*
Antimony ..	Tons	.5	N.A.	.7	.7
Semi-manufactures	,,	22	,,	50	N.A.
Enamelware ..	Pieces	24	24	25	25.2
Cement ..	Tons	1800	2075	2500	2815
Refractories ..	,,	210	214	225	269
Paper	,,	90	110	110	110
Plywood	Sq. ft.	N.A.	30000	63000	100000
Caustic Soda ..	Tons	10.5	10.5	13.5	17.6
Soda Ash	,,	29	N.A.	35	54
Super-phosphates ..	,,	60	60	75	113
Sulphuric acid ..	,,	80	100	100	150
Power alcohol ..	Gallons	16000	20000	20000	9144
Ammonium sulphate	Tons	17	N.A.	35	N.A.
Abrasives ..	Reams	N.A.	122	122	145
Electric lamps ..	Nos.	13000	13350	14350	18.00
Dry Cells	,,	130000	132000	142000	187200
Power transformers..	KVA	100	102	175	225
Electric motors ..	H.P.	100	100	150	200
Electric fans ..	Nos.	200	250	250	300
Diesel engines ..	,,	.8	.8	1.2	5.2
Storage batteries ..	,,	172	172	268	268
Cycle tyres	,,	N.A.	N.A.	4500	6000
Cycle tubes	,,	N.A.	N.A.	4500	6000
Bicycles	,,	50	52	60	94
Cotton textiles ..	Spindles	10000	N.A.	10500	10366
Hydrogenate oil ..	Tons	150	N.A.	200	N.A.

DIFFICULTIES AND OBSTACLES

In spite of the fact that comparatively large sums have been spent for economic development, the results have not been encouraging. Among the causes that have come in the way of success, the following may be mentioned.

Partition

We have already mentioned the partition of the country as one of the causes. Naturally when territories whose economies have been integrated for a very long time are separated from each other, economic changes that inevitably follow the making of two regions into two separate sovereign States make the transition period extremely difficult. The shock and the disturbances of this transition can be minimized by mutual understanding and goodwill on both sides of the frontier. Unfortunately as the partition took place amidst scenes of anger and hatred there was little room for such an understanding. The partition was followed by large streams of evacuees which disturbed the economies of both the countries as many of these evacuees performed essential tasks in the national economy and were not easily replaceable. Further as most of them tried to settle in urban areas, the economies of these already over-crowded areas were rudely shaken. Both the countries had to spend large amounts of money on rehabilitating the evacuees. The ill-feeling which these events created was responsible for keeping the defence expenditure in both the countries at a high level, thus reducing the amounts available for economic development. It is hoped that the recent pact between the two countries will gradually improve relations.

Non-availability of Capital Goods

The task of world reconstruction after the war proved more protracted and immense in magnitude than was expected. As far as Western Europe was concerned, it was greatly facilitated by the granting of Marshall Aid. This very grant of Marshall Aid, however, with the priorities that it implied, meant that countries which were not considered as fit recipients of Marshall Aid were to receive a poor share of the scarce goods and materials of the world. It thus happened that even when the Government of India, the Provincial Governments and the private industries had ample financial resources including reasonable amounts of foreign exchange, they could not get the necessary raw materials or capital goods from abroad with which the task of reconstruction could be speeded up. This meant prolongation of wartime hardships and suffering which in turn further deteriorated the economic situation.

Limited Availability of Sterling Balances

A common feature of both private and Government plans has been that it was assumed that the large amounts of sterling balances which had accumulated to the credit of India on account of the method of financing the allied expenditure in India, would be available for the purchase of capital goods for the economic development of the country immediately after the war. The post-war situation of the United Kingdom which made it difficult for her to make these balances convertible into goods as required by the creditor country was not realized at the time. Besides, the peculiar difficulties of India herself, which made it necessary for her to spend whatever sterling releases she could get mainly on food imports were not foreseen. Part of the sterling releases had also to be utilised to meet the adverse balance of payments caused by the changes in India's trade after the partition. The quantum of sterling balances was reduced by certain capital payments to the United Kingdom and transfers to Pakistan as her share.

Inflation

India had inherited from the war, like most of the other countries of the world, a great rise in prices and also a large inflation potential. The large development expenditure, though small in relation to requirements was likely to give a further inflationary impetus. The great structural changes in the Indian economy which took place as a result of wartime and post-war inflation added to these difficulties. The small agricultural producers who in the past were compelled to sell foodgrains in order to acquire enough cash to pay either land revenue or interest on their past debt found both these charges greatly reduced in real terms because of the increase in prices. They also found that there were insufficient amounts of industrial goods to be obtained in return for their foodgrains. The inevitable result of this was to make them reluctant to produce and part with foodgrains. Monopoly procurement including requisitioning of foodgrains which were practised in some provinces was just enough to keep the situation under control. Imports of foodgrains on any considerable scale was out of question in view of the post-war scarcity. In other fields imports on a liberal scale were tried and to some extent they had an anti-inflationary effect. Before however, any noticeable effects on the economy as a whole could occur due to scarcity of foreign exchange, the Government had to clamp in import controls once again with the result that prices got a further impetus. Devaluation that came in September 1949 had naturally the effect of making the position worse. The situation throughout needed delicate but firm handling; but the Government of India showed little recognition of this. Afraid of post-war unemployment, it did not pay adequate regard to the need for anti-inflationary measures, abolished the E.P.T. prematurely, and was not prepared (along with the Provincial Governments) to take taxation measures more in keeping with the shifts in income and wealth. It was reluctant even to continue the preventive measures already in force. Against the advice of most of the economists, it embarked on a decontrol experiment in November 1947. The price reactions were so adverse that soon after prices were again controlled, but at a much higher level. In spite of this experience instead of boldly recognizing the role of controls in conditions of scarcity, the Government adopted an apologetic attitude towards controls instead of enforcing them rigorously.

Lack of Experience

It must be noted that Economic Planning was put into operation in India soon after Independence. She has highly spirited and enthusiastic public leaders at the helm of affairs. They however did not have experience of such affairs. In their first flush of enthusiasm they under-estimated the difficulties of development and tried to concentrate too much on fair distribution. In addition to this a number of declarations on industrial policy were made whose contents greatly varied from time to time, but the net effect of which was to make the position of industrialists uncertain. The result of inflation combined with uncertainty and excessive zeal for social justice was that the investment market became panicky and almost all genuine investors withdrew. Industries became a plaything of the speculator who was not at all interested in production or its quality. Trade and speculation became more attractive than industrial investment, and Government loans became so unattractive that investment in Government loans which had been as high as Rs. 2,500 millions during the war years declined to 25 per cent (570 millions) during 1949-50. In this atmosphere economic development based on private enterprise became very difficult.

Defective Planning Mechanism

As we have seen earlier, various methods to secure co-ordination among the plans of the Provincial Governments and between these and those of the Centre had been recommended and tried to some extent, but none of them seemed to have succeeded. It has been acknowledged that "the programme was originally conceived without reference to any estimate of the resources or the needs of a nation as a whole (the Advisory Planning Board had brought out in its report as to how the resources budget had been entirely neglected); and since then, though it has gone through successive revisions, it has not acquired coherence or unity of purpose in the process. The Government of India, has, through grants and loans ......exercised a certain amount of control over them in the initial and subsequent stages. The control, such as it has been, has, however, been exercised only over individual schemes, and each provincial programme, as a whole, has remained, what it was originally, a collection of departmental development schemes unrelated to an over-all estimate of what the country or each individual province needs or can achieve with available means." The plans of the Central Government were in no better position.

The reason for this chaotic state of affairs seemed to be the absence of an adequate organisation at the highest level. Planning is so intimately connected with activities of all other Departments that the Planning Department, in a backward economy must have overriding authority over the rest in practice to be effective. For a time there was some hope of such a possibility when a Minister was in charge of Planning and Development during 1944-46. But this department had no executive powers, and it suffered from the want of co-operation from others. With the abolition of this Ministry in the latter part of 1946, Development and Planning became the plaything of rival Departments with none wholly responsible for their entire outcome. A much better alternative would have been an Expert Planning Commission, which would have no direct executive powers, but which, if assured of continued interest by the more important members of the Cabinet, might come to enjoy sufficient respect so as to ensure adequate regard for its views. The Advisory Planning Board recommended in December 1946 the creation of such a body, but it was not till very recently (April 1950) that a Planning Commission was created.

Capital Formation

The level of consumption in the country is low, as the average income is low. Saving in real terms is therefore difficult; and capital formation required for large scale planning is not possible. Foreign capital or foreign aid or both are essential for rapid development. But there are as yet no signs of substantial foreign investment.

Long-Term vs. *Short-Term Plans*

The inadequacy of capital creates difficulties for long term planning. The growing population results in increasing pressure in the utilisation of limited resources. Any large scale expenditure which does not result in immediate increase in production of essential articles tends to be inflationary. The need for short term plans to make up for the scarcity of essential goods in the near future is therefore urgent.

A large part of the Provincial Development Programmes consisted of long-range programmes. From the item-wise analysis of expenditure already given, it is obvious that a large part of the expenditure was devoted to irrigation, electricity etc. which could not have any effect in the short term. This would also be obvious from the fact that in 1948-49 about 50 per cent of the expenditure on development was on capital account. It is very difficult to say how much of this expenditure was well advised, but naturally nothing immediate could be expected from it. In the meantime, smaller schemes which might have a better short term effect were ignored because of these spectacular plans. The result was that the general economy deteriorated.

Role of Private Enterprise

The Industrial Policy Statement of April 1948 defined the relative spheres of state and private enterprise in industrial development. Certain key industries were reserved for the State. In others, future development was to be initiated by the State. The State would undertake such industries on its own or invite the co-operation of private enterprise. The position would be reviewed after ten years to determine whether existing private concerns in any such industry should be nationalized. In the remaining industries private enterprise had full scope, but had to work under Government regulation and control.

Industrialists are not quite clear about their position in the new Policy. They find on the one hand that measures of social justice in the interests of labour are increasing their costs, which are becoming rigid without proportionate increase in labour efficiency. On the other hand, they find that the scope for private enterprise is limited and in the limited sphere in whch they have to work there is increasing interference by Government, which in practice means by Civilian Officers who are as a rule not conversant with the needs and techniques of business and industry. Investment in industrial enterprise seems to have acted as a disincentive. In consequence, the burden of development became more a responsibility of the State, as private enterprise became hesistant so far as positive action was concerned.

Lack of Adequate Statistics

Any effective administrative action whether in the realm of controls or planning presupposes fairly reliable statistics. In its absence, decisions regarding policy as well as judgements regarding the efficacy of certain steps to achieve a desired goal become extremely difficult, and opportunistic policies tend to have the upper hand. India has suffered from a woeful inadequacy of basic statistics regarding production, national, income, etc. This lack is nowhere better illustrated than in the realm of Indian agricultural economics which has aptly been described as a gamble in statistics. While glowing accounts of the increase in area under cultivation as a result of the Grow More Food Campaign are published by various

Provincial Governments from time to time, the crop production statistics compiled by them bear no evidence of the success of such campaigns. The Government of India have published from time to time figures of food requirements of the Indian population, and one would think that their food policy was based on such figures; but when driven to a corner recently they admitted that these were so untrustworthy that their food import policy was only based on the requirements of the rationed population under rationing rules and the likely procurement figures based on provincial estimates. It may be mentioned that Sir T. C. Gregory, then Economic Adviser to the Government of India is reported to have advised against Economic Planning because of the want of adequate statistical data.

Administrative Machinery

The Indian administrative machinery was built up mainly with a view to discharging the police functions of the State. While in this respect its efficiency has been great, it has not easily adapted itself to its recent role of administering economic controls or of the execution of economic development schemes. In the general lowering of moral standards during the war, it has not found it easy to withstand the greatly increased temptation which the changed situation offers. The Indian Government is perhaps unwise in demanding too much of it. For example, recently even in public corporations civil servants have been put in key positions. Unless an efficient and honest Economic Civil Service is built up, the task of economic development would be very difficult. Whereas large amounts are spent for the development of scientific and technical education, nothing is being done to give a corresponding impetus to train young men in Advanced Economics and Statistics including research in them. It is assumed that the ordinary Civil Servant is competent to handle work relating to economic administration arising out of development plans.

THE PLANNING COMMISSION

From the summary of Indian Planning that has been given above, it should be obvious that Indian Planning has not yet come to grips with the more fundamental problems. So far the trial given to planning has been for a short period only and that period has been one of big political changes. It has also been one of acute economic difficulties created by inflation and post-war shortage all over the world. It is only now with conditions a little more settled that India can be said to have a chance to try to tackle the real problems in planning. She has begun already by setting up a Planning Commission presided over by the Prime Minister which will co-ordinate all plans, Provincial and Central. According to the terms of reference the Planning Commission will:

1. make an assessment of the material, capital and human resources of the country, including technical personnel, and investigate the possibilities of augmenting such of these resources as are found to be deficient in relation to the nation's requirements;
2. formulate a plan for the most effective and balanced utilisation of the country's resources;
3. on a determination of priorities, define the stages in which the plan should be carried out and propose the allocation of resources for the due completion of each stage;
4. indicate the factors which are tending to retard economic development, and determine the conditions which, in view of the current social and political situation, should be established for the successful execution of the plan;
5. determine the nature of the machinery which will be necessary for securing the successful implementation of each stage of the Plan in all its aspects;
6. appraise from time to time the progress achieved in the execution of each stage of the Plan and recommend the adjustments of policy measures that such appraisal may show to be necessary; and
7. make such interim or ancillary recommendations as appear to it to be appropriate either for facilitating the discharge of the duties assigned to it, or on the consideration of the prevailing economic conditions, current measures and development programmes, or on an examination of such specific problems as may be referred to it for advice by Central or State Governments.

Unlike some of the earlier efforts at planning, the effort on this occasion is more systematic and shows greater promise of success.

In order to see that the work of the Commission is co-ordinated with that of the Executive, adequate links have been provided. The Prime Minister is the Chairman of the Planning Commission as of the Cabinet. The Secretary of the Cabinet is also the Secretary of the Planning Commission. Among the members of the Planning Commission are well known persons experienced in different walks of life and together they make a good team, though experts have not been included in it.

The co-ordination of the work of the Planning Commission with that of the Provinces is being organized; the machinery has not yet taken shape. It is to be hoped that the mistakes of the past will be avoided and that the Planning Commission will be able to do its work without interference.

Immediate Outlook

In one respect however, the condition now is less propitious than that at the end of the war. The foreign exchange position has considerably deteriorated. Though the world situation now permits of effective international aid, the chances of India obtaining this on any significant scale are not bright. At one time it seemed that foreign capital, both from international institutions and from private agencies might easily fill in this gap, but as it will appear from the figures of foreign capital announced by the Finance Minister, these hopes have not been realised. The three loans given by the I.B.R.D. have been on such terms as are likely to cause a heavy drain on the foreign exchange position. Private capital has come but in drops. Capital from the new world has been specially shy in coming. American capital which sought entry in India during 1949-50 amounts to less than Rs. 600 thousand. Unless something is quickly done in this direction, we may soon be near the stage prophesied by the Advisory Planning Board. They had observed that in view of the difficult times through which we were passing, "unless concrete results are obtained soon, all our vaunted plans instead of leading to the general improvement which was expected of them, will scarcely make good the ground lost during this period of transition." It is only quick and effective international aid combined with determined steps at home that can check the deterioration and set Indian economy firmlv on the road to progress. Given these, there is no doubt that the Indian economy is capable of a large-scale expansion. The problem however is as to whether the pace of economic development can be sufficiently rapid as to meet the high expectations of the Indian people, and to make it worth while for people to limit the size of their families. The question also is whether it is possible for the Governments in democratic countries to so regulate the economic atmosphere as to make rapid expansion of economic activities by private parties possible without too detailed controls and regimentation. If rigorous controls are essential, how can we ensure an administrative machinery, which in its lowest rungs will be above the huge temptations which private parties in an unequal society can always lay before them? Industrial progress in the past in most of the countries has been slower than that needed by India to tackle effectively her population problems. Also such progress has been brought about at the cost of social justice. Factory Acts, Minimum Wages, Progressive Taxation, and large scale Government transfer expenditure have come as a rule with a time lag. In the case of countries like India the process is different. We had our Factory Acts before we became an industrial nation. We have Minimum Wages and might have Fair Wages before long. There is naturally a great deal of enthusiasm in ratifying the various conventions of the ILO. Even if we try to do away with the abuses of the past like the Zamindari system of land tenure, we must give fair compensation for it. Will it be possible to achieve a rapid rate of investment in spite of all these tendencies towards a more equitable distribution which may hamper growth of savings? Already in India, as in some of the other undeveloped countries, we had the benefits of an enlightened administration with peace, order and security and all that it implies, without its concomitant factor of economic progress. The result has been that we have a density of population higher than any industrialized country of a parallel size. Will economic planning be able to achieve progress in a reasonable time to overcome the existing obstacles? Economic planning implies a co-ordinated attack on economic and social problems and raises hopes among the people. The responsibility of those in charge of planning and execution of development schemes is all the greater, because frustration of such hopes may prove dangerous.

Role of Agricultural Economics in Indian Economy*

I AM deeply grateful for the honour done to me by electing me as President of this Session of the Indian Agricultural Economics Conference. I have had the privilege and the opportunity of watching at close quarters the way in which the work of this conference and particularly of the Indian Society of Agricultural Economics has grown from slow beginnings. I have seen the struggles and the obstacles through which it has passed, before it could occupy an acknowledged position in its own field. In this connection you will allow me to pay a tribute to the untiring zeal and devoted work of Sir Manilal Nanavati who, as President of the Society, has brought to bear his wide knowledge and life-long experience of the subject as well as his numerous personal contacts on the work of the Society. Since Sir Manilal took over this work, the Department of Economics of the University School of Economics in Bombay, and particularly its Agricultural Economics Section, have been in close contact with the work of the Society. We are proud to treat Sir Manilal as the Hon. Professor of Agricultural Economics in the School. The only complaint which sometimes I receive from the members of this Section, is that they are overworked because of him. But his personality inspires a compelling response from all those who come in contact with him. It will not be inappropriate, if I take this opportunity to review the state in which we are in connection with the study of and research in Agricultural Economics and make a few suggestions.

Paucity of Economic Data

As is well known, though efforts at planning in India were first made by private organisations, the first official step in this con-

* Speech as President, Thirteenth Annual Conference of the Indian Society of Agricultural Economics at the Travancore University, Trivandrum, 26th December 1952.

nection was taken by the Government of India in 1944 when the Department of Planning and Development was constituted with Sir Ardeshir Dalal as the Member in charge. Sir Ardeshir was one of the authors of the Bombay Plan which, along with the National Planning Committee, was responsible for creating planning consciousness in the country. Sir Ardeshir expected that the Government of India would have at its disposal adequate material by way of statistical and other information for the purpose of planning, and that to the extent to which it was deficient adequate machinery would be created to make up for it without delay. He naturally looked for guidance and help in this connection to Sir Theodore Gregory, then Economic Adviser to the Government of India. Sir Theodore pointed out the paucity of data for the purpose of planning and advised that under the circumstances, planning in India was not possible. It was a sad commentary on the state of affairs in the country then, that a person of the eminence of Sir Theodore, who was especially brought out to train suitable Indian staff for giving economic advice to the Government and for creating suitable machinery for the collection of scientific data as the basis for such advice, should have damped the enthusiasm of the Planning Member in this manner. A Departmental Committee consisting of Officers and Economists in Government Departments with Sir Theodore Gregory as Chairman was appointed to devise ways and means to improve the statistical machinery of the Government. One does not know the fate of this Committee. In the meanwhile, several departments dealing with economic affairs were created in the different Ministries of the Government of India. At the same time several Provincial Governments created Departments of Economics and Statistics to help in the collection and interpretation of economic information, and the Reserve Bank of India enlarged the scope and activities of its Department of Research and Statistics. This move, in a way, had some adverse effect on the Universities inasmuch as some of the trained staff in the University Departments of Economics was employed by Government at more attractive scales of remuneration, and as the Government Departments began to increase their activities, younger qualified recruits in this subject found employment in these Departments more attractive than in the Universities. Research activities in the Universities in Economics in general and in Agricultural Economics in particular, suffered in consequence.

Tendency to Ignore Economic Facts and Analysis

Before things could take a better shape, we had the uncertain political situation in the country soon after the cessation of hostilities in 1945. This was followed by Independence in August 1947, accompanied by the partition of the country. The new economic situation which was thus created had to be handled with great care and foresight. Those responsible for the partition agreed to it on political grounds without realising its economic consequences and significance. Those who came to power were, however, anxious to bring about rapid reforms of the type that they were advocating while in opposition. Some of these reforms affected the basic economic life of the country such as changes in land tenure, tenancy legislation, relief from agricultural indebtedness and efforts to introduce schemes of improvement for the development of agriculture such as large irrigation projects, reclamation of land, and development of rural banking. The stagnant condition of agricultural life in the country and the systematic neglect of the farmer and his work became the concern of the well-meaning politician now in power. It was believed that by passing quick legislation for this or that reform affecting land and finance of agriculture, the millenium would follow. In his anxiety to achieve rapid results, the politician was impatient to the extent of ignoring facts or even of making efforts at obtaining facts. Wherever facts were available, he was equally impatient regarding its correct interpretation; he was willing to trust his own practical sense instead of the trained mind of the expert. As a result of this, we got legislation for the abolition of zamindari without the means to implement the same or without the realisation of its reactions on production under the existing circumstances. The effects of the various Debt Relief and Money-lenders' Acts were neither foreseen nor examined. We also noticed wild schemes of simultaneous self-sufficiency in food, in cotton and in jute at a time when we were seriously in deficit in each of them, showing total ignorance of the elementary facts of the situation or want of capacity to appreciate the fact that with a limited area under cultivation it was not wise to make such an assumption. The inter-relationship between different crops, both with reference to production and prices, was ignored both in public discussions and executive decisions. Nowhere was this tendency more apparent than in the field of prices, where the changing mood of the political leader more than economic facts or economic interpretation decided the issue, either of fixation of prices or of changes in policy such as control or decontrol.

Confusion of Thought

In the complex economic situation created by the partition and later by the merger or union of former Indian States, the above tendency succeeded in adding confusion. The confusion was so great that any one trying to understand in simple, clear terms, the policy of the Government of India as a whole or of any given State Government in matters affecting agricultural progress in the country, found himself at sea because he was faced with contradictions and conflicting measures. It was under this background that the Planning Commission was appointed. It was charged with the function of evolving a co-ordinated plan of economic development for the country. The task of the Commission was not at all enviable. It did not have adequate data on many aspects of its work, particularly in the principal economic activity, viz. agriculture. It was not allowed time to make up for this deficiency because it was asked to produce a report at short notice based on the existing inadequate material. Both in the Draft Outline of the Five-year Plan issued last year and in the Final Plan issued recently, the Commission has proceeded on assumptions, perhaps with full awareness of the uncertainty involved in the same. For example, it has assumed that prices in general in the country will not rise; if at all, they will slowly reach a downward level. For this basic assumption they are naturally in favour of effective price control and have pointed out that as food happens to be responsible for 60 per cent of the budget of most people in the country, control of prices is essential for the success of the Plan. It was rather paradoxical for those interested to find that at the time when the Planning Commission was working out its plan on this assumption, a psychology of decontrol was being created in the country by responsible persons. If any evidence were needed of the chaotic conditions in which our basic facts are and of the queer lack of unanimity as to their interpretation it was provided by the recent debate on food controls in the Parliament. In view of this the remarks of the Planning Commission on controls in their Final Report do not inspire confidence. If in matters so vital to the well-being of the people, we are so ignorant and so uncertain, one can imagine the extent of disregard of facts, in several other questions, which though less urgent are none-the-less significant for sound and successful planning.

Controls

In this connection, I would like to make a few observations on controls in general and price control in particular. In a country suffering from inflationary pressures and desirous of undertaking a large-scale development programme, controls—particularly those governing prices—have a significant function. The Planning Commission has advocated the continuance of certain price controls. Sections of the business community, however, believe a relaxation of controls would serve to increase industrial production. It is difficult to find much substance in their argument. For example, when the government experimented with partial control of the sugar industry, manufacturers had to sell a certain percentage of their output to the government at a fixed price; the remainder could be sold in the free market. A noticeable increase in sugar production resulted, but at the cost of reduced acreage in food-grains. In the same way, the increased foreign demand for oil-seeds led to a reduction in the acreage devoted to cereals. Unless much land is reclaimed for cultivation, or unless new irrigation works permit an increase in the cultivated area and in the yield from existing acreage, the prospect for improved agricultural output seems to be limited in the short run; in other words, an increase in prices of agricultural commodities would not lead to a rise in aggregate output. Higher production depends upon large-scale capital investments of a type far beyond the reach of the ordinary farmer.

As long as the aggregate supply of most commodities falls woefully short of total demand, and as long as the possibilities of a speedy expansion in their over-all production are sharply restricted, the nation must depend upon price controls to allocate resources in accordance with the pattern of social priorities established by the government. The complaints of private business on this score are justified in so far as the controls have operated unsatisfactorily because of administrative defects and a lack of integration among the various controls. An improvement in administrative efficiency would go far to abate prejudice against controls, which are necessary for the smooth operation of the economy.

Neglect of Agricultural Economics

In a country like ours which is predominantly agricultural and in which we are faced with the problem of providing the elementary needs of a growing population, one would have expected that systematic attention would be paid to the collection of correct data on all agricultural problems, to their analysis and interpretation on scientific lines and to a continuous examination of the inter-relationship of different agricultural problems *inter se*, as well as with the other sectors of the economy. One would also expect that those in authority would do everything in their power to encourage such work by all possible means so that the country might be fully aware of the exact situation, and whatever steps were taken either by Government or by private parties were taken with knowledge, and therefore, with reasonable prospects of success. Some of the unfortunate tendencies referred to above would not even be expected under normal conditions. But they have to be mentioned to show that such unexpected things do happen in our country. It is a tragedy that a country which is spending crores of rupees for the development of scientific and technological studies and research, and can boast of some of the most imposing structures with the most well-equipped laboratories in the world, neglects the basic facts of our life in the field of agricultural economics and allows such vital problems to be the playthings of the politician, who thereby treats the vast mass of the population in the country as a living laboratory on which to experiment with his fads, which though exalted by the term practical wisdom, are sometimes based even on intuition. Already there is clear evidence of unemployment among technically trained persons; but without paying any attention to this economic fact more institutions for technical education are being created costing crores of rupees. Economic progress in the modern world depends considerably on technological studies and research, but it has to be remembered that unless there is a parallel progress in the field of economic information, economic analysis and interpretation we shall have a lop-sided development resulting in shocks and inevitable failures.

In this connection, I may refer to the view of a foreign expert of the status of Prof. Ashby, Director of the Oxford Institute of Agricultural Economics, who was invited by the Indian Society of Agricultural Economics in 1949 to India. He referred to the amazing unconcern of the Government in this country and observed: "Having regard to (*a*) the area of agricultural land (*b*) the size of the agricultural population, (*c*) the importance of agriculture in the national economy—its actual and potential contributions to national wealth—I am appalled at the small provision made for investigation and research in Agricultural Economics....Recognising that India is a relatively poor country, it is still true that in comparison with other applied sciences of agriculture, Agricultural Economics has been starved."

The weakness of the existing organization for the collection of basic information is well known. The persons in charge of the work at the village level are ill-qualified and low-paid. The work of collection and presentation is done mechanically. There is complete absence of the research angle. In fact there is a tendency among Government Departments to confuse collection of economic statistics with economic analysis and interpretation. Though some efforts have been made in recent times to improve the collection of economic statistics, there is no change in the attitude of Government, so far as improvement in arrangements for economic analysis and interpretation are concerned. It is not realised that the handling of economic statistics by the lay politician may do more harm than good, if the data are not properly analysed and interpreted by the economist.

In a way, the British administration took more pains in such matters. For example, the Settlement Reports—apart from their political implications and anxiety to increase revenue receipts—were very thorough and comprehensive and contained a detailed assessment of the prevailing economic conditions. The Deccan Agriculturists' Relief Act was subjected to systematic periodic scrutiny and results were published which revealed all its drawbacks. The volume of similar legislation has now increased manifold. But the corresponding efforts at collecting the basic facts relevant for the purpose have not increased. There is also a striking unwillingness to avoid all scrutiny and evaluation of the working and the effectiveness of the new legislation and other administrative acts. And when independent efforts are made at such an evaluation they are frowned upon. For example, the Bombay School of Economics in collaboration with the Reserve Bank conducted an investigation with a view to discovering obstacles to the Grow More Food Compaign. When the results were published their validity was stoutly contested from official quarters. Subsequently, the Government of Bombay was compelled to appoint an official Committee to look into the question, and I learn that all its major findings amply supported our conclusions. People may lose faith in the capacity of legislation to effect change, if legislation is found either persistently unsuitable or is generally left unimplemented or worse still, if unexpected results emerge from it. The need for continuous examination of the effects of rapidly growing legislation relating to Agriculture is obvious.

By now some of the Departments of Economics and Statistics in the Central and State Governments have been considerably expanded. The Department of Economics and Statistics in the Central Ministry of Agriculture and the Bureaus of Economics and Statistics in State Governments have large staff. While considerable attention is paid to the compilation and publication of statistical data in a routine way, one wonders whether these Departments are encouraged to do correct analysis and interpretation of the data and help effectively in the formation of policy. One feels that those in charge have to watch the changing mood of the politician and the administrator and adjust their work to suit the same rather than in the interests of truth. It would be appropriate to have a searchlight on the working of these departments including the methods of recruitment of their research staff, and opportunities available to them to do independent analysis of the problems before them, and the extent to which their work influences policy. These remarks also apply to the Department of Research and Statistics in the Reserve Bank of India, which has done some good work and which is perhaps the most expensive of similar departments in the country with an estimated expenditure of Rs. 10 lakhs a year and is still going strong. I may be permitted to mention here that the country owes a debt of gratitude to Sir Chintaman Deshmukh who as Governor of the Reserve Bank took special interest in its Department of Research and developed it. Not being subject to the exigencies of the fluctuating finances of a Government, the Reserve Bank could set apart liberal funds for the purpose. While some of the work done by this Department is creditable and some of its members have proved worthy of their task, one may say that there is considerable room for improvement in the working of this Department, including the methods of recruitment of its staff. The method of recruitment and promotion of the research staff both in the Reserve Bank and in Government Departments is a matter of concern to those of us who are engaged in the training of research workers in Economics in general and in Agricultural Economics in particular. Instances are not rare in which persons with ordinary foreign degrees are preferred to those who have done approved research work in the subject concerned in Indian Universities.

Economic Analysis and the Plan

In spite of the fact that more than 40 per cent of the proposed expenditure of the Five-Year Plan is to be devoted for agricultural development, few efforts have been made to carry out competent research both as a preliminary to the Plan as well as for its subsequent evaluation. A good deal of the work is based on vague assumptions and beliefs. For example, for rural electrification, it is assumed that once electricity is produced rural areas would be able to absorb the electric energy. The question whether the farmers will have the necessary equipment and resources to utilise electricity even if it is available at low rates is not asked. Similarly, the lack of co-ordination between electricity planning and industrial planning is well-known. This has resulted in the paradoxical situation in which large electricity schemes were planned in areas where industrial possibilities were not even considered, and expansion of electricity supply was not thought of in existing industrial areas where the demand was rapidly growing. It was left to non-official research workers to point out this anomaly before some adjustment could be made. Similarly, regarding the agricultural targets in the Draft Outline, their correlation with the available financial resources was not properly examined. The same is true of minor irrigation projects for which sufficient provision was not made in the Draft Outline. In this case also, it was left to private research workers to point out the defect. Similarly the fact that the average cost for bringing an addiional acre of land under cultivation varied widely in the case of tanks and tube wells and also from one area to another was not studied. Though this was pointed out, it is not known whether these correlations have been properly examined. Though in the Revised Plan, the Commission shows awareness of the problem and realises the importance of detailed cost and benefit estimates, it does not seem to have considered how the work is going to be done.

The most glaring example of the absence of economic analysis and interpretation is in connection with the recent food policy to which I must again refer. The National Sample Survey is reported to have calculated on a sample basis that agricultural production is underestimated by 25 per cent. One wonders whether we should rely on the accuracy of a small sample in a country with such diverse agricultural conditions for this conclusion. On the same analogy, production in 1948 must also have been under-estimated by 25 per cent and therefore, decontrol ought not to have led to higher prices. Apart from this, it may be pointed out that what is relevant is not merely the collection of statistics of production, but how the economy would behave and how the distribution of grain would be affected, if controls were removed. In other words, the question to be asked is, what is the amount of agricultural surplus that would be marketed by the community in the absence of procurement and comprehensive control? The discussion of such a vital matter as food control by lay politicians in Parliament on the basis of such statistical calculations without proper economic analysis and interpretation of the relevant issues, is a sad commentary on the prevailing confusion re: the treatment of economic problems in the country at the highest level. In this connection, we may also draw attention to the fact that in the wake of the decontrol policy in Madras, economists predicted that prices would rise though the lay public were beguiled into the belief that they would not rise, so much so that the Madras step was hailed as a bold one to be imitated blindly by the rest of the country. It is wellknown now that prices have substantially increased in spite of the fact that stocks were released on the market from imported grains.

Need for Independent Economic Analysis

It may be pointed out that economic problems are often mixed up with political issues and that it is not unusual to find that political considerations often weigh in deciding economic policy. The harm done to the country at large in consequence of this confusion is not realised. The lay politician often relies on economists and statisticians employed in Government Departments not only for his material but also for his brief. He does not always expect them to tell him the truth; he wants them to find arguments to support his conclusions arrived at on non-economic considerations. In view of this, in a democratic constitution, it is essential in the interests of truth that economic analysis and interpretation should be beyond the influence of those in power and should be conducted by non-official academic institutions on scientific lines. The research workers in such institutions should be placed in such a position that they would be free to tell the truth without fear or favour, so that all parties in the country might at least have a common basis on which to work. In view of the fact that the State in India is trying to develop into a Welfare State, and that democratic planning is being rapidly organised, it is hoped that the importance of this objective will be realised by all concerned. If this is realised the importance of encouragement of research in Agricultural Economics in the Universities and independent research institutions would be easily appreciated.

Arrangements should also be made to remove the existing barriers between Government Departments and the Universities by organising more active co-operation and exchange of personnel. As in other countries, academic persons should have opportunities for consultation by Government departments, and research workers in Government departments should have opportunities to work in the Universities to have that independent and scientific outlook on their work which they lack. One of the reasons for the existing barriers between these two types of workers is the wide gap in their respective emoluments leading to a superiority complex among those in Government departments and elsewhere, which leaves no impetus in them to do quality work, and which is bound to be resented by the University research worker, who prefers his independence to money.

The Role of the Universities

It will be easily conceded that the most appropriate parties to undertake the study of and research in Agricultural Economics are the Universities. It is their function to arrange for imparting instruction and spreading knowledge about this subject. It is also their function to train workers who can help in the dissemination of correct information and problems relating to Agricultural Economics, and, above all, to carry out research in the subject. Besides the Departments of Economics of the Universities, there are a few research institutions which can also do similar work of one type or another. So far as collection of primary data is concerned, the Government must improve its own administrative machinery for the purpose. Some of the primary data are collected as a by-product of administration. In other cases, special machinery has to be attached to the Government Departments for the purpose. Whereas this is true of routine primary data, in those cases in which Governments require special studies or surveys or enquiries for specific purposes, the Universities are obviously the most appropriate parties for carrying out the work. So far as the interpretation of primary data or of material specially collected in special inquiries is concerned or their correlation, research workers in the Universities should be entrusted with the task. Among the advantages of doing so are: (1) that the work in the Universities would be without bias and, therefore, more accurate and reliable; (2) that the Universities would thus get an opportunity to train young workers in this type of work who would be useful to the country in similar work in future; (3) that besides helping the Universities to build up in this manner their research activities, on the whole the work would be cheaper, as any effort to create *ad hoc* research organizations by Government proves not only costly but also involves administrative bias and, above all, unnecessary delays. In a democratic constitution it would be easy for all parties to have confidence in the results of the work of the Universities in matters of this kind than in a Government Agency, which may be under the control of a given political party at any moment of time.

This suggestion naturally leads to the question: are the existing University Departments of Economics and similar organisations in the country equipped for the task? The only answer that can be given to this query is that the continuation of the present attitude of ignoring the Universities in work of this kind, adds to the existing neglect of the Universities in their efforts to develop research in Agricultural Economics. Apart from other special funds, which should be earmarked for this purpose, even the diversion of funds which are now being spent by the Government for *ad hoc* enquiries to strengthen University Departments would result in permanent advantages to the country as a whole. Whereas continuity and tradition would be gradually developed in this type of research work done by the Universities, in the case of *ad hoc* enquiries by Government such experience is often lost. I would, therefore, suggest that immediate steps be taken for strengthening the existing Departments of Economics in the Universities, by the addition of separate Sections in Agricultural Economics to them. The courses and syllabuses should be suitably revised to enable those interested to pursue this study. Scholarships and Fellowships should be liberally endowed to enable qualified persons to undertake research in Agricultural Economics. Small sample research projects should be undertaken by these Sections on their own in their respective areas to train research workers. For this they should have adequate funds at their disposal. Both the Central and State Governments should first think of utilising the resources of the Universities, for any given enquiry in which they might be interested, because by doing so they would not only get their work done at a smaller cost and more efficiently, but would also provide training to young workers in future. Once this arrangement is set on foot in a proper manner, it would be possible to expect private donations to flow into the same channel.

Finance for Research in Agricultural Economics

I may be reminded that this is all a question of funds and that the funds at the disposal of Government are limited. But if the basic facts and tendencies in the economic life of the country are not correctly known and interpreted for those in authority, the expenditure which they want to incur for development would be wasted. Compared with the total expenditure earmarked for Agricultural Development in the Plan, the percentage that would be required for the purposes of developing study and research in Agricultural Economics would be insignificant, if we take into account the immense advantage likely to result from that effort. What is lacking is not so much funds for the purpose, but the desire and the will to understand and appreciate the problems as well as the approach suggested here. Instead of keeping the Universities as water-tight compartments and condemning them as academic or unpractical, if efforts are made to see that the life of the people is reflected in the work of the Universities and that the results of such work and such training are utilised with advantage in Government policy and measures, we shall have that harmonious and well-balanced development for the progress of the country for which we all aspire.

In making this suggestion, I may refer to the experience of the U.K. and the U.S.A. where Universities and research institutes are liberally assisted by Government and generously endowed by private donors for work of this kind. It is also true that the work of the Universities is kept free from political bias so that all parties are able to rely on their conclusions. Besides, there is close co-operation between the research departments of the Universities and those of the Government which is conspicuous by its absence in this country.

I have said that Government does spend sometimes lavishly on some pet schemes of research in an unco-ordinated manner. It sets up *ad hoc* bodies to do the work because it does not have the correct approach on the best methods of carrying out its work. In order to make my point clear I shall try to give some illustrations. Several illustrations could be cited of this tendency; I shall, however, satisfy myself by referring briefly to only four of them.

1. *Inquiry Regarding Agricultural Workers.* The Ministry of Labour, Government of India, undertook an All-India Enquiry into the conditions of Agriculural Workers in June 1949. Among other things, the enquiry was intended to collect data regarding unemployment, earnings, cost and standard of living and indebtedness of agricultural workers. After a preliminary enquiry which covered 27 villages and 3,000 families, the method of enquiry was revised and the rest of the enquiry was conducted with the help of State Governments. I understand the total expenditure spent on this enquiry exceeded Rs. 10 lakhs. Instead of entrusting the work to different University Departments of Economics, it was laid down that the organization created by the Ministry of Labour for

the purpose should ask University Professors and students to give voluntary assistance in the collection of data. I remember, while this was in progress, that the person in charge of the Bombay Office of this organisation wrote to me letters asking me in the name of the Government of India that the University Professor and some students should be at his disposal for collecting the necessary information. The person who wrote did not seem to be competent to handle the subject-matter of the enquiry, much less to deal with scientific workers in seeking their co-operation. He was also not aware of the conditions under which University Departments functioned and the way in which they could co-operate in such an enquiry.

2. *National Sample Survey.* In connection with the work of the National Income Committee, I understand that the data are to be supplied by a separate organisation called the National Sample Survey. Among the fairly wide objects of this survey is the collection of dependable data on different socio-economic aspects of rural life in the country. The number of schedules to be filled is large, and some of them are very detailed and quite impressive. What I am concerned at the moment is the way in which this is organised from the point of view of the encouragement of studies in Agricultural Economics in the Universities. I understand that a large sum of Rs. 35 lakhs has been set apart by the Government of India for the purpose and has been placed at the disposal of the Indian Statistical Institute, Calcutta. As I do not have first-hand knowledge of the way in which things are done, I have tried to find out the position as best as I could, and subject to correction, I would like to make the following observations. In the first place, this enquiry should have been conceived not merely as a statistical enquiry. It is essentially an economic enquiry, though its form may be statistical. I am not aware whether competent Economists have had any effective share in the planning and execution of the work. I am not aware whether the work is being carried out on some uniform pattern of organisation in different parts of the country. I can, however, say with confidence that the University Departments of Economics have in most cases been kept in the dark. One and a half years have already gone since the survey started its work. We do not know to what extent it has helped the work of the National Income

Committee. We are not aware whether this survey is likely to become a permanent organisation, because we find that under this assumption, it is trying to take up other work for which it is obviously not suited. One would like to know how the large funds at the disposal of this organisation are spent, whether there is any financial control over it and whether still more funds are likely to be given to it.

3. *Rural Credit Survey.* The third enquiry to which I would like to make a reference is the Rural Credit Survey now being carried out by the Reserve Bank of India. Arising out of the recommendations of the recent Committee on the Development of Rural Banking, the Reserve Bank is now anxious to play its part so far as rural credit institutions are concerned. It appears that the Reserve Bank was anxious to complete the enquiry in record time, and came to the conclusion that the only way to get its research staff and other parties associated with it to do the work in time, *i.e.* in 9 months from the start, was to provide the necessary drive. I understand that for this purpose, a small committee of five persons has been set up by the Reserve Bank two of whom are administrators and one of whom is the Chairman. I am aware that in a few centres the co-operation of the Universities or Research Institutes has been sought. But these appear to be exceptions. It is not easy for me to understand why the Reserve Bank which has a very costly Department of Research and has done some useful work, should not have thought of parallel Departments of Research in the Universities as the appropriate parties to co-operate in this work. So far as the expenditure incurred for this purpose is concerned, I understand that it is likely to be about Rs. 15 lakhs.

4. *Evaluation of Community Projects.* The Planning Commission has recently set up an organisation for the Evaluation of the Community Development Projects in the country with the help of the Ford Foundation. I am glad that we have at the head of this organization one of our valued colleagues, Prof. D. G. Karve. This organisation is supposed to be independent, though it is a branch of the Planning Commission. If the Commission really wanted it to be independent, I submit in all humility, that the work ought to have been entrusted to the Universities. With a small staff at the Centre to co-ordinate the work, Prof. Karve would have been really independent in his work if he were functioning in co-

operation with the Universities, with whom he has worked all his life. I am also surprised that the American authorities in general and the Ford Foundation in particular, did not think of this, in spite of the fact that the Universities would be first considered for such work in the U.S.A. I venture to suggest that even now it is not too late to make the necessary change, because the work has hardly begun. It must be conceded that the different Universities in the country would have greater and more lively interest in the Projects in their respective areas, that they would have greater local knowledge and facilities and that they would be able to recruit and train local investigators without difficulty. The amount of expenditure spent in his way would have been uilised with greater effect, better results, wider training, and above all, for encouragement to the Universities to develop research in Agricultural Economics.

Indian Society of Agricultural Economics

In the somewhat dark picture regarding the difficulties experienced by Universities to develop the study of Agricultural Economics that I had to paint, there is a silver lining. This is provided by the work of the Indian Society of Agricultural Economics under whose auspices we are meeting today. For the last 12 years this Society has made an attempt to convert itself into a research organisation. It has published several valuable research publications and its quarterly journal has now an established reputation both in India and outside. It has also created interest in the subject by its Annual Conferences, and by keeping contact with similar bodies in other countries including the International Conference of Agricultural Economics. In spite of indifference or want of response from the authorities, the Society has continued to persevere in its efforts to draw pointed attention to the need for suitable encouragement of the study of and research in Agricultural Economics. Not being disappointed at the apathy of Government, the Society at the instance of its President and Mr. Elmhirst, President of the International Conference of Agricultural Economists recently made certain concrete suggestions to Government calculated to rouse interest in Agricultural Economics, not only in the country generally but also among those in authority. The first suggestion was that the Government of India should invite a well-known Agricultural Economist to advise them regarding the Role of Agricultural Economics in the Ministry of Agriculture as well as in the rest of the country. The Society suggested the name of Prof. Theodore Schultz in this connection, and we are happy to find that as a result of this Prof. Schultz is likely to be in India soon. Let me extend to him on behalf of all of us a most cordial welcome to this country and assure him of our fullest co-operation. Let us also hope that the advice that he may be able to render will be followed up by the Government of India without delay.

The second suggestion made by the Society was that the Government of India should sponsor an invitation to the International Agricultural Economics Conference to hold its next session in India. The object of this suggestion was that the meeting of International Experts on this subject in India to discuss world problems in Agricultural Economics, would rouse the necessary interest in the country in general and in those in authority in particular, so that it might be possible to remove the prevailing apathy towards the subject and bring about the desired progress. I am glad to be able to say that the Government of India did send its representative to the recent International Conference at Michigan and an invitation was extended. Unfortunately there was some delay in doing so, and it was not possible for the International body to accept this invitation for the next session which they have decided to hold in Finland. I have no doubt however, that the invitation of the Government of India will stand and be repeated at Finland for the meeting thereafter.

The third suggestion of the Society was for making a special financial provision for research in Agricultural Economics. So far as the source from which the necessary finance should come, Sir Manilal Nanavati has repeatedly made a useful suggestion *viz.* that a certain percentage of the profits of the Reserve Bank should be constituted into a Reserve Fund for creating the necessary organisation at the Centre for the development of agriculture, including research in Agricultural Economics. This principle is in operation in Australia. In fact in an agricultural country like ours, what is novel is that such a provision has not yet been made. By doing so the work for the development of this subject will be independent of the changing financial situation of the Government, and there would be continuity of resources from which to finance such a desirable object. It is expected that there would be unanimity of opinion on such a proposal, and that all concerned would whole-heartedly support the early implementation of this suggestion from so experienced a person both in Agricultural Economics and in Central Banking as Sir Manilal Nanavati.

In the first place, the Government should see that its own work in this connection is put on a proper footing. There is a long-standing need for having an Economics Wing of the Indian Council of Agricultural Research, so that the Economics of the various scientific schemes suggested for the improvement of agriculture are properly studied as well as certain problems of an all-India nature are effectively examined. The same applies to the Department of Economics and Statistics in the Ministry of Agriculture and similar organisations in the States and the Reserve Bank.

Besides, the Government should encourage independent research. The Government of India would be failing in its duty, if they did not rise to the occasion and did not decide without delay to provide adequate funds to existing University Centres and organisations like the Indian Society of Agricultural Economics for the development of the study of and research in Agricultural Economics. Besides providing funds in this manner to strengthen the existing University Departments, I do hope that instead of indulging in the costly luxury of *ad hoc* economic enquiries in rural problems by administrative personnel, who have little interest or capacity to do the work, the Governments at the Centre and in the States will appreciate that to get such work done with the help of the University Departments would be not only cheaper, not only more efficient and more accurate, but would also be in the national interest inasmuch as it would provide training and experience to a large number of young workers.

Conclusion

In conclusion, let me say that in this rapid survey of the role of agricultural economics in our country, if I have been frank, it is in the interests of the subject for the development of which we have met today. I have no malice against any institution or person whom I may have criticised directly or idirectly, and if I have emphasised the part that the Universities should play and can play in this national work, it is based not only on the experience of other countries, but also on my own experience and observation both as a research worker in the University of Bombay and as one who has had opportunities to know first-hand the working of Government Departments and Institutions. I am fully aware of the existing deficiencies in the Universities. But it is more a reflection of the studied neglect of the past, than a cause for ignoring the Universities in this national work.

While emphasizing the role of the Universities and academic workers, I would like to address a few words to brother-economists. We should be aware of the increased responsibilities that we have to shoulder under the new environment in the country. We are in a position partly by influencing the work of the younger generation trained under us and partly by contributing to the knowledge on the subject by our own researches, to render substantial help in the formation of correct economic policy in the country. This requires devotion to the subject and hard and sustained work. The time has come when the Universities and other employing authorities in academic institutions should give to the economists working under them adequate opportunities for research work and make it worth their while to do independent work of this nature. Though there is considerable room for improvement in the outlook of the employing authorities on the one hand, and in the work of the academic economist on the other, I venture to suggest that some existing institutions have reached a high level of efficiency and standard of work to be able to undertake research projects of the type referred to above. In fact, they have been entrusted by Government with some research projects and their work has been appreciated. I need not give illustrations, lest I may overlook deserving cases, but I may say that there is no reason why many more such institutions cannot be developed in the country in the different University centres.

In all such development, Agricultural Economics should have an important place. In the existing Departments of Economics in the Universities, we find that due attention is not given to this subject by those in charge. Whatever may have been the position under the British regime when some felt that there was no room for original research work in Agricultural Economics due to the static condition of our rural economy, we must recognise that the entire scene is now rapidly changing. The various reforms for improvement of agriculture which have been already introduced and the various schemes of development of agriculture included in the Plan indicate the pace at which changes are occurring and are likely to occur in the life of the people. Add to this the consciousness among the rural folk due to adult suffrage and the work of the political parties, thus increasing their desire and urge for a better existence which were hitherto absent. The land policy as outlined in the Plan, the various schemes of irrigation that are contemplated and particularly the river valley projects, the community development projects which aim at all-round development of rural economy including the outlook and methods of work of the farmer, are but few illustrations of fundamental and rapid changes which are about to take place. This opens up a vast and also unlimited scope for research and investigation beyond the capacity of Government Departments. Those interested in Agricultural Economics are now provided with huge experiments the like of which they have not seen before. If we can utilise these immense possibilities for work each in our respective areas, we shall be able to contribute to a better understanding of the new forces which are set in motion. Because of the nature of the problem, there is also room for joint efforts in this work for social scientists not only in Economics but also in Sociology, Psychology and Politics. We must be ready to view these dynamic forces in their proper perspective. We have thus opportunities to contribute in our humble way to the thought on the subject so that timely changes in policy and measures may be adopted. I have every hope that in spite of difficulties, we shall rise to the occasion and prove worthy of our new responsibilities.

The time is also overdue when workers in this field should organise themselves more effectively so that their voice can be heard in the appropriate quarters. Our existing arrangements by which we meet once a year in Conferences of this type though useful, are not adequate for organising scientific work and scientific opinion in Economics in general and in Agricultural Economics in particular. Some more effective machinery is called for, for the purpose, and I trust both the Indian Economic Association and the Indian Society of Agricultural Economics will give due attention to the problem of co-ordinating research activities in the country and of bringing about greater cohesion and contacts among research workers.

Let the academic scientific worker in Economics have his due place in the new scheme of things in the country; let him play his legitimate part as an independent worker above party politics, and let him contribute to a correct understanding of the complex forces which operate in the economic life of the country in a detached but independent manner. All thinking persons will agree that for the building up of New India, unless we strengthen the Universities to do this work properly, we shall not have that independent critical examination of economic problems, which we need so badly. We boast of political independence but tolerate intellectual paralysis; we confuse independence of thought as hostility to the Government of the day and therefore unpatriotic; we want to abolish caste from our social system and yet create new castes in the intellectual sphere; we treat the academic research worker in economics as a person whose shadow shall not fall on the politician or the administrator, lest the practical wisdom of the latter be polluted by the theories of the former; we do not realise that the so-called wisdom of the practical man is the unsystematic and often unconscious theorising on his limited individual experience, and that the so-called unpractical theories of the scientific economist are the result of systematic thought based on the widest possible experience in the subject concerned. I trust this unfortunate tendency is only a passing phase and that the academic workers in Economics in general and Agricultural Economics in particular will have their rightful place in the growth of New India.

PART III

TECHNICAL PAPERS ON PLANNING AND DEVELOPMENT

(jointly with P. R. BRAHMANANDA)

1. Technical Knowledge and Managerial Capacity as Limiting Factors on Industrial Expansion in Underdeveloped Countries

Paper submitted to the Round Table Conference of the International Economic Association held at Santa Margharita, Italy from 28th August 1953 to 2nd September 1953 on "Factors of Economic Progress".

2. Investment Pattern in the Second Five Year Plan

3. Institutional Implications of a Bolder Plan

Working papers submitted to the Panel of Economists, Planning Commission in March 1955 in connection with the preparation for the Second Five Year Plan.

4. The Size of Nations and Dynamic Adjustment: Problems of Developing Countries

Paper submitted to the Round Table Conference of the International Economic Association held at Lisbon, Portugal in September 1957 on the "Size of Nations".

5. Price Stabilisation *versus* Fiscal Stabilisation

Article published by Kyklos (International Review for Social Sciences, Geneva) in its symposium II on Stabilisation and Development of Primary Producing Countries in Vol. XII—1959.

6. Capital Supply and Growth—Source of Savings

Paper submitted to the Round Table Conference of the International Economic Association held at Gamagori, Japan on Economic Development with special reference to East Asia in April 1960.

Technical Knowledge and Managerial Capacity as Limiting Factors on Industrial Expansion in Underdeveloped Countries*

THE rate of a country's economic development depends on many complementary factors; deficiencies in any of these may slow down or even inhibit economic growth. Underdevelopment is often attributed to a low rate of capital accumulation; certainly, shortage of capital compels changes in technique and organization so that existing resources can be used to best advantage. Technical knowledge and managerial capacity are both necessary and complementary. Mere technogical knowledge is of little avail; managerial efficiency in an underdeveloped economy in large part determines whether full advantage is taken of new techniques. The more efficient management is, the greater the demand for technical knowledge.

The essence of technical progress is to reduce the volume of resources needed to produce a given output. The relative efficiency of different technical developments thus depends upon how scarce the resources saved are. An economy where a particular factor is scarce, or which urgently needs new techniques, calls technical knowledge to its aid. But new methods will not necessarily be found. Otherwise existing international differences in development would be less. Technical knowledge has not developed autonomously in underdeveloped countries, because certain essential conditions are not satisfied.

Technological advance can occur at various levels. It can come from experienced workers, from research departments of large firms, or from independent specialized laboratories and research

* Paper submitted to the Round Table Conference of the International Economic Association held at Santa Margharita, Italy on 28 August 1953 to 2 September 1953 on "Factors of Economic Progress". (Jointly with P. R. Brahmananda).

institutions. How far the individual worker can himself modify known methods or invent new ones depends upon the extent of specialization. In underdeveloped economies there is too little specialization; nor does the high labour turnover allow long-period concentration. Again, whether industrial or state resources can be devoted to technical research depends on general economic development. Poor countries have no surplus resources for such long-term investment. Most firms are small and lack research departments; nor do specialized research agencies develop autonomously. The state's responsibility in developing technological knowledge is widely recognized; but since the state is poor, underdeveloped countries inevitably depend in part on accumulated technical knowledge in advanced countries.

Technical knowledge can be broadly classified as:

1. Knowledge with economic possibilities, which can be utilized in the socio-economic environment, but which is not available because developed countries will not impart it, or will do so only on conditions. This occurs particularly with international combines which have pioneered industrial expansion in underdeveloped countries, and whose technical knowledge is closely guarded. Again, a country might industrialize without its own citizens knowing how to construct or operate particular industries. This would raise serious problems if friction caused foreigners to leave, which partly explains the attitude of underdeveloped countries to foreign capital.

2. Knowledge available on reasonable terms, but which is useless without changes in industrial organization or social policy.

3. Knowledge which is available, but which requires easy access to capital. Here, known technology is of little value, unless it develops more suitable methods.

4. Knowledge which could be used only if the country has sufficient capital. First, one must establish training institutions. But in underdeveloped economies existing institutions often cannot be used because of high training costs, uncertainty in employment, and caste or class rigidities. Expenditure on technical training is a long-term investment, which few families can afford. A literary education is preferred; those who can afford technical education usually seek it abroad. Local employers tend to prefer persons trained abroad, with unfortunate effects on home development of technical training institutions. Again, some industrialists in under-

developed countries depend on technicians trained in their own firms rather than at universities. Apprenticeship is not common, and technical colleges do not own factories. Qualified men tend to be under-used and have to accept jobs where their hard-won specialized knowledge is of little avail.

The desire for higher technical education, implying great specialization, depends on both size and certainty of demand. Unless many industries are expanding, highly specialized individuals risk unemployment.

Some underdeveloped economies have powerful obstacles to labour mobility. Communities are divided into watertight compartments, perhaps by caste systems. Such obstacles persist, despite changing social opinion, largely through vested interests. Those who are better off consolidate their relatively high standard of living by preventing the flow of talent, though democracy is slowly eliminating this. It therefore takes some time for wage and salary differentials to adjust labour supplies. Pecuniary rewards cannot break the rigidities of tradition.

Even if technical schools and research organizations are successfully established, superior methods of production may not be used. It is difficult to introduce changes in countries with an intrinsic dislike of new methods. Old methods persist, despite their inadequacy; routine and inertia create an atmosphere unreceptive to new methods. Unless the need for improvement is keenly felt, superior methods are not used. This new attitude requires the individual to feel that conscious effort can substantially improve his living standards. The difficulties come from sheer conservatism from opposition by groups whose importance is threatened by new methods; or from opposition to the economic and social consequences of such methods.

Obviously the application of technical knowledge must lead to economies in using labour. In most undeveloped countries labour is abundant. Thus, new methods do reduce costs, but often cause unwelcome unemployment or under-employment. Admittedly the savings may enable individual firms to expand output and employment, but only much later. Initially, new methods tend to create unemployment which, if population pressure is heavy, causes serious social frictions. In fast-developing countries technological unemployment, though sometimes important, does not persist, because increased activity absorbs displaced labour. Industrial development can remedy these difficulties, but only if rapid and certain.

Again, new production methods may displace particular types of workers; for example, those in cottage industry. Admittedly, individual entrepreneurs can use superior methods, despite the dislocation and distress they cause. But, in a democracy, changes which seriously disturb the existing fabric are frowned upon. The new conception of the Welfare State sometimes prevents countries from taking full advantage of technical knowledge.

Other drawbacks of Western technology are: rapid urbanization and consequent overcrowding and slums; undue concentration of industry in particular areas; glaring discrepancies in living standards between different groups; and numerous consequent social problems. These difficulties can be overcome by expenditure on social policies; but a poor community can afford little such spending.

The socio-political environment thus tends to be unreceptive to modern techniques. There are also doubts about the practical application of improved technology. The economic unit must be large enough for the techniques to be reasonably applied. Capital must be available, also effective organization—big 'ifs' in underdeveloped economies. The unit of activity often hardly warrrants applying improved methods. Co-operative farms would help; but how can they be organized? Unless industries are monopolistic, technological knowledge is unlikely to be used autonomously. New techniques need new capital.

But can present technical knowledge itself help to produce more rapid industrial expansion? Past industrial development in advanced countries suggests that technical and organizational changes were linked; and that continuously expanding markets enabled industry to absorb new knowledge, and gave it freedom, despite the economic and social disturbances involved. When public opinion had crystallized in favour of a social policy to temper adverse effects, these countries were already highly developed. In most underdeveloped countries, modern technical knowledge has to be superimposed upon a retrograde system, and the social conscience will hardly give technology a free field. To desire industrialization in these countries, without wishing to pay its heavy price in supplying capital and dealing with social upheavals, is to ignore very grave difficulties.

Again, underdeveloped countries lack the appropriate technological knowledge. Each country has to work out its own salvation, and, particularly, to find out which production methods are feasible for it. In this sense technological knowledge is a limiting factor.

The following techniques seem best for underdeveloped countries: (*a*) those which can be quickly learned; (*b*) those requiring little initial investment and no increase in the size of firms; (*c*) those reducing the 'gestation' period; (*d*) those requiring less investment in specialized and skilled workers, being appropriate to current educational standards; (*e*) those saving scarce resources other than labour; (*f*) those expanding production horizons, and increasing supplies such as minerals or electricity. The limited resources available for acquiring technical knowledge necessitate careful choice of fields in which to become proficient. Natural aptitudes, expected requirements in various fields, and activities in which specialization is desired, show the fields of knowledge appropriate for concentrated development. Without careful planning, resources may be dispersed. The choice between pure and applied research is also important. Scarcity of resources makes it desirable to seek knowledge with immediate practical application.

Again, what type of specialist technical training is most useful? Should it be based on a wide general training, or should specialization start early? In backward countries, specialization might be preferable. The pace of industrial expansion in backward countries depends on modifying Western techniques and creating a suitable organizational framework. Here managerial capacity has a significant role.

Managerial capacity must be distinguished from innovation or entrepreneurship. Managers direct existing enterprises; innovators cause radical, discontinuous, changes in the economic environment. The manager's function is to adapt production as efficiently as possible to changes in external conditions, including changed production methods, forms of organization, markets and legal systems. The 'optimum' organization is continuously changing with the economic environment. Co-ordination is essentially dynamic; its efficiency determines the reserves which firms can create. Thus it limits future expansion. Further, the speed with which firms adapt themselves determines the rapidity of social change.

Deficiencies in management limit expansion in two main ways:

1. Management becomes more difficult as firms expand; entrepreneurs prefer limited development. With more adequate managerial talent, individual firms might grow faster. Such limits on expansion occur at two extremes. First, firms denied specialized managers suffer from a deficiency in managerial capacity. Since management has to be performed anyhow the choice lies between a specialized manager, able to adopt highly-scientific management methods, and the native, untrained, ability of owners or their nominees. Such firms could attain greater efficiency if assisted by specialized management. Second, firms may grow so large that even the best managerial talent cannot cope with them. In underdeveloped countries the former limitation is more important.

2. Fewer new firms may be established because entrepreneurs are lacking. How is management related to enterprise? In most underdeveloped countries entrepreneurs are scarce enough; the position only worsens when they become entangled in actual management. This happens when enterprise and management are sufficiently diversified. If proprietors prefer to manage their own firms, then, from the community's point of view, the more they perform actual management the less their time for starting or expanding enterprises. Modern management is highly complicated, and specialization on management or entrepreneurship is essential. Development in backward countries depends too much on a small group of leaders; they should not fritter away their resources. Why do not entrepreneurs realise this? It is a vicious circle. Efficient managers are scarce. Entrepreneurs therefore cling to responsible functions. Yet unless there is a sustained demand from entrepreneurs, the best men do not specialize in management. Until proprietors trust in managers, such a specialized cadre will not develop. There are, broadly, three stages in developing the management function. First, the entrepreneur himself is the manager. Second, as responsibilities increase, he may delegate them; but not if he is old-fashioned, or disapproves of decentralizing responsibility, or cannot find or afford specialized managers. In any case, a firm's progress may be hampered by insufficient personal interest or organizational ability. As a result,

the owner's energy may be dispersed between several concerns, all run inefficiently. Gradually, as the concerns grow, the owner will probably have to delegate his functions. Thus, third, the management function becomes subdivided, and the manager allows greater functional specialization.

The attitude of industry generally, the rate at which firms expand, and the conscious need for functional specialization, all largely determine the demand for managers. If most firms are small and moderately poor, the demand for specialized managers is limited. 'Average' managerial capacity is abundant, but specialized management can only be used after the business has become fairly large. Somewhat later, diminishing returns set in and co-ordination exceeds the individual's capacity. Since management is an admixture of diverse talents, the supply of efficient managers is limited. The indivisible nature of managerial capacity and the predominance of small firms explain why the general level of managerial efficiency is relatively low in underdeveloped countries. Yet if large corporations developed, the demand for specialized managers might fall. The demand for managers depends on the number of individual firms and on their rate of growth.

As firms grow, they may find it desirable to delegate management to an external agency looking after several concerns and with a financial interest in them. This system makes specialized managers unnecessary in individual firms—and large-scale management is more economical. But the system can lead to abuse. An agency interested in several competing firms may use its funds so that their respective interests are set at naught. Again, when some industrial development has occurred, such agencies hinder growth by preventing the separation of ownership from control, and prevent specialized business leaders and managers emerging. Hence the Managing agency system in India has become outmoded.

To make good deficiencies in managerial capacity, one first needs to teach entrepreneurs how to employ specialized talent and to encourage its development. If reliance on family relationships cannot be reduced, adequate training should be given to managers. Even in advanced countries, entrepreneurs often look down on scientific training. They are doubtful of qualified persons' ability to adapt themselves. Industrialists in advanced countries are beginning to realize that scientific management pays; but not yet in underdeveloped countries.

Again, the scale of rewards must attract the right kind of managers. In underdeveloped countries government service takes the best talent, partly because of better conditions and higher income, more because of the high social status of government service. To attract good men, private business must offer unduly high rewards, great security and possibilities of advancement.

In developed economies, changes in ownership or control do not cause large management changes. In underdeveloped countries, the tendency to appoint relations to key positions does frequently cause changes in top management. New men come from outside the firm, giving little opportunity for advancement to those inside. The consequent uncertainty and lack of incentive helps to perpetuate inefficiency.

Managerial talent also develops slowly, because of the general 'unenlightened' attitude of entrepreneurs. Industrial development depends on capital, and hence on the pattern of wealth distribution. Since there are few investment institutions, industrial advance largely depends on the attitude of wealth-owning groups. If they prefer short-term gains, even the best manager has limited scope. Indeed, interests of owners and managers may diverge. The latter stress the continuity of the concern and its efficient organization. The rewards of this are reaped only after much time, and often lead only to intangible returns like increased prestige. Managers would like to create reserves for expansion; proprietors only judge managers by their ability to earn immediate profits. Unless owners are enlightened, management has little scope and good managers will continue to be scarce.

Private enterprise in an underdeveloped economy can hardly offer the same opportunities as government service. Firms can only give security within their own organization. Unless industry generally is highly developed, and promotion chances are reasonable, too little talent will enter industry, and the best of it will go to the larger, well-established firms, which by definition, need it less. Average industrial efficiency will not increase. Small wonder, then, that in many underdeveloped economies foreign-owned industry attracts the best talent. Again, social prestige in business may not tempt able men. If standards of education of businessmen—and morale and standards in private business—are low, social status in industry will suffer.

The remedy is to separate management from ownership and enterprise; to make management a profession; to improve conditions of work; to increase rewards, and to raise morale. This would help to attract the right type of manager. Managers should have the latest information about business conditions and methods, if necessary from specialized agencies. Established houses may thus gain little. They may even stand to lose because less-established firms will develop; but the reserves of developed firms can enter other fields. The considerable outlay on specialized management leaves the majority of small firms, unable, at present, to use modern organization methods. Specialized agencies able to perform various management functions should be developed, and their services made available widely and cheaply, until firms grow big enough to employ specialized talent. Yet no outside agency can alter the internal problems of firms, which must themselves see that their employees are trained in scientific management.

Investment Pattern in the Second Five Year Plan*

THE problem to be discussed is the relative role that is to be assigned to industry as against agriculture, and within industry to heavy industry as against light industry, and within light industry, between labour-intensive fields of activity and capital-intensive fields of activity. In other words, what should be the pattern of investment in the Second Five Year Plan?

2. The main criticism that was levelled against the First Five Year Plan was that a relatively low priority was accorded to the development of capital goods industries.[1] The Plan could be defended on grounds of the emergency conditions that prevailed at the time. A major effort had to be devoted towards filling up of the structural gaps created on account of the Partition, and the undertaking of measures to provide a more or less long-term solution of the food problem. Moreover, the Commission had to consider a number of schemes which were already under way. Our point was not that so much importance was given to agriculture, but that provision should have been made towards the establishment of those industries which would enable the economy continuously to step up its output of food through an increase in the ability to plough resources towards irrigation, multi-purpose projects, etc. The neglect of heavy industries ancillary to agriculture was considered a defect not because of the lack of emphasis on

* Paper submitted to the Panel of Economists, Planning Commission, March, 1955 (Jointly with P. R. Brahmananda).

[1] The idea that heavy industries should get predominance in the Second Five Year Plan is being heavily canvassed in certain quarters. We may be permitted to point out that this was among other things the central point of criticism re the First Five Year Plan in *Planning for a Shortage Economy* by Vakil and Brahmananda (vide Chapter X, pp. 130-139). It may also be pointed out that the above work emphasised the development of capital goods industries ancillary to agriculture as against the current plea made in certain quarters for an indiscriminate expansion of heavy goods industries.

industrialization, but because it was only through such industries that a continuously increasing marketable surpuls of food could be built up to meet the requirements of a growing population, thus enabling a larger extent of industrial potential to be built up. The Planning Commission, however, seems to have missed the theoretical perspective governing the above criticism. It may be pointed out that the central problem of the Indian economy, namely, the slow rate of growth of industrial employment is due to the slow rate of increase in the supplies of marketable surplus of food. The problem is not merely one of lack of appropriate organization facilities in the industry; nor is it one of lack of innovational abilities; and not even one of lack of credit. No doubt, these and other factors may tend to explain why the performance of the economy does not reach, at different periods, the capacity limits. The process of a continuous building up of complementary facilities in the industrial sector becomes dependent upon the rate of growth of expansion of the marketable surplus of food. This, in its turn, depends upon the rate of growth of production and the rate of growth of internal requirements, the former depending upon the paçe of expansion in the construction of capital assets and utilisational measures which increase productivity, and the latter depending upon primarily the growth of population, particularly, the rate of increase in the pressure on land. From this point of view, a long-term solution of poverty and unemployment in India is to be sought through two types of efforts. On the one hand, we should continuously build up our agricultural basis; on the other we should build up the necessary organisational machinery in industry which automatically utilizes effectively the conditions of increasing the marketable surplus that are created as a result of the first set of measures. Mere efforts to develop a number of industries of diverse types, with no corresponding improvement in the conditions governing the availability of marketable surplus will lead to the emergence of excess capacity in the industrial sector. The problem takes a peculiar shape in which while we know fully well that the rate of industrialisation has been slow, we are not able at the same time to keep the industrial units at a level where there capacity is fully utilized. The problem here of course is one arising out of a lack of markets as well as capital. It is in such a quandary that India finds herself to-day. It is from this point of view that we had emphasised in 1951 the need to develop certain heavy industries ancillary to agricultural production. (Manufacture of equipment necessary for irrigation and power plants, earth-moving equipment, equipment for fertiliser plants, intermediate goods like steel, cement, etc.) This would enable the economy to have a larger rate of development of irrigation and multi-purpose projects, which in turn would solve the problem of provision of wage-goods capital, a deficiency of which is the central bottle-neck preventing a higher rate of industrial expansion and at the same time provide a growing market for various types of consumer goods, whose growth in turn would provide the market for the development of heavy industries, manufacturing equipment of consumer-goods. It may be pointed out that this approach outlined by us in 1951, is different from the approach which puts a blind emphasis on the development of heavy industries of all sorts.[2] Reference may be made to similar lack of co-ordination in Electricity Planning with industrial planning leading to waste of natural resources. The very ideal of planning presupposes such co-ordination and one is surprised at the desire of some people to advocate the growth of heavy industries without regard to the demand for their products.

3. It is obvious therefore that we must concentrate on the development of heavy industries which are ancillary to agriculture, particularly those which will help increase the rate of construction of irrigation, multi-purpose projects, etc. A continuous state of excess capacity in these industries would enable us to have a continuously increasing supply of marketable surplus of food. The question that arises here is whether during the period of the Second Five Year Plan the emphasis on agriculture, directly or indirectly, should be lessened. Those who argue from this point of view have the recent food situation in their mind. Food production has gone up by about 11 per cent as compared to last year, and by 20 per cent as compared to the targets laid down in the First Five Year Plan. The burden of food imports too has eased considerably. The problem appears to be one of how to dispose of the quantities of food that have accumulated with the farmers and the middlemen. The optimistic approach that has been posited for the Second Plan derives its strength mainly from the above situa-

[2] Vide *Economics of Electricity Planning* by Vakil and Brahmananda.

tion. It may be pointed out that we are not at all certain whether the improvement in the food output, is of a permanent character. The Third Progress Report of the Five Year Plan is not clear on the point whether the improvement is of a transitory character. No doubt, a number of short-term measures like provision of fertilizers, introduction of new methods of cultivation, better supplies of seeds and manures, the innovation of new organisational leadership in the villages and a number of other reasons have helped to increase food production, but these different measures are complementary to the windfall in the form of good rainfall which has blessed the economy during the last two years. It has been found that the aggregate food production may vary as much as 20 per cent, depending upon variations in the monsoon. The other measures raise the level of peak output during periods of good rainfall. They do not, however, help raise the level of food production when rainfall is not favourable. From these points of view, unless we are definitely clear that the ghost of the food problem has been once and for all exorcised, it will be hazardous to ignore the need to step up continuously agricultural production. We would, therefore, suggest that unless we are definitely certain about the permanent character of the improvement in the food situation, it would not be proper to embark on a type of industrialisation which neglects agriculture over a fairly long period of time.

4. In this connection, it may be pointed out that the system for an expansion of heavy industries is based on the experience of the Soviet Union which concentrated in the first few years on the development of heavy industries and later on, on the development of consumer-goods industries including that of agricultural production. It would be dangerous to argue on the basis of the experience of a country which had had a different economic background to face in planning. May we point out that the problem in the case of the Soviet Union in regard to agricultural production was more one of deficiency of marketable surplus rather than one of overall production; whereas in the case of India, we have both the problem of a relatively lower production as well as a lower proportion of marketable surplus. The Soviet measures towards collectivisation of agriculture and co-operative farming were designed on the one hand to divert surplus labour from the rural areas and on the other to increase the extent of the flow of marketable sur-

plus. Nor did the Soviet Union face during its earlier planning period the problem of expanding agricultural production on the basis of long-range capital-intensive schemes in the form of irrigation and multi-purpose projects. Further, the technical problem confronting the Soviet Union during the period of the plan was more that of lack of complementary capital assets like livestock and tractors, rather than that of lack of assured supplies of water. Moreover, the absolute growth of population in the Soviet Union in any given year is one-third of that in India. We should not assume that all is well with the Soviet economic situation now. The Soviet Government appears to have recognised the importance of agricultural production and measures are being undertaken to bring about increases in agricultural productivity. After all, the time has not yet arrived to give any final ex-post verdict on the issue whether the investment pattern chosen in the Soviet Union for their plan was of the optimum type. No doubt, every economy has to take certain risks, but then would it not be appropriate to point out frankly the nature of the risk that an economy has to undertake, and put it directly before the public, so that those who have to bear the burden may well know what they have bargained for? In this connection, it may also be pointed out that the international climate under which the Soviet industrialisation process was carried out was not favourable for the imports of capital equipment into that country. Fortunately, the conditions in the case of India are somewhat better. The above reasons are sufficient to prove the doubtful validity of the Soviet experience under conditions facing India today.

5. Another point worthy of consideration in this context is that the growth of heavy industries should be keyed to the rate of growth of consumer-goods industries. In the ensuing discussion, we shall proceed on the assumption that heavy industries ancillary to agricultural production will find an important place in the Second Plan. The question to be considered is whether other types of heavy industries which provide capital equipment for consumer-goods industries, besides food and other wage-goods industries, should be given any importance at the present juncture. Here, the question is what has been the rate of growth of demand for consumer-goods (besides food and other wage-goods) in India in the past? The demand for equipment arises on account of: (*a*) replace-

ment and (*b*) expansion. The replacement demand depends upon the rate at which equipment is wearing out and the life composition of the equipment of consumer-goods industries is significant; mere replacement demand cannot serve as a basis for the development of heavy industry in the particular fields. In so far as the expansion demand is concerned, the problem is one of how the general level of incomes is rising in the economy. The final demand for various types of consumer goods must ultimately depend upon the quantity of marketable surplus of food and the condition governing its supply. Neither small-scale industries nor the large-scale consumer-goods industries can develop at a rapid rate, unless the surplus over and above the consumption needs in regard to food and other wage goods is large and is growing at a high rate. The demand for products of heavy industries is ultimately derived from the demand for consumer-goods, the demand for which is ultimately derived from the marketable surplus of food and other wage-goods. Thus, it is ultimately the growing agricultural base which enables indirectly the development of heavy industries. If the problem of providing marketable surplus does not exist, however, and we are fairly certain that for a relatively long period of time we are not going to be in difficulties in regard to the available food supplies, we can think of accelerating the rate of growth of heavy industries, which in its turn would provide the basis for the expansion of consumer-goods industries. Moreover, the problem is one of having conditions under which a continuously increasing excess supply of food can be created. Only if we had very large capital resources at our disposal, or if we are assured that continuously increasing quantities of food would be available to us through external loans or that the foreign exchange position is continuously improving so that we can bank upon large imports of food, we would be justified in expanding heavy industries other than those which are ancillary to agriculture.

6. In this context, it is suggested that a detailed study be carried out to ascertain the extent by which the demand for consumer-goods has increased. It is not correct to assume that there are no capital goods industries of any sort in India today. In some fields there are. In some fields the problem is not one of commitments on imports of capital equipment for consumer-goods industries, but one of utilisation of the capacity that is already available

within the country for the manufacture of equipment. Further, we must find out the experience of the capital goods producers in the economy and asertain whether their expectations are realised or not. The trouble that we are facing in regard to the Shipbuilding Industry is sufficient to dispel blind faith in all types of heavy industries by themselves. The excess capacity that prevails in a number of engineering industries is again a pointer in this direction. Moreover, a number of consumer-goods industries are also facing the problem of under-utilisation. There is clamour for sharing of markets and reservation of spheres. Under these conditions, if a super-structure of heavy industries is to be built, should it not have some relation to the economic background in the country? We have already shown that mere development of heavy industry by itself is not going to solve the problem of demand for products of these industries.

The case for an indiscriminate expansion of heavy industry is further weakened if we take into account the present international situation. In so far as it is possible for us to import capital equipment of various types for different consumer-goods industries and a sellers' market for these goods obtains abroad, we should not be unduly worried as was the case with the Soviet Union. It may be possible for us to enter into agreements with International public bodies and private organisations abroad for assuring ourselves of effective supplies of these equipments. Moreover, the embarkation on a plan for heavy industry and the diversion of substantial resources in this field would involve as a corollary a long waiting period. It is justified provided the results are promising or in keeping with the requirements. Capital resources available to the economy are meagre enough; their utilisation in one field implies their non-availability to others.

8. The problem is not one of having substantial surplus resources which we have to utilise now. It follows that the greater the importance given to indiscriminate expansion of heavy industry, the less the importance that can be given to consumer-goods industries, capital-intensive or labour-intensive. In this connection, it has been suggested that expansion of consumer-goods industries which involve capital-intensive methods of production, should be kept under check. Under this suggestion, the pressure of demand during the period of the Plan arising for various types of

consumer-goods should be met by the development of small-scale and cottage industries. This argument has an appeal however superficial, to the producers of small-scale and cottage industries. Let us examine whether the argument is consistent and the supposed benefit in the cottage and small-scale units would at all arise. The problem is not posed as one of choice between heavy industries and consumer-goods industries as such. The problem is one of whether substantial portions of resources should be diverted to large-scale expansion of heavy industries in the Second Plan. We have seen earlier that the demand for consumer-goods, whether produced by large-scale or small-scale units, in farms or in towns, depends upon the rate of expansion of marketable surplus of food. If we neglect continuously the need to step up agricultural productivity, the problem would be one of sharing out stagnant or a slightly increasing market between large-scale consumer-goods units and small-scale consumer-goods units. If the large-scale consumer-goods units already derive their supplies of capital goods from within the economy, then a policy in favour of small-scale and cottage units would involve under-utilisation of capacity in these industries. Well, what is the purpose of the development of capital goods industries? Will the new capital goods that are to be manufactured meet the requirements of small-scale and cottage units? Unless we are clear on this point, we may be proceeding on a wrong track on the basis of incorrect appreciation of facts and logic of the situation. What happens if the small-scale and cottage units find that they are unable to compete on a level of efficiency with the large-scale units already in the economy? What happens if the latter derive their supplies of equipment and technical skill from within the economy? What happens if the organised consumer-goods industries are in a position to develop markets at a fast rate in other countries? Should the products of small-scale and cottage units be equal in efficiency in this respect? What about the need to maintain continuously increasing supply of foreign exchange? Are we aware as to how much of our foreign exchange is earned by the consumer-goods industries? How are we to obtain the foreign exchange for the development of heavy industries? Are we agreed that we do not require imports of various types of consumer-goods during the period? Can the small-scale and cottage units provide the entire requirements assuming that such imports are banned? To what extent is it true to say that it will pay in the long run to bring about a rapid increase in the consumer-goods industries? Is not our position similar to that of Britain in the 19th century? Should the levels of efficiency built up cumulatively over a long period of time in a number of our organised consumer-goods industries be set at nought? If we halt the process of expansion of consumer-goods industries now, what will happen when our heavy industries are built up? Is not the purpose of the latter to provide equipment for the consumer-goods industries? Should heavy industry be desired for itself or as a means to a higher standard of consumer welfare? These and other questions crop up when once we probe into greater detail about the currently fashionable arguments for an indiscriminate expansion of heavy industries. It may be emphasized that the need for the development of heavy industries ancillary to agricultural production was emphasised by us long ago, but what we are contending against at present is not the development of such industry, but the development of heavy industries, which emphasises vaguely an indiscriminate expansion of heavy industries, on the basis of arguments which have no support either from facts or from logic valid under conditions facing us here and now, and which derives its justification only from hasty imitation of the experience of some other country with obviously different economic conditions.

9. Let us remember that we have no strong economic basis for an all out expansion of heavy industry and a blind following of other countries' experience in this context should, if it is at all agreed upon, be based on the political implications, from a long-term point of view, of the above approach. Otherwise, we would be taking a veritable leap in the dark. We would be putting the economy under certain constraints, which may envisage more and more of such constraints until we are prepared to accept the institutional corollaries that will become inevitable at a later stage. It is obvious, therefore, that in the investment pattern under the Second Five Year Plan more emphasis should be given to heavy industries ancillary to agriculture, while the development of heavy industries to provide the requirements of other consumer-goods industries should depend upon detailed studies of the rate of growth of demand for various types of consumer-goods. The pos-

sibilities of obtaining cheap equipment during the period of the Plan and the alternative cost of utilising the capital resources in other fields should be explored. Secondly, a substantial stepping up of the expansion of consumer-goods industries built up for export markets is an urgent need of the hour. Nothing should be done in the Plan period which negatives the cumulative progress in these industries over a period of four or five decades. In the third place, small-scale and cottage units should be developed by encouraging those industries which provide cheap equipment for them. The Japanese experience which concentrated on manufacture of low cost capital equipment of various types is preferable to that of the Soviet Union. What is required here is the minimisation of the impact of indivisibilities. Technological progress should be concentrated on this and more can be gained through a close study of the Japanese experience. The small-scale and cottage units should no doubt be helped; such help, however, should not be of a permanent character, but should enable these units to stand on their own legs at least at a later stage. A high rate of technical progress is a vital pre-condition to the success of economic development programmes. In the case of India, the need to retain and develop export markets is also a vital consideration. It is not a question of the enumeration of those industries which have already developed; it is also a question of ascertaining which industries have potentialities in this field. Unless we know the latter, we may be denying ourselves the advantages of industrialisation. Finally, a programme of economic development in the country has to be correlated to the requirements of providing a growing volume of employment. By definition, heavy industries do not provide large employment. If, however, we can get cheap imports of equipment, and consumer-goods industries within the country can be developed at a faster rate, the volume of employment can be continuously stepped up. There will be great scope for both large-scale and small-scale units. The growth of demand for consumer-goods is determined by the growth of marketable surplus. Continued use of substantial resources on improvements in agriculture would automatically create conditions for expansion of consumer-goods industries. Under the international situation facing us today, we have less difficulties in regard to imports of equipment. It is quite possible that a sellers' market may emerge here. The strategy of economic development should be utilised at each step to gain the advantages that accrue at a given conjuncture, internal and external. It is on these grounds that it is suggested that the Second Five Year Plan should continue to lay predominant emphasis on the stepping up of agricultural production and programmes to step up agricultural productivity. It should also utilise substantial portions of resources for development of heavy industries ancillary to agriculture and create conditions under which more and more of consumer-goods industries of all types including small-scale as well as cottage units can be established. It should utilise a considerable portion of resources for the manufacture of cheap and low-cost equipment and for the provision of power for small-scale and cottage units.[3] It should concentrate on expanding industries which have built up export markets and at the same time explore the potentialities of those industries which can built up export markets anew. This, in essence, appears to be the ideal investment pattern under conditions facing India today.

[3] Vide Appendix on "A Positive Policy for the Development of Small-Scale Industries".

APPENDIX

A POSITIVE POLICY FOR THE DEVELOPMENT OF SMALL-SCALE INDUSTRIES

1. FROM the conceptual point of view, we have to distinguish between large-scale units and small-scale units in any given industry. The terms 'large-scale industries' and 'small-scale industries' give the impression that there are some industries in which the industrial units operate on a small-scale. The real problem is one of competition in each of the industries between large-scale units and small-scale units.

2. It is difficult to divide the different industries according to those which are predominantly suited for large-scale production and those which are predominantly suited for small-sale production. This is because we cannot be definite about the changes in technology and what form they are going to take.

3. In a growing economy in which new techniques are being invented or industrial units come to know of the potentialities of the superior techniques, there is bound to be a transition from inferior methods to superior methods. Generally, it happens that the superior methods require a considerable amount of initial expenses in the form of outlay on capital equipment, technical skill, organisation expenses, etc. Large-scale economies arise because of indivisibilities. Small-scale units are not so efficient because they operate with methods which are uneconomic compared to the methods that large-scale units can employ.

4. It is possible, however, to split up some of the economies which large-sized units are able to reap. Some of the indivisibilities are conventional or institutional. Changes in the legal framework as well as in technology go to some extent to reduce the impact of indivisibilities. The following examples can be given:

(*i*) It should be possible for small-scale units to get access to easy and cheap sources of credit.

(*ii*) Small-scale units should be enabled to consult technical experts and engineers at a low fee. Large-scale units can employ their own experts, whereas small-scale units cannot afford the expenditure.

(*iii*) The legal and other organisational overheads that are associated with the inception or operation of any enterprise can be reduced if advice and service on these matters are made available to small-scale units at a relatively low fee.

(*iv*) The small-scale units should be in a position to get access to power, coal, oil and other resources as well as transport facilities at a relatively low rate. Several of the large scale units can have their own subsidiary plants for these purposes.

(*v*) Small-scale units should be enabled to get a clear knowledge about the advantages of different productive processes and of changes in techniques of production. Large-scale units can have their own laboratories or research units. They can also afford the cost of outlay on adoption or invention of new methods.

(*vi*) Capital equipment, land and other facilities should be available at low costs.

5. The above are some of the ways by which it is possible to reduce the impact of indivisibilities. To a considerable extent, the initiative in the supply of facilities and services must come from the State or some body which is initiated by the State. The difficulty is that for some time to come the outlay on the starting of such organisation will not be self-financing. From the social point of view, considerable gains can be reaped by the above process.

6. The above represents a constructive approach towards the problem of increasing the competitive efficiency of the small-scale units on a long-term basis. The current approach accepted by the Government is however in the opposite direction. It seeks to perpetuate the difficulties of small-scale units by giving them subsidies and other advantages which, however, do not solve the problem but only postpone it. The point is that the community as a whole is bound to benefit if the cost of production of different commodities are lower than what they are. This requires that production must be carried out on the basis of the best available techniques as well as organisation. This does not, however, presuppose that there should always be large-sized units in every industry. Several of the difficulties which small-scale units are facing arise on account of the impact of avoidable indivisibilities. That is why the approach of the Government should be to encourage the invention of methods of production which involve lesser initial outlay in the form of capital equipment, organisational expenses, etc. This requires a new approach in regard to the problem of the appropriate technology suited to underdeveloped countries like India.[1] Any other method can only be a palliative. It must be remembered that India has to compete with products of other countries if she has to maintain or expand her export market. This by itself necessitates a careful approach towards the problem of efficiency. Secondly, from the point of view of the consumers, it is iniquitous that the gains of superior methods of production should be denied to them. Technical progress which connotes a continuous improvement in the method of production has been an important factor in the raising of the real incomes of the individuals in advanced countries. Whatever little progress India itself has achieved has also been to a great extent due to the gains arising out of technical progress. Any policy which comes in the way of adoption of the best available method of production places a serious obstacle

---

[1] Vide "Technical Knowledge and Managerial Capacity as Limiting Factors in Industrial Expansion in Underdeveloped Countries," *International Social Science Bulletin,* 1954 and "The Structure of Capital in Indian Economy" *Indian Economic Journal,* October, 1954.

to the progress of technique. What is suggested in this note is that the Government should see to it that improvements are brought about in technique and organisation in order to better the competitive efficiency of small-scale units. This requires that the Government should conduct detailed inquiries on the factors responsible for low level of efficiency in all the small-scale units in different industries. At present, the policy has been based upon emotional and unscientific approach towards the subject. What is needed now is more of facts and research into the reasons responsible for disparities in the levels of efficiency of large-scale and small-scale units. It is not proper to delude the small-scale units that they can continue to exist on whatever the level of efficiency of their operation. At one stage or another, they will again be put into difficulties. This problem has to be faced now and then and it is no good postponing it expecting a fortuitous solution at a later date.

Institutional Implications of a Bolder Plan*

Introduction

INCREASING attention is now being paid towards the problem of the scale and pattern of effort in the Second Plan. There are three approaches: (1) The method and type of efforts pursued in the First Plan may be continued with marginal adjustments here and there. (2) The Second Plan may be patterned on the model of the experience of the Soviet Union. (3) The Second Plan may be formulated on the basis of an approach which emphasizes the institutional and other organisational base which already exists in the economy, and which works out a rate and pattern of effort after fully taking into consideration the working of the economic mechanism of the country. Experience of other countries can be utilised provided we modify it in the light of our conditions.

2. It is suggested that the important lessons of the First Plan are: (1) Observed results do not show correlation with planned efforts. (2) While national income is stated to have gone up, savings do not show any appreciable rise. The generally assumed correlation between income and savings does not appear to hold true. The assumption that when once incomes are increased, savings go up and hence the cumulative process is started is not valid in India. (3) The economy as it is constituted does not have reliance to go through unassisted either during periods of shortfall in food or during periods of excess. (4) While national income has gone up, employment has not proportionately increased. Thus, the assumed correlation between income and employment holds true only within limits. The economy has the twin problems of achieving a high rate of growth of incomes and a high rate of growth in employment. (5) The working of the Plan has revealed that the analysis behind the formulation of the Plan was

* Paper submitted to the Panel of Economists, Planning Commission. March, 1955 (Jointly with P.R. Brahmananda).

ad hoc and could not take note of the forces which bring about development in the Indian economy. (6) Finally, we now find ourselves in a situation in which we are not definite whether the economy is expanding, whether such expansion has cumulation behind it and whether it is expanding in the right direction. All this leads to the conclusion that the first approach, however appropriate for the First Plan needs to be changed for another which is more suitable. The second approach which emphasises heavy industry, a greater extent of regulation and regimentation and utilises the coefficients and relationships as derived from Soviet experience is far removed from the realities of the Indian situation than the first. Further, it does not at all take into account the peculiarities of the Indian economic scene. Moreover, here the physical targets are estimated without stating clearly the institutional and ideological implications. It appears to be out of tune with the prevailing climate of opinion in India. The only alternative is to adopt an approach which places cardinal emphasis on the elements of strength and weakness in the Indian structure and which draws up a Plan best suited to our conditions. It is the objective of the present paper to outline such an approach. There are several related issues which, for the sake of convenience, are dealt with separately. For example, the paper on "Investment Pattern in the Second Five Year Plan" deals with one such problem. We deal with some of the other problems in appendices to this paper as under:

1. Problem of Increasing the Rate of Procurement of Marketable Surplus.
2. Measures to Utilise Idle or Under-utilised Labour Power.
3. Measures for Built-in Flexibility.
4. A Positive Policy for Employment.
5. Policy towards Labour Welfare Measures.

The objective of this paper is to enquire into the possibilities of raising the rate of effort during the period of the Second Plan. In considering the possibilities, we must take into account the nature of the difficulties that had to be faced during the period of the First Plan. It is also sought to indicate the nature of the adjustments in the institutional pattern which become necessary if the bolder plan is to be worked through.

3. A bolder plan implies the stepping up of the rate of plough-back of resources in investment; in other words, the proportion of savings to national income must be raised. At present, the savings ratio is approximately between 5 per cent to 7 per cent. If we can raise it to about 10 per cent, we would have increased our scale of effort by more than 50 per cent. On the other hand, we should see that the increased savings are utilised in those forms which enable us continuously to step up the rate of effort at each stage. Another aspect of the problem is to work out an inventory of under-utilised or unutilised resources in men and material and to devise appropriate technological and organisational measures and combine them in such a way that the total national income is raised. While these measures are being attempted, a bolder plan would require corresponding efforts to prevent or check a rise in the rate of growth of demand on resources for consumption and the utilisation of resources on unproductive investment. Simultaneously, the plan must provide for as large a rate of increase in employment as possible.

4. Let us take up each of these problems in turn. How to raise the rate of savings? Now, the different units undertaking investment in the economy are: agencies of the Government, industrial and public utility units of the private sector and private individuals. The total Government expenditure on economic development may be split up into different categories on the following basis: (*i*) Items of expenditure which are output yielding, the output having a marketable value. Here, a further category of division according to the gestation periods may be drawn up. (*ii*) Items of expenditure which are welfare yielding. (*iii*) Items of expenditure which are welfare yielding, but may lead to output at a later stage. In general, a broad division of Governmental investment between productive and unproductive can be made. If the proportion of productive investment to total investment is higher, then other things being given, the rate of growth will also be higher. The implication is that a bolder plan would require a low ratio of direct investment on unproductive items. We are not suggesting that unproductive investment should not be undertaken at all, but as we shall indicate later, different forms of orga-

nisation should be evolved with a view to increasing the quantum of welfare yielding services, but at the same time involving less units of scarce input. Assuming that productive investment would dominate Government plans, there is the further problem of how to choose among these investments and what should be the price policy to follow. It is suggested that both in the choice of investment as well as in the methods of operation, the central policy should be to maximise the ratio of net revenue to capital. The net revenue is the surplus available after all expenses which vary with the scale of output are made good. A high net revenue ratio would mean more of resources available for plough-back. For this, each unit of Government should work as a commercial concern. The principle of maximisation of net revenue, given the environment, should apply. This does involve a change in the managerial and administrative set-up. It is suggested that the Government take the assistance of the private sector in the field. The maximisation of profits is not an ideal to be looked down on its own, particularly when these profits are required for ploughing back. If both the State units and private units follow a similar policy, then it would be easy to find out the reasons for the difference in the level of efficiency and mistakes can soon be rectified. In so far as private industrial units are concerned, the principle that is actually followed is one of maximisation of net revenue, but then the question to be asked is whether all that could be ploughed back is being done. To a considerable extent, the resources for reinvestment are provided from within the firms. The general policy of the Government should be to enable as much maximisation of the rate of reinvestment as is desirable. This should be looked upon as an independent objective desired for economic development irrespective of ideological considerations. The State may, however, regulate the direction of reinvestment by a system of appropriate taxes and subsidies. A point which may be mentioned here is that an underdeveloped economy of the type of India depends for its growth at this stage not merely on the nature of the activity conducted by large-scale units. The predominant form of organisation for a long time to come would continue to be one of small private companies, limited or unlimited. The quantitative importance of this may be limited, but under conditions facing India, these units can perform a more effective role than what they are doing at present. The problem is not merely one of comparison between large-scale and small-scale units. It is a question of providing appropriate incentives by which small units tend to grow at a faster rate. This requires a new approach from the point of view of Company Law, Industrial Legislation and Tax Administration. It is submitted that we are giving too much importance to largeness as an ideal by itself. A multitude of small firms is the strongest source of growth in an economy. The problem of capital and organisation should not be looked at from the aggregate view-point. It should be looked at primarily from the point of view of units which compose the structure as such.

5. There is no doubt that a policy of profit maximisation or net revenue maximisation followed at each level would lead to an increased rate of investment. What about raising the rate of savings of private individuals? It is suggested that the Government should not object if in a policy of appropriate mobilisation, more is available to the general pool of savings, though it may not directly take the form of contribution to the tax revenue as such. What is required is a general tax on expenditure with discriminatory rates on particular types of expenditure. There is no reason why an appropriate system cannot be worked out to suit Indian conditions.[1] The tax incidence may be made to vary depending upon the contribution of individuals towards various types of investment, both Government and private.

6. Is it possible to raise the rate of savings through greater emphasis on taxation and on borrowing programmes? To take the former first, the question is whether the tax system as such is not weighing too heavily in the case of the urban sector and not so heavily in the case of the rural sector. The problem is not one of differences in the living standards between the two sectors. On account of the vastness of the rural sector, appropriate types of taxes must be devised which tend to get some contribution from these areas. In this context, more can be achieved through the

[1] A detailed discussion of how the tax weapon can be utilised to bring about appropriate allocation adjustments in the economy is given in "Towards an Optimal Tax Policy in a Retrogressive Economy", *Journal of the University of Bombay*, July, 1954.

price system than through the orthodox tax machinery. The general character of the products consumed by the vast majority of the rural sector is fairly well-known. If a network of State trading institutions can be built up and appropriate policies are followed, the economy being divided into different regions, it should be possible to get more from the rural areas than what we are at present getting. The central problem for a long time to come in this field will be one of how we can get a larger extent of real marketable surplus than what we are getting now. This is mainly a problem of organisation and the extent by which we can step up the rate of investment would ultimately depend upon how we are able to devise appropriate organisational changes. (Vide Appendix I on "Problem of Increasing the Rate of Procurement of Marketable Surplus".)

7. In so far as borrowing programmes are concerned, there is considerable scope for de-standardisation. Regional planning boards can be set up whose main function should be to mobilise savings available within the different regions and to utilise a part of these savings for investment which directly benefits the regions. The rate of interest may be made to depend upon the productivity of the investments. In some cases, the contribution of the people in the sector may not be on a cash basis. It may be on an effort basis and it should be possible to take the responsibility for maintaining the workers during the period of the work, at the same time offering additional advantages in the form of pieces of land and other productive assets when once the projects are completed. This type of system would be an alternative to forced labour. If regional planning authorities can be set up in different parts of the country, their work being coordinated with the work of the Community Projects and National Extension Services, it should be possible to tap a considerable portion of underutilised labour power in the rural areas through a system of voluntary loans of various types of effort and kind contributions. What is necessary is that the results of the efforts should in the first place have some significance for the individuals concerned who make the contribution. A number of local projects can be devised. The regional planning authorities should have a multitude of schemes in each of the regions. At each stage, it should be possible to take in hand some of these.

8. We have referred earlier to the need for a reduction of outlay on unproductive items by Government authorities. After all, a significant portion of developmental expenditure by the Governments on such items is on roads, health services, housing, education and social welfare. Most of these services can be performed at low cost provided the under-utilised labour and skill resources of the public are utilised in these fields through a system of appropriate social incentives. More attention than hitherto is to be given to activities which involve the application of individual initiative in fields in which there are no monetary returns. The problem is one of devising appropriate methods by which the young and the old of the country can devote part of their working time or leisure for activities which, while they involve some exertion on their part, would lead to more proportionate returns to the community. If a spirit of voluntary work could be created and it pervades the different parts of the country, it would be possible to economise on expenditure which is primarily unproductive and which does not contribute to material output. The resources directly available for capital formation could be augmented in this field. (Vide Appendix II on "Measures to Utilise Idle or Under-utilised Labour Power".)

9. A more important problem facing economic planners is that concerning the mobilisation of surplus labour power in rural areas and their transformation into fields of activity which would lead to capital formation. The crucial question which determines the employment potential here is the quantity of potentially available marketable surplus of food and other wage goods. The quantity of marketable surplus in its turn depends upon the level of production and the extent of internal requirements in the farms. In the short run, whenever there is a sudden expansion in output, the internal requirements being more or less constant, the problem for the farmers is the disposal of the produce. If, however, we have appropriate institutional devices to mobilise the marketable surplus and utilise it in the form of additional employment of labour power, periods of excess production of food would be transformed into periods of rapid capital formation. The lack of an appropriate credit system, insufficiency of innovators, the lack of managerial capacity, inability of the system to make quick adjustments, all these are coming in the way of such a transforma-

tion. There is no doubt that a part of the excess production will have to be retained as buffer stocks, but provided short-term productive opportunities exist and these opportunities tend to be self-liquidating, initiative will be taken either by the State or by the private authorities to utilise the food and the surplus labour power in appropriate productive channels. The main problem here is one of organisation. The economic system as it is constituted in India to-day gets into difficulties when there is a little short-fall in food production and also when there is a little excess. A little less or a little more creates serious problems. This is because corresponding changes in the rest of the economy are not taking place in such a way that the incidence of excess or shortage is absorbed in the most productive manner possible. More attention than hitherto should be given to working out a system of appropriate organisational arrangements so that periods of surplus production are automatically converted into periods of boom. If the suggestion is accepted, then measures for built-in flexibility have to be worked out. (Vide Appendix III on "Measures for Built-in Flexibility".)

10. This leads us on to the problem of employment. For sometime to come, this is going to be the most important economic problem facing the planners. A positive employment policy for the economy has to be based on an appreciation of the working of the economic mechanism in India. The Government of India has set up a target of 12 million jobs. It is not known how this target was fixed. On the basis of the analysis outlined above, we can say that cxpansion in employment requires efforts towards mobilisation of the marketable surplus of wage goods and corresponding activities in the rest of the economy. It is not appropriate to view the problem of employment as being capable of solution only on the basis of long-term measures. As unemployment is most acute among the educated urban middle classes, whose services when properly channelised can become the greatest source of strength to the economy, we must provide a quick solution to the problem. The current situation in the economy is such that such a solution *can* be found. (Vide Appendix IV on "A Positive Policy for Employment".)

11. Another problem related to the above is that of devising an appropriate policy towards labour both in respect of welfare

measures as well as wage rates. Here again, a new approach is called for in the interests of rapid capital formation as well as of the need to provide a larger volume of employment. (This is discussed in Appendix V on "Policy towards Labour Welfare Measures".)

12. Finally, a few words about incentives. In an economy which wants to develop fast and in which the public sector takes an active role, it is natural that wide differences in living standards would be objected to. This is so particularly when we want to mobilise the incipient labour power or skill power in the vast majority of the population. But then, the crucial question here is whether the objection is to differences in living standards or to differences in ownership of wealth. These two should not be confused. What society naturally objects to is the conspicuous differences in living standards which appear more glaring in an economy in which the rich were, as it were, merely islands in an ocean of poverty. If, however, the resources available with the richer groups, or those who are relatively better off, get utilised in the form of capital formation beneficial to the community, there should be no difficulty whatsoever. Such a suggestion would imply a considerable set of restrictions on the pattern of consumption as well as investment of the relatively better off groups. The more such restrictions take a voluntary form, the better the atmosphere will be from the point of view of the community. This fits in with the basic philosophy of Gandhiji and Vinobha Bhave; a philosophy which the Congress has accepted. The issue is vital because on the successful resolution of this dispute will depend the future of mixed economy. It is in this context that the role of the private sector should be visualised. More can be achieved here through a system of appropriate leadership. It would be beyond the scope of economics to discuss the implications of these suggestions, but there is no reason why we should lose hope in this respect. The greatest need of the hour in the country to-day is that of social innovation. This is primarily the task of leadership; looking at the past history of the country, there is no reason why we should despair on this score.

APPENDIX I

PROBLEM OF INCREASING THE RATE OF PROCUREMENT OF MARKETABLE SURPLUS

AS pointed out in the text, the central problem in the economy for a long time to come will be that of obtaining from the rural sector as large a quantity of marketable surplus of food as possible. The lower the cost of marketable surplus in terms of the alternative commodities that have to be given in exchange for it, the higher the possible rate of development. The requirements of food of the food producers would depend upon: (1) The internal consumption requirements which in turn depend upon the produce necessary to pay for the labour and other services necessary for the production of the given output and that necessary for the maintenance of the dependents. These two items, however, get mixed up. Given the state of technique and organisation, there is, however, a minimum requirement in terms of what is necessary for the labourers and what is necessary for the performance of the given amount of work. The rest would be outlay on unproductive consumption, or more appropriately on unreproductive consumption. (2) Requirements for hoarding and stock: This depends upon the size of internal requirements and the possible variations in it. It also depends upon the state of expectations regarding the availability of foodgrains, expectations about rainfall and so on. A part of most of the hoarding, therefore, bears a constant proportion to output, whereas another part fluctuates depending upon the state of expectations. (3) The residue is that which is available for disposal on the market. This depends upon the cash requirements of the farmers for carrying out their operations, the standard of living in terms of the non-food goods to which they are accustomed, the requirements in terms of accessories for agricultural production and finally, the requirements in terms of outlay on capital formation or sudden bursts of conspicuous and social expenditure on consumption. It is not correct to assume that a larger aggregate produce must always imply a larger absolute quantity of marketable surplus. Very often, expansion of output may be brought about on marginal farms and by intensive or extensive cultivation which yields no surplus whatsoever. Even though the total output of the economy is increasing, the quantity marketed may increase very slowly, or may not do so at all, or may even decrease.

2. The crucial task is how to increase the quantity of food that is marketed. In an economy which is becoming increasingly conscious of consumer-goods (other than food) and other items of expenditure, there will be a tendency towards an increase in the quantity that is marketed. The substitution of the money habit in place of the barter habit will strengthen the tendency. These are, however, long-term forces, but how to increase the absolute quantity of surplus that is marketed under short-

term periods of one to five years? Normally, the quantity that is marketed would be to a small extent dependent upon the absolute requirements of non-food goods. To the extent that the prices of the latter can be slightly raised, the quantity marketed may increase. This may be done either by an increase in total production, i.e., by exhausting the possibilities of production available to the farmers and|or by reducing the internal requirements and thus introducing some form of abstinence and|or by reducing the amount that is hoarded. Under market conditions, the prices of the goods which the farmers buy can be raised provided there is a central network of trading organisations. This can be done either through a network of State distribution agencies or through co-operative societies. The second alternative is to introduce monopoly purchases of marketable surplus of grains. The price offered to the farmers may be lower than what they would have got otherwise. There may be, however, a guarantee that the prices will not go below a particular minimum so that during periods of excess production, the farmers need not suffer a shrinkage in incomes. In an economy subject to fluctuations in output due to seasonal conditions, such a measure may introduce a greater extent of certainty and may actually be welcomed by the farmers. If we adopt this course, we would be procuring more of marketable surplus than we would be doing otherwise.

3. The two alternatives suggested above are not mutually exclusive courses of action. It is possible to combine both. After all, the requirements of consumption goods by the farmers are well known, and it is possible to ascertain through trial and error how far savings can be introduced. The State should introduce both distribution agencies who sell consumer and other goods to the farmers and buy the food produced by the farmers. The tertiary sector can thus be enabled to play a central role in capital formation. Further, a number of other measures can be devised. The State can be prepared to offer loans to the farmers in exchange for surplus of foodgrains. Another measure is to encourage the consumption of goods other than cereals in short supply, that is, to bring about a balanced diet. This too can be brought about through price adjustments. The network of distribution agencies suggested will help to popularise non-food goods among the farmers and will gradually introduce the idea of a higher standard of living in their minds. There can be a number of other functions which the distribution agencies can perform. The important point here is filling up of certain organisational deficiencies. As stated in the text, it is not proper to assume that the food problem has been solved once and for all. The problem of procuring adequate quantities of food is important not merely from the point of view of subsistence requirements, but also from the point of view of providing employment. If the State can directly get access to marketable surplus of food, it can utilise the powers of credit control to bring into fruition the desired schemes of capital formation.

As regards hoarding, when once the public come to know that there is an assured supply of foodgrains, the incidence can be reduced. Under a free enterprise market economy, part of the price paid for food during periods of shortages or expected shortages is like premium paid for surrendering liquidity preference. It is only conditions of assured supply of food for a fairly long period that will overcome the preference for hoarding. The problem is institutional as also psychological.

Appendix II

MEASURES TO UTILISE IDLE OR UNDER-UTILISED LABOUR POWER

1. Different calculations have been made about the extent of completely or partially idle labour power in the economy. A part of the idleness is due to seasonal conditions. A major part is due to absence of economic opportunities. A part is also due to lack of balance within the structure. If we give up the conventional assumptions regarding preference between leisure and work, a considerable surplus of potentially available labour power in skilled, technical and manual fields will become available. The question is how best to harness these resources towards desirable channels.

2. In the first place, an inventory of different types of surplus labour power according to categories has to be worked out. In the second place, we must find out what types of incentives or institutional arrangements are necessary to harness the above. Some part of the labour power can be harnessed only through monetary incentives in the form of money wages or a system of taxes and subsidies. If a discriminatory wage policy is followed a given portion of the idle labour power in different rural areas can be harnessed provided further that the projects are spectacular in character from the point of view of the units and are expected to yield quick results which have some correspondence to the efforts. Some part of the labour power can be harnessed through incentives in kind. If the Government can directly get access to marketable surplus of food and other requisites of labour, a pool of these commodities can be built up in different regions and policies of employment expansion can be stimulated. A part of the labour power can be utilised through incentives in the form of attractions of a rising social status. The Government can introduce a system of rewards and prizes, the responsibility for their distribution being made dependent upon enquiries at the regional level. A good portion of the resources going towards unproductive consumption and unproductive investment can be diverted towards socially desirable fields provided a systematic policy in this regard is worked out. Centralisation here would not be an advantage. A part of the labour force can be mobilised through community welfare incentives. Here, the persons who perform the work have other alternative sources of income, but they are prepared to work more because they believe that that region or the community for whose welfare they are striving, satisfies their ideals. Here again, the problem is one of working out the potentialities in different regions. Finally, a part of the labour power can be mobilised provided such mobilisation takes a mass form. Here whereas one individual may be unwilling, when once enthusiasm is created in the group, a

considerable amount of work can be done. This is a function of leadership and appropriate utilisation of the springs of local patriotism which lie dormant in the rural parts of India is a task for the leadership to perform.

3. A final word about the types of fields to which the labour power channelled in the above manner has to be diverted. It would be best if the method of utilisation of labour power which involves considerable money burden and hence a real burden, is for fields which tend to become self-financing. Output that is produced must be marketable; then alone will the process become cumulative. It would not be appropriate to utilise money incentives for mobilising the labour power which is diverted for welfare yielding purposes. In this connection, it may be pointed out that the system of incentives that is evolved should concentrate on creating within the economy a nucleus of leadership, both in social and in economic fields. Whereas leadership in the economic field is mostly self-financing, and more often than not, more than self-financing, and is undertaken with the clear objective of economic rewards, leadership in social reform and allied fields does not have the above advantage. Social innovation which brings about adjustments in the social structure (propaganda for reduction in unproductive consumption, changes in the pattern of unproductive investments, introduction of the idea of birth control, introduction of a greater extent of mobility, etc.) is, therefore, as important and as vital as economic innovation. In fact, the contours within which economic innovations function are set by the tempo of social innovation. In our country, unfortunately, sufficient importance has not been given to this and there is no positive incentive in the system which favours the emergence of leadership in social reforms as such. Adequate attention should, therefore, be given to the encouragement of social innovations.

Appendix III

MEASURES FOR BUILT-IN FLEXIBILITY

1. Over a period of years, it has been noted that agricultural output, particularly of food, is subject to wide fluctuations owing to the vagaries of the monsoon. There are years when an increase in total production by a particular extent, given the internal consumption requirements which do not substantially change year by year, lead to a more than proportionate variation in the quantities of marketable surplus of food. A principle similar to that of acceleration is in operation here. This explains why there is a sudden and steep variation in the price level of food. In a similar way, a decrease in output leads to a more than proportionate decline in marketable surplus, and hence, causes a significant pressure on the price level. Thus, even marginal variations in production either way have a more than proportionate effect on the price level. The question is: Is it not possible to evolve such organisation in the economy so that periods of excess production automatically generate a boom in capital formation, thus enabling the stepping up of the trend of growth of agricultural and other output? It should also be possible to build up buffer stocks during these periods so that the incidence of general shortage during periods of decline in production can be minimised. When once it is accepted that for a long period to come fluctuations in agricultural output are inevitable, it should be possible to evolve such institutional arrangements that they lead to certain desirable results in the economy.

2. Let us first take the case wherein there is a sudden expansion in output of food. There is bound to be a certain lag before the increased output leads to a reduction in wholesale prices and then in retail prices. A fall in retail prices in food should, under autonomous conditions, lead to a decline in money wage rates. This is because, given the level of money wage rates, a fall in the prices of food, the expenditure on which is the largest portion in the budget of a working class family, will make the workers better off in real terms. Assuming that a fall in money wage rates takes place, the employers find that, other conditions being given, conditions are propitious for an expansion in the level of industrial and other activity, and hence in the volume of employment. Such an expansion is conditional upon the prevalence of an optimistic state of expectations and the availability of adequate credit. There are thus a number of links before we can assume that a sudden increase in the output of food would automatically lead to an increase in the volume of employment, and hence in the rate of capital formation. The analysis of the different conditions under which the movement from one step to

another step can be facilitated and speeded up provides a key to the discovery of measures which help to bring about an increase in the volume of employment under the present conditions. The central question here is one of evolving those links in the chain which lead to the above results. In the absence of these links a sudden expansion in output is dissipated either in the form of variations in the standards of consumption of food by farm producers and|or variations in the standards of consumption of employed workers, their dependents and other groups. This, it is feared, has been the actual state of the country when looked at from the historical point of view. Periods of over-supply of food did not have corresponding repercussions on employment and rate of capital formation. The additional food was just utilised for raising the standards of consumption or for spreading it out evenly. Now that we have a planned economy, it is necessary to adjust the organisational framework in the economy in such a way that periods of agricultural expansion are converted into periods of high rate of capital formation.

3. The crucial question is why the links do not automatically get themselves established. Why should a country which suffers from food shortage be not in a position to go forward under conditions of excess production of food? Let us first assume that fluctuations in agricultural output occur around a stationary trend in output. Here the problem is to utilise the excess supply of food to provide employment in a number of short-term schemes. The emphasis is on short-term schemes because we are not certain that the increase in output is of a permanent character. If each region is equipped with a number of short-term schemes which are to be put into operation when once there is an excess supply of food and if these short-term schemes are keyed to expansion in agricultural output or in industries ancillary to it, then the stationary trend will be converted into a steadily growing trend. This is one of the best things that can happen to an economy. There is no automatic process by which this is accomplished, because the problem is not merely one of availability of additional food, but of its accessability to different enterprising units and the existence of a number of short-term schemes within the range of activity of these units. It is difficult to expect these conditions to be fulfilled autonomously. That is why the natural recourse is for fluctuations in output to take the form of fluctuations in the standards of consumption. These fluctuations in the standards of consumption do not lead to corresponding fluctuations in the level of general activity as happens in the case of advanced countries. In order that the short-term schemes may be automatically taken up, there should be a unified agency in each of the regions which is provided with requisite credit facilities and is in a position to mobilise the surplus of food. We have of course assumed that there is no problem of shortage of labour which in the case of India at least is in plentiful supply. The deficiency

here is both one of lack of flexibility in credit arrangements and also that of dearth of either investment opportunities from the overall point of view as is revealed to particular units and|or of a suitable number of enterprising or innovating units.

4. In the alternative, a rise in agricultural output leading to a fall in wholesale prices and then in retail prices must lead to a fall in money wages. Now, this is a condition which is difficult to be fulfilled in an economy in which in most of the organised industries, the trade union pressure is pretty strong. There is no doubt that some sort of a situation akin to that of money illusion is at work here. Wage rates are in the short run inflexible downwards. The emphasis is on the short term because the increased output is of a short run character and unless corresponding measures are taken quickly to mobilise it by the provision of fruitful employment at each point of time, the economy would be working at a level of activity which is less than the optimum permissible and feasible. Even assuming that wage rates are somewhat flexible, expansion would depend upon the existence of a number of entrepreneurs and innovators who would think in terms of automatic schemes of new expansion under these conditions. The deficiency here again is either that of credit and|or of lack of appropriate entrepreneurial or managerial capacity. The question all along is one of converting a stationary trend in output to that of a growing trend.

5. Let us take a case wherein the agricultural output is fluctuating over a rising trend. Here, the conditions are more propitious for expansion. It should be possible for the trend rates to be further raised provided appropriate institutional arrangements are made. The same deficiencies discussed earlier operate here too.

6. Ultimately, the problem is one of sufficient flexibility in the institutional arrangements confronting the agricultural sector. If the fluctuations are in a rising trend, the problem is one of expanding the institutional arrangements so that the economy can at each unit of time work at the ceiling set by the limits of capacity. This is how the ceiling itself can continuously be raised. The optimum performance in each unit of time itself contributes towards the raising of the trend and hence of the possible ceiling. In the case of India, the sector external to the farming sector does not show sufficient resilience during periods in which there is excess production in the farming sector.

7. What about the case wherein the output fluctuates downwards? In the above paragraphs there is nothing to prevent the economy from building up stocks, these stocks not being merely maintained for purposes of meeting emergent needs by the farmers, but themselves being continuously utilised for raising the trend rate itself. The agricultural sector in India must operate in such a way that out of its own boot straps it lifts itself upwards. This requires a new approach towards the prob-

lem of fluctuations in an underdeveloped economy like that of India. The problem is not one of stabilisation of prices or of incomes. It is one of converting trends in excess production into forms of capital formation, short-term or long-term. This is the central cyclical problem for which the measures of built-in flexibility suggested in the earlier paragraphs are designed to provide a solution. The problems peculiar to each country require solutions which fit in accordance with the requirements of the countries concerned. To take over solutions valid in developed countries would be like utilisation of non-Euclidian geometry in a Euclidian world. The entire approach towards agricultural planning requires a drastic revision.

APPENDIX IV

A POSITIVE POLICY FOR EMPLOYMENT

1. AT any unit of time, the volume of employment (E) that can be potentially offered in the non-wage goods sector is equal to the quantity of marketable surplus of wage goods (M) divided by the average real wage rate (W) in terms of consumption of wage goods. Given M, if W is higher, than E, the volume of potential employment that can be offered is less than what it would have been if W was lower. Thus, E varies inversely with W. Given W, an increase in M will lead to an increase in E. Thus, E increases directly with M.

2. After all, the magnitude of actual employment is not always equal to the potential limits determined as above. Here, we have to introduce the factors concerning demand for labour as well as the impact of monetary forces.

3. Let us take the latter first. M is the difference between output of wage-goods (O_ω) and internal consumption demand for wage-goods (C_ω). An increase in M may or may not mean an increase in C_ω. The marketable surplus, therefore, is not a direct function of O. An increase in C_ω takes place when the actual C is less than the amount which individuals desire to consume. Thus, there is an equilibrium relationship between any given amount of O_ω and C_ω. This relationship will be given by:

1. The extent of unsatisfied demand for wage goods;
2. Variations in the number of dependants; and
3. The average consumption of the latter.

A substantial increase in O_ω would tend to increase M more than proportionately. This is obvious because there is a maximum limit to C_ω in any short period.

4. Let us assume that O_ω has increased and that an equilibrium relationship between C_ω and O_ω has been attained. Obviously, the market price of wage-goods, given other conditions, would tend to be reduced. But an increase in M will not take place if it is expected that the prices of wage-goods would tend to rise at a later date. The price expectations might affect the activities of producers or of middlemen.

Thus, there is what may be called a hoarding trap. Let us, however, pass over this trap and examine what happens later on. If the prices of wage-goods are reduced, then, the money value of a given quantity of M would have gone down. It is not certain that the total quantity of money income accruing to the wage-goods producers will increase, decrease or remain the same. Suppose the price of wage-goods comes down. Would there be an increase in employment?

5. There is no automatic tendency towards an increase in employment with a decrease in the price of wage-goods. This depends upon whether

the money-wage rate is also reduced. If the money-wage rate is not reduced, then, unless new employment can be offered at a discriminatory money-wage rate, total employment will not increase. A reduction in money-wage rates depends on the prevalence of a certain extent of flexibility in wage rates. Assuming that money-wages are reduced, the employers find themselves with certain augmented margins. This, among other things, should encourage expansion. Such a condition will obtain only provided the employers in general are utilizing their plants to less than the limits of capacity. This means that there must be excess capacity which can be utilized in the short period. If capacity is not fully utilized, then a stepping up of the employment consequent upon a reduction in money-wages will depend upon the attitude of the employers.

6. Suppose there are minimum wage laws or the already employed body of labour force refuses to countenance a reduction in money-wages. Expansion in employment now depends upon the employers' capacity to bring about a system of differential wage rates. The new workers will get less than the already employed workers. The policy of a closed shop under conditions of excess capacity can only lead to less of total employment. Industries or firms in which restrictions are less rigid will expand.

7. What about a permanent increase in employment? This depends upon the state of long-term expectations. Utilisation of labour force in the construction of capital assets which have a fairly long period of existence would depend upon the employers' expectations as to whether the reduced level of wage rates will continue to operate in the economy and upon the period for which it will do so. We can straight away make the following propositions.

(*a*) To the extent that the reduction in money-wage rates is considered to be enduring, other conditions being given, there will be a tendency towards the starting of new establishments.

(*b*) The expectations regarding the period during which the new level of wage rates is going to operate will determine the choice of investments. The longer the period during which the new level is expected to persist, the longer the time-horizon of the employers.

(*c*) To the extent that conditions of uncertainty heavily surround the future of employers' activities as such, any reduction in money-wage rates will not show itself in the form of an improvement in the level of capacity. It is in this sense that uncertainty about activities of the private sector comes in the way of long-term expectations.

8. Thus, it is not at all certain that a reduction in money-wages is automatically reflected in the form of a larger volume of employment. If there is no utilisable excess capacity in the short period and if expansion of capacity depends upon long-term decisions and if the stage of long-term expectations is adverse, a reduction in money-wages will not show itself in the form of an increase in employment.

9. Suppose the increase in M is of a transitory character and so also the reduction in money-wages. Obviously, an increase in employment

would now depend upon the availability of excess capacity in the short period.

10. Leaving out long-term factors, suppose there is an increase in *M* and it is believed that this increase is transitory. Suppose further that decisions will now be undertaken on the basis of rational calculations. We can say that the ability of the State to increase directly the volume of employment will depend upon the total extent of employment yielding productive opportunities, in other words, upon the extent of available short-term schemes. These short-term schemes should be profitable from the overall point of view at the new level of wage rates.

11. In a private enterprise economy or in a mixed economy, the links are more tenuous. An increase in *O* need not necessarily mean an increase in *M*. An increase in *M* need not necessarily mean a fall in the prices of wage-goods. A fall in the prices of wage-goods need not necessarily mean a fall in money-wages. A fall in money-wages need not necessarily imply a fuller utilization of capacity. Thus, there are a good number of slips between the cup and the lip.

12. Our entire analysis has proceeded on the assumption that there is some sort of continuity of economic decisions. To the extent that a further decision depends upon a state of long-term expectations, no increase in employment will follow as a result of a fall in money-wages. In an enterprise economy, it is not merely the potential availability of *M* that matters, but also the availability of credit. If credit supply is inelastic, then an increase in *M* may or may not be followed by an increase in employment. The supply of credit depends upon the banking practices and conditions governing distribution of capital which itself depends upon the potential creditworthiness of the borrowing parties. In an economy in which there is continuous growth, a substantial increase in *M*, given other conditions, will lead to an increased credit supply, because not merely would more credit be demanded, but more of it would be forthcoming. If, on the other hand, conditions of continuous growth do not obtain, then there is no guarantee that the needs will be satisfied. Hence, there is no increase in employment. The problem of credit supply is, therefore, qualitative as well as quantitative.

13. There is no doubt that an increase in output of wage-goods would immediately show itself in the form of increased demand for all types of goods available within the wage-goods of the rural sector. Given profitable opportunities of further employment, the employment expansion can be had here, but if potential opportunities are meagre, then there is no relief to employment. The crucial factor is the availability of short-term productive opportunities. The lower the rate of interest, the greater the range of such opportunities actually available. A dear money policy under conditions of abundant *M* will not help provide a solution to the unemployment problem.

14. Would not a fall in money wages lead to reduced demand? There is no doubt that under Keynesian conditions, this should be so. Under

conditions of underdevelopment equilibrium, a fall in money-wages accompanying a fall in prices of wage-goods, which arises as a result of increased output of wage-goods, does not lead to a worsening of the conditions of workers. It, however, enables the increased *M* to be reflected in the form of increasing overall employment.

15. As a result of above discussion the following policy conclusions can be derived in regard to the current situation in India:

I. (*a*) The increased marketable surplus must be reflected in the form of low food prices and low money-wages.
(*b*) There should be liberalisation of conditions governing credit expansion.
(*c*) The state of long-term expectations must be rendered favourable from the point of view of the private sector.

II. In the alternative, the State can itself directly get access to the marketable surplus thus short-circuiting the market mechanism and expand employment by utilizing labour on a number of short-term or medium-term schemes. The initiative may even be left to the local rural agencies.

16. A positive policy of employment expansion must be based on an awareness of the working of the economic mechanism in an underdeveloped economy like that of India. The Government of India has formulated plans for expansion of employment opportunities by about 12 million jobs. If the analysis in the text and in the Appendix is correct this target is only the statement of a wish and not a planned target. Expansion of employment in our economy requires efforts of a particular character of which there is little evidence in what is being done. It is not correct to consider the unemployment problem as being remediable by only long-term measures. As shown above the problem is capable of solution here and now, if we are clear of the working of the economic mechanism in the present conditions of the country.

Appendix V

POLICY TOWARDS LABOUR WELFARE MEASURES

1. An important point of difference between the process of economic development of newly industrialising countries like that of India and that of currently advanced countries during the periods when they industrialised, is the increasing importance that is given in the former countries towards a number of labour welfare measures. The modern social conscience will not tolerate an iniquitous policy regarding labour. The question, however, is whether the welfare measure can be so timed and patterned that their impact on the rate of growth as well as on the pattern of growth can be transformed into the best desired type.

2. In India, particularly in the post-independence period, a number of measures have been undertaken to improve the lot of the workers and strengthen their bargaining position vis-a-vis the employers. The form that these measures have taken cannot be said to be the best under the circumstances. The central difficulty here is that the welfare commitments have been imposed on individual undertakings or groups of undertakings and the burden of these commitments is made to be dependent upon the strength of the labour force employed in these units. Further, a number of measures have been taken to prevent retrenchment without notice or without appropriate pay adjustments. The method for settling labour-capital disputes has resulted into a polarisation of the views between labour and capital on each of the issues. These tendencies have cumulatively placed an additional premium on the employment of capital-intensive methods. If the burden of labour welfare measures is transferred to the State itself, the contribution from the different parties being taken through a system of general or discriminatory taxes, the special prejudices against the utilization of labour-intensive equipment can be overcome to some extent. The general pattern of policy in these issues may correspond to that which is being followed in the U.K. The Planning Commission or the Labour Ministry can send a team to the U.K. to make an intensive study of the methods of evolving a welfare state as in operation in the U.K. and to enquire into the appropriate modifications that can be made under Indian conditions. There is some truth in the statement that the labour welfare policy of the Government is indeliberately causing difficulties to labour itself. Further, while the interests of the employed labour force are being cared for, those of the employable but unemployed labour force are not being looked after.

3. Another difficulty is that the method of settlement of labour-capital disputes has led to considerable uncertainty regarding the process of accumulation of reserves within firms. In India as in advanced countries, the process of internal accumulation has an important role to play in capital formation. To some extent, unproductive utilization of funds

either in consumption or in investment, can be prevented if appropriate adjustments are made in the labour policy.

4. A reference has been made earlier to the need for safeguarding the interests of the unemployed workers. In advanced countries, where a well developed employment market already exists, standardization of wage rates and methods of settling issues associated with labour, do not have a corrosive effect on growth. In the case of India, however, the need is to evolve a policy suited to a country with heterogeneous labour groups and types of employment opportunities. A policy of de-standardisation which would, within limits, permit considerable wage differentials between regions and between groups of workers, would lead to a fuller extent of utilisation of economic opportunities.

5. What about the wage policy? It is obvious that, given fixed wages, a fall in the prices of consumer-goods would lead to a rise in the real income of the workers. The unemployed workers, however, may be willing to offer themselves for employment at lower real wages. The employed workers may not object to the procedure provided the reduction in their standard of living takes the form of higher prices of goods which they buy rather than that of a reduction in their pay packets. There is considerable scope for utilising the technique of indirect taxation or credit expansion to bring about a larger volume of employment and thus satisfy the labour interests without affecting their sensibilities. There is no doubt that the wage rates in India have tended to be inflexible downwards. An alternative measure would be to permit differentials in wage rates and to follow, as stated earlier, a policy of de-standardisation.

6. There is no doubt that the measures suggested above would help to increase the indirect contribution from the employed workers towards economic development. But, then, under what conditions would the workers acquiesce in the above strategy? The question here is the extent by which the consumption standards of the relatively well-to-do group in the economy can be related. This is the problem of incentives and is not incapable of solution.

The Size of Nations and Dynamic Adjustment: Problems of Developing Countries*

I

THE relationship between geographical area, population size and the level of economic efficiency and the rate of development is one of the leading topics of current economic discussion. The issue has gained considerable political and practical importance because of the various efforts being made both among the developed and the under-developed countries to work out new patterns of market alignment. This Paper concentrates attention upon the analysis of the way in which the factor of size in respect of both population and area can affect the nature and rate of development. Section I differentiates between the economic and political concepts of "nationhood". Section II examines the nature of the supposed links in the relationship between size and the level of economic efficiency. Section III works out the concept of optimum size of a nation, taking into account the crucial economic factors. Section IV examines the various possible types of effects which differences in size along with other factors can exert upon the dynamic processes. Section V examines the special problems of underdeveloped countries vis-a-vis size. It briefly deals with the possibilities and implications of market expansion programmes. Section VI draws attention to the economic consequences of the pursuit of a policy of aggressive "nationhood".

Among political scientists there is considerable discussion about what exactly constitutes a nation. Various factors like geographical contiguity, ethnic and racial homogeneity, common heritage in regard to cultural and other values, allegiance to a common politi-

* Paper submitted to the Round Table Conference of the International Economic Association held at Lisbon, Portugal in September 1957 on the size of Nations (jointly with P. R. Brahmananda).

cal head, prevalence of common aspirations and ambitions, etc. are included in the concept of nation. The clarification of the above concept from an economic point of view has not, however, received due attention. For example, mere geographical, racial, climatic, cultural or political factors alone are not important here. The economist's concept of nation would include some assumptions concerning the absence of tariff barriers within the geographical limits of a nation, prevalence of a high degree of mobility between different groups and sectors in the economy, the existence of a certain similarity in regard to the strength and intensity of reactions of various forms of economic stimuli and such other factors. In other words, the term "nation", when looked at from an economic point of view, assumes the existence of a fair measure of *economic homogeneity*. This would imply that the different sections of the people have somewhat similar outlook in their want and preference patterns in regard to commodities and jobs; that a fair degree of uniformity would prevail in regard to the response of individuals and different groups regarding changes in prices, wages, interest rates, profit rates, tax changes, etc.; and that there would be some similarity in regard to the choice structure between effort and income; and so on.

The term "Size" is somewhat ambiguous and may refer to either area or population. Large-sized countries may be sparsely populated, while small-sized countries may have high density. From the economist's point of view, geographical size, other conditions given, has significance because of the possibility that a large-sized country would be possessing a larger quantity of natural resources or a greater diversity in their supply and conjunctural advantages in climate. Thus, the larger the size, the larger the resource base, and, other conditions given, the greater the *capacity* to have a larger-sized population. On the other hand, if we emphasize the population aspect in size, we find that some countries with a small geographical size have a very large-sized population though with low per capita incomes and poor productivity levels. A large-sized country may, however, have a relatively smaller sized population but with high per capita standards and productivity levels. Thus, contradictory trends in living standards and productivity levels will be found if we try to correlate them positively with the geographical area and size of population.

The economist, however, emphasizes the significance of geographical and population size upon the size of the market. The concept of "market", however, has both demand and supply aspects. A country large in size and in population may, however, have low incomes, just as another country small in size but also large in population may yet have low incomes. Thus, the level of per capita income is, or perhaps can be, more important than the size of population or the geographical area. From the point of view of potentialities, mere large population or even large size may be of limited significance. In fact, largeness in size may even become a handicap in this respect. There is, however, the possibility that a larger geographical size would, other conditions given, connote a richer supply base, and if the supply base is also rich from a potential point of view so that there is a large gap between the actual levels of utilisation of resources and their potential supply, a larger population might connote the possibility of higher incomes and hence of a larger-sized market. Other conditions given, if resources are abundant in relation to population, productivity levels can potentially rise, and the economy has considerable scope of expansion, the process having increasing returns.

Thus mere geographical size is by itself not very significant even if we assume that there is a fairly similar degree of economic homogeneity between the countries of equal size. Further information about the relative endowment of different countries in regard to natural resources both in quantity and quality is needed We want to know whether there are substantial climatic differences; whether the size and growth of population are fairly similar; whether the pattern of institutions, sets of laws, socio-religious customs, etc. are similar and so on. These different factors are closely inter-related and it would be difficult to single out any particular factor as *the* determining influence. Hence, so many diverse factors affect the economic well-being of different countries that it is extremely difficult to isolate the factor of size in ascertaining its impact upon the dynamic course and prospects of an economy.

Thus, we find in actual practice that two countries with equal size in the world to-day might have very great differences in regard to the current levels of standard of living and the potentialities for the same in future. We also find that some of the countries with a smaller size have been able to have very high standards of living. They have attained high levels of improvement in methods of production technique and have large capital stock as compared to countries much bigger in size. Nor even among the developed countries does it follow that the capital stock is proportionate to geographical size or population or that the actual standards of living tend to remain the same or grow with size. In fact, we cannot draw any definite conclusion that a small-sized country is invariably worse off in relation to a large-sized country or that small sized country is invariably better off than a large-sized country or that the size of a country is a matter of indifference. It is just not possible to derive the level of development given the size.

II

At the outset it may appear that a large-sized country, other conditions equal, would have greater advantages as against a small-sized country. For example, firstly, whatever the size of a country, some minimum expenditure has to be incurred in regard to the maintenance of administration. Administrative overheads do not increase proportionately with size. It is true that a small-sized country is put to some handicap in this respect because of the indivisibility in this item of expenditure. Secondly, whatever the size of the country, certain minimum expenditure has to be incurred in regard to defence. It is very difficult in modern days to distinguish between military expenditure purely needed for defence and that which is necessary to maintain the country militarily ahead of others. Military expenditure is not necessarily proportionate to size. A small-sized country is again at a disadvantage here. Thirdly, there are a number of items of expenditure on transportation, communications and other public utility services which are generally a function of size. Here again, a small country is to a certain extent at a disadvantage. Fourthly, a country's position in regard to bargaining vis-a-vis other countries is not determined purely by economic forces. Relative size might play an important part in this case; in other words, there might be special advantages in the case of a large-sized country. The most important advantages arise, however, from the spread of the cost of the establishment and maintenance of various economic institutions. They arise from the common currency, credit and exchange arrangements resulting from an integrated monetary and banking system. The large costs of the establishment and operation of scientific laboratories and the technical training institutes can also be spread out. Another factor is the possibility of the development of specialization. It may also be possible to diversify the economic structure.

The purely economic argument in respect of size runs as follows:

(*a*) The larger the size of the firms, the lower the unit cost of production. This is because of economies of scale, which arise on account of indivisibilities.

(*b*) The larger the aggregate market, the larger would be the size of the firms. Here the assumption is that an increase in the size of the market would imply an expansion in the size of the firms. This in its turn would lead to the gains arising on account of the economies of scale.

(*c*) The larger the size of a country, the larger would be the aggregate market. The assumption here is that the larger the size, the larger would be the resource base, and the larger the population, the larger would be the magnitude of demand.

Hence the argument about the superiority of a large sized nation based upon the above three critical links. Firstly, there must be economies of scale, which cannot be exploited if the average size of the firm is small, given the aggregate market. Secondly, an increase in the size of the market must lead automatically to an increase in the size of the firms. Thirdly, an increase in the size of a country must lead to an increase in the size of the market. If the reasoning is to be valid, it is necessary that it should not at all be possible to reap the economies through mere reorganisation, with given size in regard to the market. In other words, a number of economies are oriented purely to the aggregate size of the firms.

It is difficult to acquiesce in the view that all the above links would necessarily hold. For example, it is not clear as to whether the size of the firms is positively correlated with the size of the nations. In a broad sense, it is true that there *are* economies of scale to the *economy* in the sense that an expansion in size gets over various types of indivisibilities. The argument in respect of positive correlation of efficiency with size must assume that it is not possible to overcome the indivisibilities through any other method other than an expansion of the size. Perhaps, the most difficult link to be satisfied is that between the size of the market and the size of the country. It is clear that a mere increase in size may or may not connote an actual expansion of the market as is the case with several underdeveloped countries facing acute population pressure. As pointed out earlier, what the economist's argument emphasises is that an increase in size would connote an increase in the capacity to produce and secondly, the existence of such conditions that the above increase in income is realised.

III

Assuming, however, that the above links do operate, it appears that for a large country, there are increasing returns arising on account of indivisibilities (as also certain windfall advantages). From this, it may be reasonable to infer that as in the case of individual firms, there is an optimum size for a country from an economic point of view. Such 'optimum' has normally to be subjected to various qualifying considerations.

A preliminary clarification of such an 'optimum size' needs to be given. Assuming that the average density of population remains the same, if there is a slight *increase* in the average net product per worker, then the current size of the country may be said to be less than optimum. If a slight *increase* in area and population with constant density leads to a *decrease* in the per worker productivity in the long period, then the size of the country is more than optimum. Here, of course, we exclude the impact of changes in technology and in methods of production due to reasons other than variation in size. Further, the use of the term "slight increase" in area and population, implies that the average resource potentiality of the increment of land is the same as that of the existing land, and that qualitatively, the increment of population is similar to that of the existing population. We are also assuming away the complications arising on account of the possibility of new barriers in transport and communications, etc. Thus, the concept of optimum size is subject to the same limitations as the concept of optimum population. The change in productivity is, however, to be reckoned after taking into account the adjustments arising as a result of the change in size. A certain time-lag is inevitable here.

If a country, however, *has* to invest in various indivisible administrative, economic and political overheads, and if the cost of these overheads could be distributed over a larger base on the assumption that the size could be slightly increased, there is obviously a possibility of increasing returns. The country's size is less than optimum. On the other hand, if there are diseconomies in organisation and there is a possibility of violent exposure to crisis, if the size is increased, then a reduction in size would be beneficial. It is very difficult to cite cases wherein the size of a country is more than optimum, for, very often, the problem is that of possibility of improvement in productivity, if the size of population could be slightly decreased, or population remaining the same, if the geographical size could be increased. If, therefore, the per capita product can rise with a slight increase in size, population being the same, then obviously the country is less than of an optimum size with respect to geographical area. If, with a given population, a slight decrease in size could lead to a rise in average product per worker, then the size is more than optimum. This would be the case wherein the administrative and other overheads could be slightly reduced in the long period if the size could be reduced somewhat. With a given geographical area, a slight increase in population might lead to a rise in per worker productivity. Here, the country is less than of an optimum size with respect to population as there are vast potentialities in land and other forms of natural resources. Another case would be wherein with a given size, a decrease in population would lead to a rise in per worker productivity. This case is similar to that wherein with a given population, a slight increase in area would lead to a rise in product per worker. In these cases, the country's size with respect to either population or area is less than optimum.

The concept of optimum is useful only in abstract discussion. In the real world, however, it is difficult to attach practical and quantitative significance because any given country's pattern of activities and of specialisation tend to be historically orientated towards the needs and requirements of the trading world as a whole.

IV

It is necessary, therefore, to examine the relationship between size and the reaction tempo and patterns in different countries in the light of various dynamic changes under different sets of assumptions. Let us assume that different countries differ in respect of size; the size of population is proportionate to geographical size; the supply of agricultural land in terms of quantity and quality is also proportionate to size; the supply of other forms of natural resources like minerals, water, hydro-electric potentialities, etc. is also proportionate to size; the composition of population in regard to age structure, sex ratio, etc. is similar in different countries and is not affected by variations in geographical size; the conjunctural advantages arising out of climatic and other reasons are also similar in different countries. In such a situation, would the relative difference of sizes matter in respect of rates of capital formation, patterns of techniques, adjustment capacity of countries in respect of emergencies, both economic and non-economic, etc.? Would the potentialities of growth in these different countries be *also* affected by the size factor?

The answers to the above queries would yet be not unambiguous. Inspite of the rigid framework of assumptions, the critical factor would be whether the size factor would by itself lead to particular forms of production functions as well as levels of costs and returns. The classical analysis as popularised in Smith's *Wealth of Nations* emphasizes the possibility of increasing returns with enlarged population sizes. As other factors would relatively be proportionate to population, a larger population would, on this analysis, give more room for specialisation of talents. The quality of labour would improve; productivity levels would rise; there would be thus scope for considerable division of labour. In such a case, country *A* whose size is double that of country *B* would manifest any or a sum of the following characteristics:

(*i*) The capital stock in country *A* would be more than double that of the capital stock in country *B*. The per capita wealth would, therefore, be higher in country *A* than in country *B*.

(*ii*) The level of real wages in country *A* would be higher than in country *B*.

(*iii*) The rate of capital formation and/or the rate of rise in real wages would be greater in country *A* than in country *B*. From the familiar Keynesian hypothesis about the relationship between consumption and income, one may say that the large-sized country would be subject to business fluctuations of a larger amplitude. As the relationship between consumption and wealth from a long period point of view is not clear, it is difficult to say anything more precise about the course of business cycles in the two types of countries.

Another important factor in this connection is that some diseconomies might emerge beyond a stage when population size increases. From an aggregate point of view, the problem of coordination would be important in this connection though, if the other factors are available and are proportionate to size, it is not clear as to when and how increasing returns would end. The other advantages arising out of a large-sized per capita wealth and income would be available in the case of large-sized countries. The latter's capacity for bearing through a programme of forced savings arising out of needs of war and military preparations would be greater. Further, the large-sized country would be in a better position to carry through rapidly programmes of new changes in technology. Thus, there might be a certain extent of cumulation in the rate of growth of levels of living and/or of wealth in the case of the large-sized country.

The above conclusions would be true provided the rigid framework of the assumptions is satisfied. In the real world, it is never so and there are wide differences between different sized countries in respect of the population size and structure and composition, availability of land and other forms of natural resources, geographical and climatic advantages, etc. In fact, it is only in the context of a proportionate availability of other factors and conjunctural advantages that size might happen to be the important factor.

It is necessary, therefore, to relax the framework of assumptions and to move some steps nearer reality. Let us first take up the case of availability of agricultural land. It is not true that the size of country *A* which is double that of country *B* would also be equipped with double the quantity of agricultural land. The term "land" has to be interpreted here in such a way that qualitative factors are subsumed. In other words, population and other factors being given, a country double the size of another may or may not have proportionate advantages in the supply of agricultural land from the qualitative and/or from the quantitative points of view. Let us first assume that country *A* is relatively deficient in respect of land. Obviously, the next question emerges as to whether the volume and rate of growth of production of food and of agricultural raw materials for industrial purposes would be adequate, taking into account population needs. It may be that at any point of time, the shortage of land in relation to the size and growth of population may not have an immediate impact upon economic well-being. The land limit might enter at a later stage so that if population growth is given, a large-sized country deficient in land in the above sense might at a later stage come into serious difficulties on account of diminishing returns or of a continuing crisis in regard to production of food and agricultural raw materials. This may be reflected in the emergence of long period pressures upon the country's balance of payments. Any underdeveloped country which is forced to depend upon imports from other countries in regard to supplies of food and agricultural raw materials would tend to face an economic situation of anxiety, particularly in foreign trade. The scope of adjustments is not great and the country's policy will have to be conducted within certain rigid contours.

Assuming that it is possible to overcome the obstacles arising on account of diminishing returns and the increasing pressure of population on land, through changes in technology, it follows that the rate of growth of living standards would in any way be still lower than would have been the case if the land supply was relatively larger.

Thus, if the supply of land is not proportionate to size, and population variation *is* proportionate, a large-sized country would tend ultimately to get into difficulties. It might be necessary in such a country to set in motion forces which would reduce the rate of growth of population. Such a country will have to be further dependent upon the emergence of land-saving innovations and upon foreign trade to a greater extent than a small-sized country.

Let us now take up the case wherein the size of population is proportionate to geographical size but in one case the supply of land is relatively abundant. Here obviously, a country with a larger amount of land will have better economic prospects.

It might be that in fact the size of population is too meagre in relation to land supply so that potential development would be conditional upon an increase in the rate of growth of population or immigration. There may be increasing returns in such a process. Here, of course, a country with more abundant land is potentially worse off in a sense that it cannot utilise to the maximum extent the available resource opportunities.

The next factor is the availability of resources other than land. The mining and mineral resources are, to some extent, independent of size. Country *A* which is double country *B* will not necessarily have double the quantum of mining and mineral resources. If population and other factors are proportionate to size, obviously the rate of development of a large-sized country would be affected adversely. The same factors as in the case of land would be valid here too. A large-sized country with a large population will have to think in terms of synthetic substitutes if it has to overcome the shortages.

On the other hand, it may happen that a large-sized country may also have abundant resources not merely of land but also of other types, but is not in a position to utilise its advantages fully because supply of population is not sufficient. In such a case, there might be increasing returns with a rise in population growth or through immigration.

The next factor to be taken into account is the distribution of geographical and climatic advantages. A large-sized country would not ordinarily have adversities in weather. It may happen that a large-sized country would be in a better position to resile from adversities due to climatic reasons like draughts, floods and unequal distribution of rainfall over the year, etc. This would be so because in a large-sized country except on rare occasions, there would not be a short-fall in rains in all areas. So also with regard to other climatic adversities, there is always a possibility of counterbalancing forces. Thus, such a country would not be so much worse off during periods of climatic adversities.

Similar comments may be made in respect of the distribution of rivers, mountains, etc. Mere size is not the only important factor in all cases. It may be that a small country may be most favourably equipped in regard to climatic and weather conditions and a large country may so lie within a particular geographical range that it has absolutely no advantages arising on account of this.

The above remarks also apply in regard to conjunctural advantages like proximity to the sea, availability of hydro-electric resources, etc.

It may be that the population of two countries may be proportionate to size, but because of geographical reasons within the country, the different parts of the large-sized country are not easily accessible to each other. There are natural barriers in the way of mobility of men and materials. If these barriers are of a strong character and their impact has been felt over long centuries, there might be wide differences in the characteristics of labour. This would imply that a large-sized country would just consist of a number of economically heterogenous parts. In such cases, the advantages of size may all be nearly lost. To overcome the disadvantages, large expenditure on transport and communications and preliminary educational overheads may be necessary. From this, the next step is to consider cases where differences due to religion, language, caste, customs and such other sociological factors might be preventing the attainment of a higher degree of economic homogeneity.

Another interesting case would be that of two nations which are equal in size but one is different from the other in that geographical contiguity is absent in one. Here obviously, the potentialities of increased returns would be limited and there might be various indivisibilities which tend to detract resources from productive investments.

From the above discussion, it appears that more detailed data about the various aspects of an economy is needed before one can generalise about the relationship between size and economic well-being. It may be, and it is so in practice, that a small-sized nation *may* be at the spearhead of industrial advance, may even be in a position to sustain a larger-sized population under higher living standards than a large-sized country can. The disadvantages due to a possibility of deficiency in the size of the market may be more than overcome by rising incomes, though the rate and the period of termination of high rates of growth would depend upon factors like availability of land, the quality of technological advance, the advantages of foreign trade, etc. From an economic point of view much of the disadvantages arising out of deficiency of size may be overcome by the creation of conditions favouring free movement of factors of production and commodities. The absence of tariff barriers as well as relative freedom in regard to movement of capital and labour would be of very great help in this connection. To the extent, however, that the feeling of nationhood is strong, there would be difficulties in the way of migration of labour. All adjustments, therefore, will have to be concentrated upon the flow of capital. The relative economic cost from the current to the temporal points of view of movement of labour as against those of capital would determine the net balance of advantage in this respect.

It may be thus generally argued that if there is freedom in regard to international movements of factors and goods and there is no restriction whatsoever upon the movement ot population, the disadvantages due to a relatively small size may be overcome. Though this might have been true during the 19th century, it does not have much validity today in the current political context. The deficiencies in regard to political size cannot be completely overcome through alternative countervailing arrangements or through the break up of the barriers against free movement. In the first place, any given nation, whatsoever its size, would tend to be worried about the possible re-emergence of tariff barriers. It might be that supplies of strategic raw materials might be suddenly cut off or become suddenly scarce. There may be a fear that other nations might develop new techniques, new products and factors. It may not be found advisable to give up the special advantages that are at present accruing to any particular nation because of certain arrangements with countries outside the 'free' area. To the extent that a policy of greater freedom is adopted in the international sphere. some nations may be afraid that they may be subjected to the serious impact of the repercussions arising on account of crises in related countries. There is also a possibility that as a result of a greater extent of freedom of trade and an enlargement of the size of the market, some countries may benefit more than others. Most of these fears and uncertainties are inherent in any process of expansion of the market which is independent of political size. The gains arising on account of a deficiency in the latter cannot therefore be completely overcome. The difficulty in any countervailing arrangement is that the relative gains and losses cannot be potentially appropriated by any one particular country. The distribution of gains and losses within a particular country would, however, not be subject to the same qualifications.

V

The special problems of underdeveloped countries vis-vis size may briefly be examined. The underdeveloped countries may be divided into three broad categories. In the first, there are those countries which are relatively large-sized in area but which have a very high density in population. These countries are less than optimum in respect of geographical size but more than optimum in respect of population. There are a number of indivisible items of expenditure which have to be incurred if the conventional requirements of political nationhood are to be satisfied. The impact of such size-orientated expenditure would be keenly felt primarily because the level of income is low, and the annual meagre ratio of savings to income hardly permits any increase in per-capita living standards. The problem in such economies is one of the maximisation of the rate of savings. This would imply a considerable reduction in avoidable unproductive investments or consumption. A substantial increase in productive capacity might, however, require a large increase in expenditure on transport and communications. The required volume of savings may not be forthcoming within the particular country. If geographical size is given, obviously the way out would be through a reduction in population growth rates. The problem will be difficult if the existing size itself is too large so that for a fairly long period to come, reductions in population growth rates would not be of much help. Given the supply of land (determined by size), there would be possibilities of increases in agricultural production and productivity, but once again, the population factor would tend to depress the chances of any considerable increase in living standards. The population factor in market expansion takes the form of an increasing pressure upon diminishing return activities like agriculture. Hence, actually, as per capita and per worker productivity would tend to be depressed below that level which would have been attained if population, size and growth rates had been less, mere large size in respect of population connotes no scope for increasing returns. The country's resource potentialities may be vast in absolute terms but in per capita terms they may be fairly meagre, and the potential limits up to which standards can be raised would also be low. Such a country might seek expansion outlets in other countries. It may import land-orientated products and export manufactured goods. But then, the scope is not much inasmuch as at low incomes and low productivity levels, the level of specialisation would be low. Owing to the low rate of accumulation, the country's capacity to produce on competitive terms those goods which are largely demanded in other countries would be meagre. Foreign trade, therefore, does not offer much of a way out. The position becomes chronic if, because of population pressure, the country is forced to import land-orientated products without sufficient capacity to produce the required quantities of other goods in exchange.

In category two, can be included those underdeveloped countries which have a large geographical size but have a relatively low volume of population. There is scope for increasing returns if population size could increase. At present, the country's size of population is less than optimum. In such a country, the current levels of income and productivity may be low; the vast potential resources might however remain unutilised or under-utilised because of the insufficiency of population. The size of the market is too meagre to permit large-scale specialisation and the needed industrial diversification. There are no intrinsic supply difficulties, particularly in respect of land-orientated products, but the question is one of the need of accumulation of a large quantity of capital before accelerated rates of income growth can be obtained. Immigration and accelerated population growth rates would have beneficial repercussions upon the economy.

In the third category may be placed those underdeveloped countries whose geographical size as well as population are not much out of proportion with each other, but whose absolute size is small so that very large overheads are to be incurred upon the maintenance of the convention of nationhood. A number of such countries together might constitute a potential base for large-scale expansion and each might gain in the process of integration.

Let us examine briefly the implications of market expansion schemes with reference to underdeveloped countries:

(*a*) Two or more underdeveloped countries, all of them having acute population pressure and hence relatively deficient in land, and with meagre industrial and technological base get into an integrated 'market expansion' programme. In this case, it does not appear that there would be substantial gains from the integration. The different countries are relatively deficient more or less in the same factors. A country which is slightly more developed than the others might, however, derive considerable advantages in such expansion schemes, but this aggravates cumulatively the inequalities between the different countries. No wonder that from the economic point of view, underdeveloped countries geographically contiguous to each other do not much relish the idea of integrated market programmes. Another complicating factor is that in the world, as it is today, a number of underdeveloped countries have close relationships with some developed country or other, and it is difficult to fashion out a new pattern of relationship amongst the underdeveloped countries in such a way that economic integration becomes feasible.

(*b*) An under-developed country whose size in respect of area is less than optimum, or whose size in respect of population is more than optimum, gets integrated with another underdeveloped country, whose size in respect of area is more than optimum, or whose size in respect of population is less than optimum. This particular type of integration has considerable potentialities. The relative shortage in factor endowment in the different countries can be compensated by some common arrangements. Success would, however, depend upon the degree of permissible freedom in respect of population movements. As both the countries are underdeveloped and their capacity to save is meagre, the integration will succeed most when it is possible to obtain supplies of fixed capital, technical skill, etc., from some of the developed countries. In the absence of the latter, there would be considerable opposition by the trade unions in the population-sparse country against any large-scale inflow of population from another low income country. Population movements can, however, be considerably facilitated if there is a guarantee of inflow of complementary capital from some of the developed countries.

(*c*) One or more underdeveloped countries get into integrated market arrangements with a developed country. The general picture here would be that of several developed countries having a ring of underdeveloped satellites around them. In earlier days, owing to historical and other reasons, such arrangements were frowned upon as the reflection of imperialism or of exploitation. Such arrangements, however, continue to exist despite the attainment of freedom in several underdeveloped countries in recent years. It follows that there must be strong *economic* reasons making for the continuance of such an arrangement. In fact, amongst the underdeveloped countries, there is a race as it were to get into some sort of workable arrangement for the inflow of capital and technical skill with some of the leading developed countries. In the absence of arrangements of the pattern (*b*), it is natural to suppose that one or more countries, short of capital, but abundant in labour, would tend to get into working arrangement with one or many developed countries, which have, actual or potential, capital to export. The developed countries particularly are richly endowed with those factors in which the underdeveloped countries are deficient. Any acceleration in the rate of development in the latter leads to an increased extent of dependence upon the former, though an ultimate objective of such plans might be to *reduce* the extent of such dependence. There is, however, a feeling amongst the underdeveloped countries that the process of such exchange would be more beneficial, if the relative share of benefits accruing to the underdeveloped countries could be increased.

(*d*) Finally, we may take up the case of one or more small-sized underdeveloped countries in which the relative proportion between land and population is fairly satisfactory, and which get into integrated arrangements amongst themselves with a view to reducing the impact of indivisibilities in the process. This type of arrangements would be beneficial from the point of view of the different countries. The success would, however, depend upon the distribution of gains from such arrangements and the attitudes of different countries towards one another in respect of the above.

Another complicating factor in all market expansion is that it might have different qualitative connotations. For example, if two or more equally developed countries are integrated in an economic sense, the resulting impact would be different from that in a case wherein the developed country or a group of such countries get integrated with another or a group of underdeveloped countries. In the latter case, particularly, there are large advantages in the case of commodities capable of mass production. Further, as several underdeveloped countries tend to export raw materials and minerals in exchange for finished consumers' or capital goods, the developed countries particularly may stand to gain in the process, because the supply of raw materials and minerals would be assured. If a group of developed countries integrate, there may be advantages in terms of cost of production, which leads to a fall in prices; but such gains may be mostly accruing to the inhabitants in the developed countries in the form of higher wages. The relatively less developed countries may not stand to gain so much though the demand for some other raw materials and land-orientated products would be augmented.

There are also some reasons why the underdeveloped countries have a reason to be sceptical of the benefits to themselves of such a process. For example, in the first place, this would tend to upset the schemes discussed in (*c*). If the different planets come together with a view to obtaining countervailing advantages from another highly developed large-sized planet, there would tend to be a considerable dislocation in the relationship *between* the planets and satellites. Firstly, the extent of dependence upon raw materials and processed products might tend to be reduced, if synthetic substitutes emerge or the search for them is accelerated. Secondly, part of the capital which is at present flowing to the underdeveloped countries might find an internal outlet and may not be available for export to the underdeveloped countries. In the third place, the market for some of the finished products of the underdeveloped countries amongst themselves or in the rest of the world might suffer. Integration arrangements amongst the developed countries might lead to a shrinkage in the market for the products of some of the underdeveloped countries rather than for an expansion of the market in the highly developed countries. The repercussions of such programmes, however, require much deeper study.

VI

Finally, a few words may be added about the case of a nation which is too small from the point of view of the capacity to obtain economies of scale and of mass production but which seeks to *assert*, however, its nationhood. Such a nation would like to equip itself with most of the economic and political institutions which are characteristic of a large or developed nation. For example, it is necessary to maintain a reasonably large defence force. The expenditure on this account would naturally be a first draft upon the nation's resources. A reasonably large expenditure will also have to be incurred in maintaining a foreign service with provision for embassies, consulates, etc. The foreign exchange resources would be partly strained on this account. There is also expenditure on account of the fees of membership of various international bodies. In all these cases there might be countervailing advantages. A nation might like to have its own currency and foreign exchange arrangements. Advantages due to a link with some established foreign currency might have to be given up. Expenditure will have to be incurred in establishing and maintaining a Central Bank as well as a network of commercial banks dealing in internal as well as external transactions. An independent currency would imply the need for substantial gold reserves. Here again, the advantages on account of the link with a foreign currency may have to be abandoned. If such a nation pursues also a policy of economic nationalism, tariffs may be necessary with consequent current disadvantages, though these may *prove* beneficial from a long period point of view. New industries may have to be fostered and developed though the internal market is not sufficient to warrant the large initial indivisible expenditure. The feeling of nationhood may assert itself in the form of the regulation of inflow of foreign capital or of discriminatory attitude against the growth of foreign businesses at home. In some cases the need for self-sufficiency might reflect itself in the considerably large capital expenditure upon various capital goods industries (particularly in steel). Here again, the market may or may not be sufficient to warrant the above expenditure. There may also be restrictions upon migration. Even though the country might afford to have a larger population with consequent advantages, these may have to be given up because of the pursuit of a policy of nationalisation. Immigration may be forbidden or may be selective. The feeling of nationhood might assert itself also in the giving up of certain existing cultural institutions and in the development of new ones.

Thus the desire to assert political nationhood has its economic counterparts. As a result, there might be considerable transitional costs which may or may not be counterbalanced by current or long period gains. The idea of national self-sufficiency in various economic spheres under certain conditions would definitely lead to considerable mal-allocation of resources. Excess capacity in certain fields might be a consequence of this. It may be that a particular nation may not be so well-equipped in technical skill; nor may be in possession of required quantity and quality of entrepreneurial and managerial capacity; its administrative cadre may take some time before the nationals can be completely trained. Discrimination against employment of foreigners in indigenous business and

Government might lead to certain disadvantages. The regulation of the inflow of foreign capital might create a disincentive against the flow of capital. Because of its independent currency arrangements, it may be difficult for this particular country to float loans in world markets under as favourable conditions as would be desirable. While there is no doubt that to some extent these costs are inevitable in the emerging process of a nationhood, in some cases nationalism might go too far with consequent disadvantages. Not in all cases is it true that the growth of nationhood would lead automatically to the distrust of foreigners and to the emergence of independent arrangements everywhere. The exact course of events would depend upon past experience of nationals in their relationship with foreigners, and upon current or expected political atmosphere in the international world.

Price Stabilisation *Versus* Fiscal Stabilisation*

Introduction

THE symposium on "The Quest for a Stabilisation Policy in Primary Producing Countries" revolving around Professor Nurkse's paper on "Trade Fluctuations and Buffer Policies of Low-Income Countries" has brought under discussion a wide range of issues. Professor Nurkse has tried to shift attention towards measures of fiscal stabilisation as against a "do-nothing" policy or measures of price stabilisation. The writers participating in the symposium have naturally kept in mind the background conditions of those underdeveloped countries with which they are most familiar. In the same way, we have broadly in mind the conditions in India and similar underdeveloped countries in this paper. We have specifically brought into focus the effects of different policies upon employment, income and capital formation. We agree that some form of corrective domestic action must be undertaken, whether it be in the form of fiscal stabilisation or of price stabilisation coupled with State Trading or Marketing. There is again no disagreement in regard to the need to build up buffer foreign exchange funds.[1]

General Assumptions

Fluctuations in the levels of activity of developed countries imply corresponding fluctuations in the volume of demand for the primary products of underdeveloped economies. International action in the form of price stabilisation and buffer stocks is yet in the realm of

* Article published by *Kyklos* (International Review of Social Sciences, Geneva) in its symposium II on Stabilisation and Development of Primary Producing Countries in Vol. XII-1959 (jointly with P. R. Brahmananda).

[1] Fluctuations in the output of farm crops occur also due to climatic vagaries. The problems of stabilisation arising from the same have been discussed in *Planning for an Expanding Economy* by C. N. Vakil and P. R. Brahmananda (1956).

discussion and may not be a reality for some time to come. Hence underdeveloped countries *have* to assume that fluctuations in the volume of export demand are inevitable. The problem is that of devising appropriate corrective domestic action in such a way that the maximum possible net gains are reaped in an underdeveloped economy in the wake of these fluctuations. Is it possible that through appropriate institutional adjustments an underdeveloped economy can transform the vagaries of international trade into a factor exercising a beneficial influence on the course of economic development?

In the ensuing discussion we assume that international trade has a significant actual or potential effect upon the level of national income and the rate of capital formation of an underdeveloped economy. (In some countries, though international trade forms a minor portion of the country's national income, gains and losses as a result of international fluctuations do, or could, have significant effects upon government budgets, domestic savings and investment.) We shall assume that the farm sector largely specialises in the production of export crops, so that the export sector and the farm sector are treated as identical. We shall further assume that high levels of economic activity in developed countries would imply boom conditions of demand for *all* export crops and the reverse in the case of a slump. However, in several cases cash crops and food crops are substitutes for one another, and larger production of one can only be at the cost of another.

It is again possible to visualise various patterns of dependence of an underdeveloped country upon the developed country. It may be exporting both cash and food crops; or exporting the former and importing the latter. It may be importing some cash crops as raw materials for its industries. We shall ignore these shades of difference in this paper.

The Nurkse Proposal

Let us assume that the primary producing economy faces conditions akin to those of full employment in a developed economy. The surplus labour concealed in the farms is not available in the factor market during the cyclical period. The farm producers are governed by the economic motive and would tend to expand production provided adequate returns accrue. The supply of farm, or rather export, crop output is price-elastic. (Presumably, the long-period output is more elastic than the short-period output.) Hence higher prices would imply larger production and lower prices smaller production. But in order that supply be elastic, it is necessary that factors be diverted from non-farm activity to farm activity. The elasticity of export output is higher under conditions in which the level of non-farm activity is depressed. In order that this should be so, it is necessary that higher levels of general taxation be imposed, so that the volume of non-farm disposable income is reduced. Similarly, Professor Nurkse believes that in the absence of measures of general taxation to reduce the disposable income of the non-farm sector, there would tend to be an expansion in money supply and in prices and thus in money incomes. The export boom would develop conditions of general inflation. This would tend to affect adversely the relative allocation of resources towards the export sector. Measures of general taxation enable budget surpluses to be built up during periods of export boom. During periods of export slump, factors must be diverted from the farm to the non-farm sector. As prices would be low, factors will be pushed out of farms; if budget deficits are incurred and the non-farm sector expands, it would be possible to absorb these factors. High rates of general taxation and possibly import taxes during periods of export boom would enable foreign exchange reserves to be built up. (The consumption and other import demands of the export sector must be satisfied through adequate exchange releases.) These could be utilised during slump periods. Thus, the above policy measures, i.e., building up of foreign exchange reserves as well as budget surpluses during export booms, and balance of payments deficits and budget deficits during periods of slump, would enable a primary producing economy to make the best out of fluctuations.

Farm producers would obtain higher levels of disposable money incomes during booms than otherwise. The disposable money incomes of the non-farm sector would be lower during booms than otherwise. The disposable money incomes of farm producers would be lower during slump periods than otherwise, whereas the disposable money incomes of the non-farm sector during slump periods would be larger than otherwise. Nurkse's policy implies offsetting variations in money incomes and employment between the farm and the non-farm sectors during booms and depressions. During booms the farm-sector would suck resources out of the non-farm sector; during slumps the non-farm sector would tend to suck resources out of the farm sector. Proceeding under the assumption of full employment, Nurkse's proposal thus seeks to bring about an appropriate pattern of resource allocation in order to suit the requirements of international markets. It seeks to provide an appropriate fiscal environment in which the supply adjustments could be most elastic. Professor Nurkse prefers measures of general fiscal stabilisation to those of price stabilisation. Perhaps the carrying out of Nurkse's proposal would place an under-developed economy in a better situation than would have been the case if no corrective domestic action had been taken. But it is not clear whether some form of price stabilisation coupled with the institution of State Trading and/or Marketing Boards would not be a superior alternative to measures of fiscal stabilisation. Incidentally, one must also examine in detail whether the assumptions underlying the Nurkse proposal are realistic in the context of the economic situation of an underdeveloped economy.

Specific Assumptions Underlying Superiority of Fiscal Stabilisation

There are, of course, a number of general questions underlying the fiscal stabilisation hypothesis. Do higher prices of farm crops imply automatically higher money incomes of farm producers than would have been the case with an alternative policy? Do higher money incomes of farmers imply more supply during booms? Does a primary expansion in farm incomes tend to lead to an increase in the level of incomes of the non-farm sector so that there is an increased domestic demand for export commodities? Would higher rates of general taxation necessarily imply reduced domestic demand for export crops or for the factors which help in their production?

Here again, it is not clear how *general* fiscal measures can directly impinge upon particular types of consumption. Even assuming that appropriate indirect taxes are levied, the problem is whether consumption could be curtailed in the required directions and with the required speed.

The case for fiscal stabilisation is strongest when the following assumptions hold true. The background economic situation is that of full employment of labour. This implies that there should be no reserve of unemployed labour in the rural and in the urban sectors. Further, a reduction in the demand for non-export products should *release* factors of production for export crops. This implies that resources released as a result of a reduction in the non-export sector can alternatively be used in the production of export crops. This naturally assumes away the problem of specificity and immobility of factors of production. Again, potential expansion of the non-export sector which would have taken place if high rates of general taxation had not been levied should necessarily imply additional demand for those factors of production which could have been alternatively employed in the expansion of export crops. Similarly, the expansion of export crops should necessarily imply a reduction in the volume of production in the non-export sector. Besides, measures of *general* taxation assume that the spread between the prices received by the farmers and the prices received through exports does not widen during boom periods. It is possible that variable export taxes imply largely a mopping up of windfalls which would have accrued to the trading sector. (Such a policy may possibly imply a reduction in the demand for luxury consumer goods or of imports of equipment needed in the manufacture of luxury goods.) Thus, permitting higher levels of disposable incomes in the export sector might imply higher levels of windfalls in the trading sector. It may be that price stabilisation and State Trading actually yield higher prices to the farmers and thus evoke a better and larger response during booms than would be the case otherwise.

Further, the relative superiority of fiscal stabilisation would depend upon the assumption that most of the increased incomes that would accrue to the export sector are necessary in order to evoke the required supply. Professor Nurkse does recognise that the larger exports during booms may be partly due to the release of stocks carried over from the slump. The argument would now depend upon the elasticity of stockholding in relation to the price spread between the slump and the maximum price that is expected to rule in the boom. Is the price that actually obtains in the booms the same as the expected price? It may be that stocks are more often involuntarily carried over and that part of the gains that accrue to the export sector would be a windfall. Besides, it is not clear why *selective* monetary and credit policies cannot bring about the required expansion in the export crop output and prevent expansion in undesirable spheres. One is again not certain how long it takes before supply actually responds. It is possible that expansion in the output of export crops would depend upon adequate supplies of finance as well as real resources. A higher rate of inflow of fertilisers, agricultural tools and implements, farm machinery and equipment, as well as of wage-goods in order to draw upon the reserves of labour, might be more helpful in expanding production than mere price incentives. In fact, if the above measures are undertaken, the price incentive may not be necessary at all. Naturally, we may expect the demand for various factors as well as consumer goods to *increase* when an export boom develops. It may be that with appropriate elasticity in the non-export sector, the general level of incomes and employment may go up both in money and in real terms. Part of the foreign exchange reserves may be utilised for imports of equipment, and if necessary, of wage-goods. If these possibilities exist, then the Nurkse proposal would imply lower levels of real income and employment both in the farm and in the non-farm sectors during periods of export boom. We shall revert to this issue at a later stage.

In the reverse case of an export slump, how can one be sure that supply would automatically contract in the face of falling prices, that the factors released by such a contraction would be needed for the expansion in the non-export sector and that only those activities would be expanded which would absorb the released factors? Suppose alternatively that output of non-export crops could have expanded, provided there was a relatively stable demand from the farm export crop sector for the products of the farm non-export crop sector. For example, fiscal stabilisation might imply lower food production during slumps. Professor Nurkse also leaves out of account the beneficial effects of money income stabilisation upon the rate of capital formation and the pattern of techniques adopted in agriculture.

The Case for Price Stabilisation and State Trading

Let us now examine the case for price stabilisation under a set of idealised assumptions. We assume that there exists a State Trading organisation which has a right of monopoly purchase from the farmers. This organisation keeps close watch over the international situation in regard to price trends and operates with the guarantee of (a) a set of minimum prices at which it is prepared to purchase the crops from the farmers, and (b) a range of maximum prices depending upon the extent of increase in supply that it would like to obtain from the farmers. The direct link between the State Trading agency and the primary producers may actually imply better prices on an average for the latter. There are also the gains accruing from greater certainty of demand. The State will also be supplying certain external economies to the rural producers. Now, other conditions being equal, during the period of depression the farm crops will be bought at higher prices than otherwise. It is possible that the aggregate production would be larger than would have been the case if prices had slumped. The State Trading organisation or other counterpart agencies will hold the stocks during the depression and carry them over to the boom period. As the incomes of the primary producers are higher than would have been the case otherwise, the production plans of the producers would not be disturbed because of international changes. There will be some rate of capital formation maintained even during depression. One can visualise conditions in which this is even speeded up so that when we enter the conditions of a boom, the production capacity of the producers is larger than would have been the case if there was no stabilisation of prices in the depression. Thus the supply during the boom would flow out of a larger base; to this are to be added the stocks carried over from the depression.

The State Trading organisation which accumulates buffer funds during the periods of boom might utilise these for various purposes apart from purchases of crops during slumps. It might use its profits for the development of social and economic overhead capital investments in agriculture, for the supply of various types of external economies or for financing industries which would consume the raw materials. Some buffer foreign exchange funds would also be built up. It may be also feasible to acquire buffer stocks of capital equipment as well as industrial raw materials and wage-goods. Other conditions being equal, all these measures would increase the elasticity of short-period supply during the boom.

The above policy may also have some administrative advantages.

Flexibility in fiscal policies is somewhat difficult, as quick changes in taxation and tax rates are hard to make.

Implications of Price Stabilisation

The following would be the implications under conditions of price stabilisation as compared with those of fiscal stabilisation: (a) Production of export crops during boom periods may or may not be larger; (b) Production of these crops during slump periods would be larger; (c) Farm disposable income during boom periods may be smaller; (d) Farm disposable income would be larger during slump periods; (e) Farm employment may be lower during boom periods; (f) Farm employment would be higher during slump periods; (g) Money incomes of the non-farm sector would possibly be higher during boom periods; (h) Money incomes and employment levels in the non-farm sector may be lower during slump periods.

We assume that in both types of policies measures will be undertaken to conserve foreign exchange through appropriate export duties and import taxes. Under price stabilisation, the pressure on foreign exchange during boom periods would be greater because the major portion of import demand would be related to the level of incomes and activity in the non-farm sector. Similarly, the pressure on foreign exchange during slump periods would be less than might be the case under fiscal stabilisation. Thus, other conditions being equal, price stabilisation would imply greater demand for foreign exchange during boom periods and less demand for the same during slump periods. A policy of price stabilisation in the context of a State Trading organisation would imply the building up of buffer funds. Thus an important source of saving for the economy will emerge if we adopt the principle of price stabilisation. It would be possible to determine, within limits, the extent of disposable money incomes that could accrue to the farm sector. It is left to the planning authorities to visualise the *timing* of investments as a result of the building up of buffer funds. There is also control over the *pattern* of allocation of resources, if a large quantity of resources is available at the source. General fiscal measures would not be adequate from the point of view of allocation. Further, there is the possibility of expansion in agricultural production and productivity, if they depend upon large social overhead investments or capital intensive investments beyond the reach of farmers. Thus, there is no reason why farm incomes should suffer. The fact that steady capital formation would be taking place throughout would imply a steady increase in farm capacity. (For example, capacity to produce food may be expanded during boom periods. The slump can, therefore, witness a considerable expansion of purchasing power; the needed diversification can take place without much difficulty.)

Price Stabilisation, Fiscal Stabilisation and Aggregate Welfare

How are we to judge whether price stabilisation or fiscal stabilisation would be more desirable as a policy objective? We suggest that taking the cyclical period as a whole, the following are the relevant issues in the choice between the two: (1) Would aggregate foreign exchange earnings under price stabilisation be larger than under fiscal stabilisation? (2) Would the rate of growth of national income and employment be higher under conditions of price stabilisation than under fiscal stabilisation? (3) Would the rate of growth of capital be higher under price stabilisation than under fiscal stabilisation? (4) Would the pattern of allocation of investible resources be more conducive from a longer-period perspective under conditions of price stabilisation than under conditions of fiscal stabilisation?

If more foreign exchange could be accumulated under fiscal stabilisation than under price stabilisation, the following conclusions must hold good. (1) Output of farm crops is larger under fiscal stabilisation than under price stabilisation, taking the cyclical period as a whole. (2) If output in both cases is the same, home consumption of farm crops is lower than fiscal stabilisation than under price stabilisation.

We know that by definition the supply of output during the slump periods would be larger under price stabilisation than under fiscal stabilisation. The difference between the two quantities of output may indicate broadly the volume of stocks that will be carried over to the boom. There is, however, another factor. It is possible that as a result of the planned use of the funds provided through State Trading and price stabilisation, the rate of growth of agriculture would be higher under price stabilisation than under fiscal stabilisation; hence the aggregate supply may be larger under price stabilization. It would also tend to be larger to the extent that there is a reserve of demand from domestic industry, which is encouraged because of regularity in the supply and prices of farm crops. Here again is a potential source out of which additional supply can be provided during periods of *exceptional* boom. Thus the aggregate foreign exchange earnings *may* be larger under conditions of price stabilisation than under fiscal stabilisation. (Would not the domestic cost of obtaining foreign exchange be cheaper under price stabilisation?)

Let us now consider the effects of either policy upon the rates of growth of income, employment and capital formation. A policy of fiscal stabilisation, as noted earlier, would imply higher levels of disposable money incomes amongst farmers during periods of boom and lower levels of farm money income during periods of slump. If higher rates of capital formation are to be obtained as a result, the savings accruing to the economy under fiscal stabilisation should be equal to those under price stabilisation. Most people would agree that a policy of price stabilisation coupled with State Trading would imply more savings than under fiscal stabilisation in which farm money incomes are allowed to expand first and savings are expected to flow therefrom. It is not clear why an increase in farm money incomes should not imply (*a*) an expansion in the volume of money balances held; (*b*) an increase in the demand for gold imports; (*c*) an increase in the demand for consumer goods, imported or home produced; (*d*) an increase in the extent of conspicuous consumption; (*e*) repayment of debts leading indirectly to accumulation of money balances. Thus, increased money incomes of the farming classes via fiscal stabilisation need not *necessarily* imply a rise in the domestic level of income and employment; if gold imports are not possible, a higher ratio of money or goods balances in the alternative would imply lower levels of employment than would be the case when the potential resources would have been utilised for an expansion in domestic demand or for imports of equipment. Another possibility that emerges here is that there may be an increase in the demand for food; hence the marketed surplus to industry may diminish, thus affecting the latter's activity. Assuming that fiscal stabilisation would imply a reduction in the volume of non-farm disposable incomes, there would be less employment as a result in the non-farm sector. If, as noted earlier, the expansion of output in the farm sector can take place without disturbing the level of activity in the non-farm sector, there is no reason why employment and income should be depressed in the non-farm sector during periods of export boom.

On the other hand, during slump periods, fiscal stabilisation expects levels of activity in the non-farm sector to go up and assumes that such an expansion would tend to reduce the pressure on the farms. As seen earlier, it is possible that the degree of interdependence between the two sectors is not close; and further that there may be reserves of unemployed labour in the urban areas as well as in the rural areas, independent of those who are unemployed as a result of reduction in farm output. Hence the expansion in employment and incomes that take place as a result of budget deficits during slumps might have little impact upon the farm sector. Further, there is no reason to visualise that such an expansion could not have taken place in the absence of fiscal stabilisation. For, there is no reason why during a slump higher levels of farm output cannot be maintained under price stabilisation than under fiscal stabilisation without impinging upon factor supply in the non-farm sector. Appropriate monetary and fiscal measures can in any case be used to raise the levels of activity in the non-farm sector during slumps. It is possible that commodity and equipment stocks built up during booms might enable the expansion during a slump to proceed without hindrance. Here again, the question is one of appropriate *timing* of the release of foreign exchange reserves.

In view of this, it is not clear that the rate of growth of employment and income and capital formation would be higher under fiscal stabilisation than under price stabilisation. There are, however, certain other aspects to be taken into account. Price stabilisation would imply a steady stream of money incomes to the farmers and a steady stream of supply to the non-farm sector. Further, it reduces the impact of uncertainty. It permits longer-range planning than would have been the case under conditions of fiscal stabilisation. It would again tend to affect small-sized farm units more favourably than a policy of fiscal stabilisation. Hence the system of incentives would be improved. Thus, the flow of savings as well as the flow of demand would be steady under conditions of price stabilisation. The availability of foreign exchange, as noted earlier, would be steady under both policies. One could thus visualise a steady rate of capital formation as well as steady rates of growth of income and employment under price stabilisation. There is, however, one additional advantage, as a considerable proportion of the savings fund of the community would be used in a planned manner under price stabilisation. It is possible that the allocation of capital will be more in the direction in which it is socially beneficial. Thus, there are reasons to believe that there would be more savings under price stabilisation than under fiscal stabilisation. These savings would be better allocated under price stabilisation; hence the rate of growth of the economy would be higher under price stabilisation than under fiscal stabilisation.

Capital Supply and Growth—Source of Savings*

I

INTRODUCTION

PROGRAMMES of economic development can be carried out only by a rise in the rate of capital formation. Such a rise is conditional upon an increase in the ratio of savings to national income.[1] The objective of this Paper is to provide the necessary facts relating to savings in India during the First and the Second Five Year Plans.

At the outset, some characteristics of the Indian economy may be noted. India is an underdeveloped economy in terms of per capita income. Agriculture is a major occupation, providing nearly half of the national output. The corporate sector is important, but only in the organised manufacturing sector. It has a number of well-developed savings and financial institutions, some fostered by the public sector. The public sector is the pace-setter in investment, and accounts for a major share in public expenditure as well as in employment in the urban areas. Finally, in India a policy of rising prices is likely to lead to pressures through trade unions for higher wages and salaries; consequently, it would be difficult to pursue over a long period a policy of development through inflation.

* Paper submitted to the Round Table Conference of the International Economic Association on "Economic Development with special Reference to East Asia" held at Gamagori near Tokyo (Japan) from 2-9 April 1960 (jointly with P. R. Brahmananda).

This paper is written in my personal capacity, and does not derive from my position in UNESCO. I am indebted to my colleagues Dr. P. B. Medhora and Mr. A. P. Murdeshwar for help in shaping the paper in its final form.

[1] Foreign aid, though helpful, cannot offset the need for domestic savings.

The main finding of the Paper is that both the government and the corporate sectors tend to depend largely upon personal savings and their growth for their development programmes. In view of this, the generally accepted savings models, emphasising the need for a rise in the share of corporate profits to national income as well as the need for a positive role for inflation in economic development, may not hold true. The problem of savings would perhaps require an approach based more on the traditional motives of thrift and productivity.

II

INVESTMENT AND SOURCES OF SAVINGS: 1951-1958

At the outset we must mention the limitations which underlie any effort to understand the pattern of savings in India. No authentic estimates of capital formation or of savings are available for the economy as a whole. Consequently, we have had to piece together various items of investment and of savings to arrive at global estimates. Attempt has been made both to provide for comprehensiveness by including all the items and to avoid double counting by eliminating duplication of items.

Net Capital Formation

An estimate of savings can be arrived at by making an estimate of investment, to finance which the savings are made. The Central Statistical Organisation (CSO) published tentative estimates of investment for the period 1948-49 to 1953-54. Thereafter, the government has published estimates of investment only in the public sector.

The Reserve Bank of India publishes statistical series on the major constituents of the corporate sector. The data presented in the various articles on 'company finances' published in the *Reserve Bank of India Bulletin* (*RBI Bulletin*) enable us to understand the volume of investment in companies in the private sector. However, the corporate sector, though dominant in the organised industries and contributing about 70 per cent of net output in the factory group of industries and mining, forms only a small part of the private sector, as the corporate form of organisation is not yet strong in small-scale industries, agriculture, trading, private transport, etc.

No estimates of capital formation in the agricultural sector are available for the whole period covered by this study. The Rural Credit Survey (RCS), conducted by the Reserve Bank of India, provides valuable data on the working of the rural economy for 1951-52. The national estimates of capital formation (and savings) based upon the RCS data, however, appear to give an exaggerated picture; hence the RCS data can be used only for qualitative analysis. The National Sample Survey (NSS) collected data on rural investment in monetary and non-monetary forms for the earlier years. For later years, however, this has not been made available to the public.

In view of these limitations it has become necessary to work out detailed estimates of investment (and savings) in order to understand their broad trends as well as the pattern of development

TABLE I

NET CAPITAL FORMATION IN INDIA, 1951-59*

(*in crores of rupees*)

	1951–52	1952–53	1953–54	1954–55	1955–56	1956–57	1957–58	1958–59
A. Total Net Capital Formation ..	662	478	586	906	1,003	1,310	1,524	1,368
1. Fixed Assets ..	482	540	642	819	962	1,090	1,332	1,353
2. Inventories ..	180	—62	—56	87	41	220	192	15
B. Public Sector ..	160	140	202	445	431	506	723	791
1. Fixed Assets ..	145	157	223	380	456	483	643	766
2. Inventories ..	15	—17	—21	65	—25	23	80	25
C. Private Sector ..	502	338	384	461	572	804	801	577
1. Fixed Assets	337	383	419	439	506	607	689	587
2. Inventories (excluding agriculture) ..	165	—45	—35	22	66	197	112	—10
D. National Income	9,970	9,820	10,480	9,610	9,980	11,310	11,360	12,620
E. A as per cent of D	6.6	4.9	5.6	9.4	10.1	11.6	13.4	10.8

* In India the financial year is from 1st April to 31st March; whenever any year is mentioned, it normally refers to the financial year, though data is not always available on this basis.

† Crore=10 million.

in India during the last few years.[2] The following Table I on net capital formation between 1951-52 and 1958-59 is a summary of Statement I (given at the end of this paper).

The Table shows that the ratio of net investment to national income increased by nearly fifty per cent during the last eight years. If the net investment rate is taken as an indicator of the stage of economic development of a country, India can be definitely said to have 'taken off'.

The volume of annual capital formation can be related to the total net value of reproducible wealth in the country. Over the last eight years, the total net value of reproducible wealth, estimated at about Rs. 13,500 crores at the end of 1950-51,[3] increased by nearly fifty per cent. The rate of growth of total capital increased from about 5 per cent in 1951-52 to about 7 per cent in 1958-59. Thus since the commencement of the Plans, national capital has started rising at a rate faster than population. But if we take all forms of wealth (including land and livestock), the rate is yet low, being about 3 per cent, as compared to the rate of population growth which is estimated at about 1.9 per cent.

Sources of Finance

No official estmates are available in respect of savings in India.[4] We have referred earlier to the difficulties encountered in arriving at estimates of capital formation for India. These difficulties are still more acute in the case of estimates of savings for the economy. One of the problems in making an aggregate estimate of savings is the need to avoid double counting. An effort has been made to overcome this and other limitations, and to arrive at dependable

[2] The Appendix at the end of the paper gives an account of the primary and derivative sources of information utilised in arriving at the various estimates in the Tables and Statements given in this paper.

[3] *Vide* paper by M. Mukherjee and N.S.R. Sastry in *Income and Wealth,* Series VIII, "The Measurement of National Wealth" (London, 1959).

[4] Cf. Dr. V.V. Bhatt: "Savings and Capital Formation in India" in *Economic Development and Cultural Change,* Vol. VII, No. 3, April 1959: Dr. Bhatt's estimates are preliminary in character. After this paper was written, a study of savings in India, "Estimates of Savings in the Indian Economy," appeared in the *Reserve Bank of India Bulletin* 14(3), March 1960. The National Council of Applied Economic Research is also engaged in a study of savings in India. The Reserve Bank of India has undertaken a more comprehensive study of savings in India.

TABLE II

SOURCE OF FINANCE FOR NET CAPITAL FORMATION

1951-52 to 1958-59.

(*Rs. Crores*)

	1951	*1952*	*1953*	*1954*	*1955*	*1956*	*1957*	*1958*	*Total*	*Per cent*
A. Total Resources	742	499	654	965	956	1,259	1,322	1,334	7,731	100
B. Domestic Savings	468	441	635	899	891	991	854	876	6,055	78
1. Personal	347	480	571	728	798	890	859	874	5,547	72
2. Corporate	39	13	..	16	54	55	20	24	221	3
3. Government	82	—52	64	155	39	46	—25	—22	287	4
C. U.S., P.L. 480 Funds	..	..	..	..	..	..	98	71	169	2
D. External Capital	94	75	48	48	75	53	110	340	843	11
1. Government	65	46	19	16	43	38	95	325	647	
2. Private	29	29	29	32	32	15	15	15	196	
E. Changes in Foreign Exchange Reserves	—180	17	29	—18	10	—215	—260	—47	664	9
F. Domestic Savings as per cent of National Income ..	4.7	4.5	6.1	9.4	8.9	8.8	7.5	6.9		
G. Total Net Investment	662	478	586	906	1,003	1,310	1,524	1,368	7,837	
H. Discrepancy between A and C	+80	+21	+68	+59	—47	—51	—202	—34	—106	

estimates of savings and sources of finance for the economy for the period 1951-59.

Table II gives a global estimate of sources of finance for net capital formation during 1951-59. The table shows that the savings ratio doubled over the period of eight years, the savings performance being better during the last two years of the First Five Year Plan, a period which had the impact of sizable harvest booms, than during the early years of the Second Plan when dependence upon foreign capital and foreign exchange reserves appears to have increased.

If we define 'take off' in terms of a big rise in the savings ratio, say, to about 10 per cent, the Indian economy cannot be said to have yet 'taken off'.

It might be interesting to note the average pattern of relationship between national income and the various categories of domestic savings. Over the period, national income has gone up at an average rate of about 3 per cent annum. If we take an average of national income over 8 years and the average of various categories of savings, direct investment formed about 3 per cent of national income; money supply about .60 per cent with currency at .45 per cent; non-institutional subscriptions, government loans, debentures, the new issue market and small savings about 1.30 per cent; fixed deposits about .40 per cent; Government savings

TABLE III

SAVINGS CATEGORIES PER 1,000 RUPEES OF NATIONAL INCOME

(*Rupees*)

	1953	*1954*	*1955*	*1956*	*1957*	*1958*
A. Money Supply ..	2.8	13.2	26.3	11.4	6.7	8.6
1. Currency ..	2.8	8.6	19.3	4.5	4.4	9.2
2. Demand Deposits	..	4.5	7.0	6.8	2.2	..
B. Fixed Deposits ..	1.5	5.4	4.3	5.5	12.3	9.8
C. Provident Funds	2.7	3.8	4.0	4.1	4.7	3.8
D. Insurance	2.6	3.1	2.9	2.3	2.7	3.0
E. Public Subscription to loans, debentures and the new issue market..	8.0	11.5	6.6	4.8	2.1	0.8
F. Small Savings ..	3.8	5.8	6.8	5.5	6.2	5.5

corporate savings about 34 and 26 per cent respectively; and provident funds and insurance form about .25 per cent each. Table III gives an idea of various savings categories per 1,000 rupees of national income.

III

PERSONAL SAVINGS

As a generator of savings, the government and the corporate sectors are not as yet important in India. But these sectors have to depend upon the market, directly or indirectly, for a major portion of their savings.

Personal Disposable Income and Personal Savings

Personal savings as a porportion of total resources have been about 73 per cent over the period. Table IV gives the detailed relationship between personal disposable income and personal savings.

The ratio of personal savings to disposable income has been rising at a fairly high rate recently. With 1952-53 as a base year, it has risen from about 5 per cent in that year to about 8 per cent in 1958-59[5], despite considerable step-up in personal taxes over the period and the fairly steep rise in prices since 1955. The crucial importance of private incomes as well as the large share of personal savings in total savings point to the significance of traditional motives in determining the growth of savings in an underdeveloped economy.

Constituents of Personal Savings

A detailed list of the various items of personal savings during each of these years is given in Statement II. Table V presents the cumulative totals for the period 1951-59.

Deposits. Most of the personal deposits are in the form of savings deposits. Personal deposits, after declining slightly in 1951, have grown fairly rapidly. A part of the increase in personal deposits is explained by the growth in total deposits and a part may be attributed to the development of the banking and thrift habit.

Deposits of the unincorporated business sector comprise deposits of small industries, registered firms and partnership concerns, trad-

[5] In the U.S.A., personal savings account for about 7 per cent of personal disposable income and form about 50 per cent of total savings.

TABLE IV

DISPOSABLE PERSONAL INCOME AND PERSONAL SAVINGS.

(*Rs. Crores*)

Year	*National Income*	*Private Income as per cent of National income*	*Private income*	*Corporate profits*	*Personal taxes*	*Disposable personal income*	*Personal savings*	*Personal Savings as per cent of Col. 7*
(1)	(2)	(3)	(4)	(5)	(6)	(7)	(8)	(9)
1951 ..	9,970	100.7	10,040	39	284	9,717	347	3.6
1952 ..	9,820	101.0	9,920	13	261	9,646	480	5.0
1953 ..	10,480	101.0	10,590	..	240	10,350	571	5.5
1954 ..	9,610	101.0	9,710	16	253	9,441	728	7.7
1955 ..	9,980	101.5	10,130	54	309	9,767	798	8.1
1956 ..	11,310	101.3	11,456	55	348	11,053	890	8.1
1957 ..	11,360	101.3	11,508	20	370	11,118	859	7.7
1958 ..	12,620	101.3	12,784	24	391	12,369	874	7.9

TABLE V

PERSONAL SAVINGS: CUMULATIVE TOTALS, 1951-1959

	Rs. Crores	*Per cent*
Total Personal Savings	5,547	100.0
A. Deposits	577	10.4
1. Personal Deposits	273	4.9
2. Unincorporated Sector	304	5.5
B. Currency with the Public	392	7.0
C. Small Savings	440	8.1
D. Insurance	221	4.0
E. Subscription to Corporate Sector's Capital	284	5.1
F. Subscription to Government Loans	124	2.3
G. Provident funds	292	5.3
1. Private Sector	122	2.2
2. Public Sector	170	3.1
H. Direct investment excluding resources obtained on credit and investment in agricultural inventories	3,217	58.0

ing concerns, etc.[6] The growth of these deposits is largely affected by changes in money supply.

From the available data, it is difficult to generalise about any significant change in the porportion of money supply held in the form of deposits. Between 1950-51 and 1958-59, total money supply increased by about 26 per cent. Out of this, the increase' in deposit money accounted for about 26 per cent. Thus, there has been no significant change in the means of monetary transactions during the period. Deposit money continues to form about 30 per cent of total money supply. This low percentage is due to a number of reasons: (*a*) absence of banking facilities in rural areas; (*b*) existence of a large number of persons in low-income groups, signifying low per capita liquid resources; (*c*) little inducement, until recently, in the form of interest rates; (*d*) low levels of literacy and general education; and (*e*) possible fears of high taxation. The Reserve Bank has evolved a system of strict supervision of the commercial banks and the possibility of defaults and liquidations is now remote.

What is remarkable, however, is the shift away from current deposits to fixed deposits, influenced partly by rising interest rates.

[6] Deposits of financial concerns of government and quasi-government bodies as well as the estimated U.S. PL 480 deposits have been excluded.

The Reserve Bank of India as well as the State Bank of India have undertaken a number of measures to widen the area of operations of banking business. The banking habit, however, has yet to make much headway in the rural areas and among the low-income groups in the urban areas.

Currency. A major portion of the increase in personal savings is accounted for by changes in currency supply. The expansion of currency has taken place largely as a result of the policy of deficit financing pursued by the government. The growth of currency with the public, among other things, is also governed by the growth in the requirements of working capital and the change in the degree of monetization in the economy.

Small Savings. Among the leading categories of small savings are: (*a*) 12-year National Plan Savings Certificates; (*b*) 10-year Treasury Savings Deposit Certificates; (*c*) 10-year Annuity Certificates; (*d*) Post Office Savings Bank Deposits; (*e*) Cumulative Time Deposit Scheme; and (*f*) Gift Coupons[7] Table VI overleaf shows details.

It is estimated that a majoı portion of small savings accrues from rural areas. For example, there has been a significant rise in the outstandings of the Post Office Savings Bank Deposits. Between 1951-55—a period of rising per capita income—the total amount collected through various categories of small savings doubled. Since the commencement of the Second Plan, however, small savings collections have risen only slightly, largely owing to the steep rise in prices between 1955-56 and 1958-59. It is expected that with a policy of price stability, the small savings movement would tend to gather greater momentum. To some extent, the success of the small savings drive reflects the potential amount of savings in the rural sector at present utilised for gold hoarding.

The small savings movement is being popularised in various ways. Agents have been appointed to obtain collections on commission. The interest rate on small savings was revised upwards during the middle of the First Five Year Plan. Small savings certificates are available in small denominations and efforts have been made to permit distress sales easily. Loans are also available on the basis

[7] Under the 1960-61 budget, a system of prize-bonds, similar to that in the U.K. has been introduced.

TABLE VI

SMALL SAVINGS: CATEGORIES

	Interest Rate	*Maximum Amount*	*Denomination*	*Remarks*
12-Year N. P. S. C. ..	4.25%	Rs. 25,000	Rs. 5, 10, 50, 100, 500, 1,000, 5,000	Income-Tax free (Hypothecation provided)
10-Year T.S.D.C.	4%	Rs. 25,000	Multiples of Rs. 50.	,,
15-Year Annuity Certificates ..	4.25%	Rs. 26,000	Multiples of Rs. 3,325	,,
P.O.S.B. Deposits ..	2.50%	Rs. 10,000 and above upto Rs. 15,000	Rs. 2 minimum required to start the account	
Cumulative Time Deposit Scheme	3.3% on 5-year account 3.80% on 10-year account	Upto Rs. 100 p.m. in 10 year account Upto Rs. 200 p.m. in 5 year account	Rs. 5, 10, 20, 50, 100	Free of Income & Super Tax
Gift Coupons ..			Rs. 5, 10, 50, 1,000	Can be exchanged for 12 year N.P.S.C.

of the small savings certificates. The certificates thus combine a number of attractions which cumulatively might increase their popularity in future.

Insurance. The total amount collected by way of insurance was rather static for a number of years but has started growing recently. Life insurance business which was left largely to the initiative of the private sector was nationalised in 1956 on the ground that the public sector should stand guarantee for the proper use of insurance funds. The growth of the insurance movement has suffered to some extent on account of the cheap money policy pursued in India for a long period. A number of measures have been undertaken to popularise the movement.

Paid-up Capital. Private subscriptions to the corporate sector have been rising recently, partly in response to expectations of high profit rates and possibilities of capital appreciation. The gross rate of profits of Indian companies amounts to about 10 per cent. Taxation has affected profit rates adversely.

Government Securities. The loan market for government securities suffered considerably on account of the cheap money policy pursued in the immediate post-war period. A reversal of this trend commenced with the beginning of the First Plan. The Reserve Bank of India which had supported the government market during the period of cheap money policy, has helped in the upward adjustment in interest rates. There has been a fairly big rise recently in public subscriptions to government loans. An improvement in the yields on government securities might tend to make more funds flow to the government sector.

Provident Fund. The development of the provident fund movement is of recent origin. Total collections, being largely a function of the size of the wage-bill and the expansion of the area of operation of the Provident Fund Act, are likely to grow in future.

Direct Investment. Apart from the above categories, there is the category of investment in fixed assets as well as working capital in small industries, agriculture and private transport. Over-all, the amount of direct investment undertaken in the economy is largely a function of levels of output and expected profit rates, as well as of availability of various forms of assistance from agencies in the public sector. A small part of the funds of the financial corporations flows to this area, as also some assistance from commercial banks. There has been an increase in the grant of co-operative credit to agriculture. With the growth of overhead facilities in agriculture, private investment may be expected to go up.

IV

DIVISION BETWEEN PUBLIC AND PRIVATE SECTORS

Table VII over leaf indicates the pattern of distribution of savings between the public and the private sectors. The share of the public sector in domestic resources has gone up from about 23 per cent in 1951 to about 44 per cent in 1958. The tentative estimates of the Third Five Year Plan indicate that the public sector's draft on domestic resources might be about 60 per cent and that of the private sector about 40 per cent.

TABLE VII

DISTRIBUTION OF DOMESTIC RESOURCES BETWEEN THE PUBLIC AND PRIVATE SECTORS

(*Rs. Crores*)

Year	*Total Resources*	*Public Sector*	*Percentage* (3:2)	*Private sector*	*Percentage* (5:2)
(1)	(2)	(3)	(4)	(5)	(6)
1951	742	95	13	547	87
1952	499	96	19	403	81
1953	654	203	31	451	69
1954	965	446	46	519	54
1955	954	400	42	554	58
1956	1,259	520	41	739	59
1957	1,322	648	49	674	51
1958	1,334	455	42	879	58

Outlay of Central and State Government

The State in India plays a major role in the economic development of the country. Both the Central and the State governments have, directly or through semi-autonomous bodies, undertaken large-scale programmes of public expenditure, a good portion of

TABLE VIII

PUBLIC SECTOR: REVENUE AND EXPENDITURE, 1951-59

(*in crores of rupees*)

	1951	*1952*	*1953*	*1954*	*1955*	*1956*	*1957*	*1958*
A. Public Expenditure of which expenditure on:	1,164	966	1,019	1,234	1,408	1,699	2,057	2,288
1. Development ..	251	269	310	343	424	451	553	610
2. Defence ..	186	192	198	201	188	212	274	283
3. Plan	259	268	343	476	615	640	846	980
4. Investment ..	160	140	202	445	431	506	723	791
B. Revenue Receipts .. of which Receipts from :	921	844	853	917	997	1,154	1,341	1,367
1. Tax Revenue ..	742	674	673	721	768	839	1,048	1,049
2. Surplus of public enterprises	46	41	50	57	59	67	78	73

which is directed towards capital formation. Table VIII gives an account of the increasing volume of public outlays as also of the growing gap between current receipts and outlays.

The percentage of public expenditure to national income has risen from about 12 in 1951-52 to about 18 in 1958-59. Expenditure on economic development, inclusive of outlay on capital formation, was about 4 per cent of national income in 1951-52 and absorbed about 35 per cent of total public expenditure. By 1958-59, the share of developmental expenditure in national income had gone up to about 11 per cent and absorbed about 60 per cent of total public expenditure in that year. Current receipts, inclusive of both tax and non-tax revenues, were about 9 per cent of national income in 1951-52, and financed about 80 per cent of public expenditure in that year. In 1958-59, current receipts formed about 11 per cent of national income and financed only 60 per cent of public expenditure in that year.

A major effort in stepping up revenue resources was made in the last year of the First Plan and the first two years of the Second Plan. A number of new taxes were introduced, including an expenditure tax, a gift tax and a wealth tax. Simultaneously, the rates of excise duty on a number of commonly-consumed commodities were raised. With direct taxation rates in India being among the highest in the world, the scope for increasing collection through direct taxation is limited.

Despite the heavy tax effort, it has not been possible to plough back for investment much of the resources from the revenue account, as expenditure on defence and administration has risen quite steeply. For example, defence expenditure rose from 1.9 per cent of national income in 1951-52 to 2.2 per cent of national income in 1958-59.[8]

A considerable part of the outlay on economic development takes the form of expenditure on improvement of education, medical and sanitation services, agricultural extension, rehabilitation of backward classes, etc. Much of this expenditure contributes to an improvement in the quality of the labour force as also to an increase in the rate of availability of technical personnel.

[8] Assuming a capital output ratio of about 2.5 : 1, defence expenditure sacrifices a rate of growth of output of about 1 per cent per annum —a luxury which a poor country like India can hardly afford.

Public Capital Formation and Sources of Finance

The outlay on capital formation on behalf of the public sector rose from about 1.6 per cent of national income in 1951-52 to about 6.3 per cent of the national income in 1958-59. The volume of capital expenditure on behalf of the public sector rose more than three times over the period. Most of the capital expenditure is on construction and social overhead capital facilities, i.e., building up of irrigation, electricity and multi-purpose projects, expansion of the transport system, etc. Apart from this, the State has taken direct initiative in the development of mining and mineral resources (particularly coal and oil), fertilizers, steel, machine building, telephone equipment, aircraft, defence equipment, etc.

It may be interesting to examine the sources of finance for capital formation in the public sector; Statement III gives the details in this respect. Salient features of the Statement are presented below:

TABLE IX

CAPITAL FORMATION IN THE PUBLIC SECTOR: SOURCES OF FINANCE

(*Rs. Crores*)

Year	*Government savings*	*Borrowings from financial and savings institutions inclusive of provident funds*	*Market borrowings from the public and small savings*	*Deficit financing*	*Foreign Capital*	*Total Resources*
1951 ..	82	3	21	—11	65	160
1952 ..	—52	37	30	81	46	142
1953 ..	64	58	3	78	19	222
1954 ..	155	75	125	91	16	462
1955 ..	39	74	107	180	43	443
1956 ..	46	96	139	239	38	558
1957 ..	—25	175	3	495	95	743
1958 ..	—22	248	72	147	325	770

Government savings over the period contributed just about 8 per cent of the resources for capital formation in the public sector. Borrowing from savings and financial institutions and provident funds contributed about 17 per cent, market borrowings from the public and small savings about 19 per cent, deficit financing about 38 per cent and foreign capital about 18 per cent. Despite the relative increase of deficit financing since 1955-56, the public sector's draft on domestic savings has gone up considerably.

Government Savings. Government savings consist of (*a*) the surplus on the revenue account, excluding surpluses of public enterprises, (*b*) the surpluses of public enterprises (the leading contributor being the railways), and (*c*) the balance available out of miscellaneous funds (excluding resources available from the provident funds). In recent years, the contribution of the revenue surplus has been negative. The surpluses of public enterprises rose only slightly, from less than half a per cent of national income in 1951-52 to about 0.6 per cent in 1958-59. Many of the enterprises undertaken by the public sector are not designed to be operated in terms of the profit maximization principle. A rise in the rates levied by public enterprises—many of which are monopolies—might tend to affect adversely demand for their products and would have to face considerable public resistance. Contributions from public enterprises might tend to increase with the addition of the new steel and machine plants to the public sector. In future, it is expected that the public will be permitted to contribute directly to the capital required for the expansion of public enterprises. There is also noticeable a tendency in favour of granting a greater degree of autonomy to the managements of public enterprises. The government has gradually come to accept in recent years the notion of 'commercial operation' of public enterprises. Strict adherence to this principle might involve a high degree of under-utilization.

Government Borrowings. An increasing part of the government's capital formation is being met through borrowings from savings and financial institutions as well as through resources made available out of the public sector provident funds.

A considerable part of the total market for government loans is sheltered[9] and consists of investments of commercial banks, the Life Insurance Corporation, general insurance business, financial corporations, the employees' statutory provident funds, other trustee funds and funds of local authorities. About 55 per cent of the re-

[9] This explains the low rates of interest at which the Government is able to borrow.

sources accruing through the growth of the life insurance fund flows to the public sector. Nearly 80 per cent of the investment of commercial banks is in the form of government securities.[10] Nearly 90 per cent of the investment of the statutory provident funds of the private sector has to be in government securities. It is also necessary to take into account the net resources available through the provident funds of the public sector. The finance corporations and local authorities also contribute to investment in government securities.

Total collections from all these sources have been rising quite steeply since the commencement of the plans. They might further grow in the years to come, depending upon the growth of resources of financial and savings institutions, particularly, of the banking system. The U.S. PL 480 funds might average about Rs. 100 crores per year, and would be an important factor in strengthening temporarily the market for government securities.

Deficit Financing. Resources obtained through deficit financing have played an important part in financing capital formation in the public sector. The following items are included in determining the extent of deficit financing: (1) resources obtained through the running down of Government cash balances; (2) resources obtained through sales of securities in the cash balance investment account of the Central and the State Governments; and (3) resources obtained through sales of ad hoc treasury bills to the Reserve Bank of India. A part of these resources is utilised for the purchase of foreign exchange; they thus lead to a running down of the foreign exchange reserves rather than an expansion of money supply.

It is usual in Indian financial circles to distinguish between deficit financing which implies expenditure abroad and which therefore has a counterpart in the additional flow of goods and that which implies expenditure at home which results in a net expansion in purchasing power. It would not be correct to regard the whole of the latter amount as inflationary. For example, during the last three years of the First Plan, because of the big increase in harvest with proportionately larger effects upon the marketable surplus of food, prices did not move directly with money supply.

[10] The receipts in this respect have been enlarged during the last two years on account of the U.S. PL 480 counterpart funds kept with the State Bank of India.

Deficit financing undertaken since the Second Plan has had an upward effect upon the price level, despite a substantial import surplus in this period. It has also led to considerable wage adjustments in the private and the public sectors. In view of this, expert opinion is not in favour of depending upon deficit finance as a major source of funds in the Third Plan.

Private Capital Formation and Sources of Finance

Excluding resources for investment in agricultural inventories, the resources available for the expansion of the private sector increased from Rs. 547 crores in 1951 to Rs. 879 crores in 1958. The average of resources for the private sector amounted during the First Five Year Plan to Rs. 495 crores per year and, for the first three years of the Second Plan, to Rs. 764 crores.

The following table indicates the sources of supply of finance for the private sector.

TABLE X

CAPITAL FORMATION IN THE PRIVATE SECTOR: SOURCES OF FINANCE

(*Rs. Crores*)

	1951	*1952*	*1953*	*1954*	*1955*	*1956*	*1957*	*1958*
A. Total Resources ..	547	403	451	519	554	739	674	879
B. Credit	61	—41	20	75	170	189	97	95
1. From Banks ..	48	—50	8	65	148	152	66	64
2. From Co-operative Societies ..	13	9	12	10	22	37	31	31
C. Loans from Financial Institutions ..	5	1	6	8	21	20	16	14
D. New Issue Market	72	34	33	60	15	44	39	41
1. Subscription to paid-up capital ..	19	33	27	43	8	43	29	32
2. Debentures ..	3	1	6	17	7	1	10	9
E. Other resources ..	309	344	398	376	348	486	522	729

Commercial Bank Credit. The supply of credit from commercial banks aggregated to about Rs. 150 crores during 1955 and 1956, largely due to the liberalisation of imports for investment purposes during these years. Commercial banks concentrate mainly on the supply of short-term credit; so only a limited amount of credit from them is available for medium-term and long-term purposes. Recently, however, a new institution, the Refinance Corporation for Industry, has been established, with the participation of the State Bank and a few other leading banks, with the specific object of financing medium-term credit. A part of the P.L. 480 funds deposited with the State Bank of India is utilised for this purpose.

Finance for Companies. The corporate sector in industry has come to depend more and more upon the banking system for credit, as the availability of internal resources for financing expansion is somewhat limited. The following table gives the sources of finance for the expansion of the corporate sector.

TABLE XI

FINANCING EXPANSION IN THE CORPORATE SECTOR

(*in crores of rupees*)

		1951	*1952*	*1953*	*1954*	*1955*	*1956*	*1957*
A.	Paid-up capital	26	14	48	22	34	54	66
B.	Free Reserves or surplus	56	18	..	22	76	78	28
C.	Borrowings	68	—20	8	68	62	148	206
	of which Borrowings from banks	30	—28	—22	38	18	130	96
D.	Other liabilities	5	..	..	44	50	90	80

A series of efforts has been made to develop a number of new institutions to meet the long-term credit requirements of the corporate sector. For example, the Central Government as well as the Reserve Bank of India took direct interest in the establishment of the Industrial Finance Corporation. The State Governments have established State Finance Corporations in each of the States. The Ministry of Commerce and Industry (Government of India) has established the National Industrial Development Corporation for the purpose of financing long-term investment in the public and the private sectors. The Industrial Credit and Investment Corporation of India was set up with the aid of the World Bank with a view to encouraging underwriting of industrial investment.

The Life Insurance Corporation as well as the general insurance companies also provide resources for investment in the corporate sector by helping in the purchase of what are known as 'blue chips'.

The fear that the annual flow of the supply of resources to the private sector might tend to diminish with the nationalisation of life insurance has proved to be baseless. The funds available through the Life Insurance Corporation have increased from year to year.

In recent years, the private sector has been able to obtain sizable amounts of resources through the new issue market, partly due to the high rate of expansion in capital formation in the private sector since the middle of the First Five Year Plan and partly to the possibility of capital appreciation. Despite heavy taxation, the rate of profit on net worth has averaged between 7 to 9 per cent during the last few years. A yield of about 7-8 per cent is a regular feature in respect of new variable dividend securities.

There is an elaborate structure of company law to protect the interests of shareholders against possibilities of mismanagement of funds belonging to companies. The Controller of Capital Issues scrutinises new issues and sanctions the amounts that can be issued. Setting up of new industrial undertakings as well as expansion of the existing ones are subject to licensing by the Ministry of Commerce and Industry (Government of India). Many of the new industrial enterprises are floated with the assurance of technical or managerial collaboration from foreign concerns.

In most cases, managing agents play an important role in financing or underwriting new issues.[11] The importance of the managing agency houses had diminished with the development of other specialised institutions for this purpose. Moreover, the Government has laid limits on the emoluments and commissions of managing agents. The fact that the managing agencies have survived, despite the legislative enactments and the establishment of new institutions, proves that they still fulfil some worthwhile economic functions.

Co-operative Credit. In recent years the State as well as the Reserve Bank of India have taken a special interest in giving a fillip

[11] It was estimated by the Company Law Administration that in the year 1951-52, 1,300 managing agencies in India, managing 1,720 companies with a total paid-up capital of about Rs. 215 crores, had subscribed Rs. 29 crores (14 per cent) of such capital. Again, out of the total loans and advances of Rs. 76 crores obtained by these concerns, the managing agencies had provided about Rs. 18 crores (24 per cent).

to the co-operative movement. The objective is to make co-operative credit an effective substitute for moneylenders who charge usurious rates of interest, simultaneously with efforts to regulate the practices of moneylenders and to fix ceilings on rates of interest. Credit facilities through the co-operative movement have increased by nearly three times during the last eight years. Loans for agriculture are given by the Ministries of Agriculture in different States. Requirements of credit too have gone up with the rapid growth of the agricultural sector and the need for credit to utilise fully the social overhead capital facilities created by the public sector in agriculture. The cultivating families which used to depend formerly solely upon their own resources for the purpose of financing growth of fixed assets did not have adequate credit resources to utilise the facilities provided during the course of the Plans.

During the course of the investigation connected with the All India Rural Credit Survey in 1951-52, it was found that there was a serious lacunae in respect of the availability of medium-term and long-term credit for agricultural purposes. Apart from land mortgage banks, there are no special institutions for the supply of medium-term and long-term finance for agricultural purposes.

Other Credit. It is generally believed in India that small-scale industries suffer from inadequate facilities in respect of credit. The commercial banks specialise in looking after the needs of the large-scale industries. The Government of India has established the National Small Industries Corporation to finance hire purchase of machines to small industries. The State Bank of India has developed pilot projects for supplying credit to small scale industries. The total assistance through the various channels was about Rs. 5 crores in 1951 and has gone up to about Rs. 20 crores during 1955-56. Most of the agencies obtained their resources either from the Government of India or from the State Governments or through floatation of debentures in the market. Apart from the above sources, the State Governments through the State Aid to Industries Acts, provide loans to a number of industries. Whereas during the First Plan the resources available though other sources provided 77 per cent, during the Second Plan, it has amounted to 64 per cent. One very common source of credit supply is the aid provided by the relatives of the enterpreneur, emphasising the crucial role of the joint family in small business even at present. Again, in urban areas, indigenous bankers and in rural areas, moneylenders play an important role in the supply of credit. Not in all these cases are transactions conducted on legal documents. There is a good deal of informal financing in private industry. This method is bound to persist until specialised institutions develop in all centres.

Recently, some general insurance companies as well as commercial banks have developed instalment credit for hire purchase of consumers' and producers' durables. It is reported that the Life Insurance Corporation may in future take direct interest in financing housing construction.

V

SOME RELATIONSHIPS AND POLICY IMPLICATIONS

It is estimated that national income grew at an average rate of less than 1 per cent per annum between 1900 and 1950; in fact, there was very little improvement in per capita income during this period. Since the commencement of the First Five Year Plan, the country has made a big effort to get out of the rut of overall stagnation. This has been reflected in a big rise in the ratio of net investment to national income, a sizable relative rise in the rate of growth of real output per annum and a considerable change in the pattern of investment. The pattern of growth of savings vis-a-vis growth of investment reveals that the household sector (comprising agriculture, small enterprises and individuals) has contributed a major portion of its savings towards the expansion of both the corporate and the government sectors. The pattern of flow of savings indicates that corporate savings particularly have proved inadequate to finance the accelerated rate of expansion of investment in the corporate sector. Though the share of the public sector in net investment has shown a big rise, the government has not been able to procure even a reasonable margin of finance from the operation of its enterprises. Thus, *the growth of both the corporate and the government sectors tends to depend largely upon the growth of personal savings.*

Prices, Real Income and Savings

In studying the changes in the relationship between national income and savings and between personal disposable income and savings, the first year of the First Five Year Plan—1951-52—cannot be chosen as the base. Economic activity during this year was characterised by the impact of the disinflationary policy initiated by the Government of India at the end of 1951 to counter the unhealthy trends witnessed in the economy during the Korean boom. During 1951-52 there was a substantial withdrawal of currency from circulation, a sizable reduction in the volume of bank deposits as a result of the credit restraint policy pursued by the Reserve Bank of India and a large unloading of government securities by the public. The savings to income ratio in that year was 4.1 per cent, and the ratio of personal savings to personal disposable income was as low as 2.9.[12] If we choose 1952-53 as a base year, we find that the savings to income ratio rose by 75 per cent between 1952-53 and 1958-59 (between 1952-53 and 1955-56 by nearly 80 per cent). Since 1955-56, the savings to income ratio has been ruling at about 8 per cent, there being a slight downward trend since the commencement of the Second Plan.[13]

The index of wholesale prices (with 1952-53 as base) was the lowest during the year 1954-55. Savings in real terms have not risen as compared to 1954-55, as shown below.

TABLE XII

SAVINGS AT CONSTANT 1952-53 PRICES

Year		*(Rs. Crores)*	*Year*		*(Rs. Crores)*
1951	..	384	1955	..	758
1952	..	441	1956	..	944
1953	..	605	1957	..	791
1954	..	927	1958	..	775

The years 1953-54 and 1954-55 witnessed a big rise in the level of agricultural output. Real income increased by 6 per cent in 1953-54 and by 2 per cent in 1954-55. It appears that the impact of the big rise in income in 1953-54 was felt in the year 1954-55. The ratio between personal savings and disposable income, steady

[12] These figures exclude change in inventories in agriculture.

[13] On the basis of the experience of 1952-53 to 1958-59, the incremental savings to income ratio works out to about 16 per cent. Incremental personal savings as a ratio of incremental personal disposable income works out to about 15 per cent.

at about 5 per cent in 1952-53, went up to about 7.7 per cent in 1954-55. Thereafter, it registered a slight fall in 1955-56, but has been rising steadily since then. In other words, the middle period of the First Five Year Plan had a big uplifting effect upon the savings ratio.

It is difficult to draw firm generalisations on the basis of an experience of just about eight years. It is clear, however, that changes in real income tend to have a big effect upon the savings ratio, though it is not possible to abstract from the effect of changes in interest rates as well as of the growth of savings habit. Contrary to conventional opinion, years of falling prices, coinciding with positive real output changes, do not appear to have any adverse effect upon the savings ratio.

TABLE XIII

INTEREST AND YIELD RATES, 1951-1959

(Per cent)

	1951	*1952*	*1953*	*1954*	*1955*	*1956*	*1957*	*1958*
A. Government's Long term loans ..	3.39	3.66	3.64	3.67	3.74	3.99	4.18	4.13
B. Yield on Debentures (Tax-free) ..	..	..	3.93	3.79	3.82	3.96	4.11	4.18
C. Yield on Preference Shares (Tax-free)	4.92	5.28	5.28	5.21	5.29	5.43	5.99	5.92
D. 3 months Fixed Deposit Rates* ..	3.00	2.89	3.00	3.00	3.38	3.68	3.90	..
E. Yield on Variable Dividend Securities (Tax-free) ..	5.18	6.17	6.07	5.09	5.01	5.68	6.88	6.27
F. Estimated amount of interest-elastic savings categories (Rs. crores) ..	26	87	109	176	178	107	187	175

* Includes fixed deposits in banks, public (non-institutional) subscriptions, government loans, small savings and subscriptions to debentures.

Interest Rate and Savings

To what extent is the supply of savings responsive to the rate of interest? The period since the beginning of the Plan has witnessed an upward movement in the structure of interest rates. Those categories of savings which are responsive to interest rate changes also have gone up, and by a large amount. Table XIII earlier shows the pattern of interest and profit rates in relation to interest-elastic savings categories.

Various factors having a bearing on savings, like a fall in the general level of prices in the initial years and later a rise in the price level, an increase in real as well as money incomes, were also in operation during the period. The change in the interest-elastic savings categories, however, was larger than the growth in real incomes, per capita and per household. Further, the savings habit would not show big shifts in the period of a few years. Hence, one might conclude that part of the increase in savings has been due to the rising structure of yields.

In a country in which the major portion of savings takes the form of individual savings, and further when expansion in savings is necessary, it is important to induce income-receivers to reduce consumption. A rise in interest rates has an important function to perform in this connection. In an economy in which the Government might resort to considerable deficit financing, a rise in interest rates induces liquid resources to be funded. To that extent there would be less potential impact upon consumption, and thus upon prices, than would have been the case otherwise.

In the strategy of planning, the Government contemplated a steep expansion in taxation to countract possible effects of deficit-financed investment upon the price level. There has been some rise in direct tax yields; the Government's policy has also been helped to some extent by the increase in savings caused partly by a rise in interest rates. If budgetary deficits cannot be avoided, the impact of such deficits upon the price-level would be reduced to the extent that cheap money policy is given up.

Food Supply and Savings

An interesting aspect of the savings problem in India is the close relation that changes in food supply have upon the volume of domestic real savings. During the early years of the First Plan, the level of food output was low. The middle years of the First Plan witnessed a steep rise in food output and a fall in foodgrain prices; the rise in the level of food output improved the balance of payments situation; there was also a big rise in the level of domestic real savings. After a lag of time, the government realised that such a situation would be conducive to a considerable step-up in the volume of deficit financing. This situation estabilised around 1955-56. Deficit financing since then has been having an upward effect upon the level of prices. Savings at constant prices (as shown in Table XXII earlier) failed to rise.

The following table shows an interesting pattern of relationship between food supply, population, national income and savings:

TABLE XIV

RELATIONSHIP BETWEEN FOOD SUPPLY, POPULATION, NATIONAL INCOME AND SAVINGS

(*Indices*)

	1951	*1952*	*1953*	*1954*	*1955*	*1956*	*1957*	*1958*
Index of:								
Food*	100	106	122	123	121	124	123	129
Real National Income	100	104	110	113	115	121	119	127
Population Growth†	100	101.6	103.2	104.9	106.5	108.2	110.3	112.4
Food Supply over and above population growth	100	104.4	118.8	118.1	114.5	115.8	112.7	116.6
Savings at Constant Prices (Rs. crores)	345	413	600	1,070	931	1,008	852	923

* Supply in any given year equalles average of production of that and the previous year plus imports of that year.

† Population is assumed to have grown at about 1.6 per cent between 1951 and 1956 and at 1.9 per cent thereafter.

Over the period, national income and food supply moved together. One can appreciate the crucial role of food supply in the Indian economy. Its significance would be very much greater if per capita food supply is stepped up at a rapid rate, for this would create economic conditions favourable for the transformation of unproductive labour into productive labour.

STATEMENT I*

NET CAPITAL FORMATION IN INDIA IN THE PUBLIC AND THE PRIVATE SECTORS, 1951-58

(in crores of rupees)

	1951	*1952*	*1953*	*1954*	*1955*	*1956*	*1957*	*1958*
A. TOTAL	*662*	*478*	*586*	*906*	*1,003*	*1,310*	*1,524*	*1,368*
1. Fixed Assets	482	540	642	819	962	1,090	1,332	1,353
2. Inventories	180	—62	—56	87	41	220	192	15
B. PUBLIC SECTOR	*160*	*140*	*202*	*445*	*431*	*506*	*723*	*791*
1. Fixed Assets	145	157	223	380	456	483	643	766
2. Inventories	15	—17	—21	65	—25	23	80	25
C. PRIVATE SECTOR	*502*	*338*	*384*	*461*	*572*	*804*	*801*	*577*
1. Fixed Assets	337	383	419	439	506	607	689	587
2. Inventories (excluding agriculture)	165	—45	—35	22	66	197	112	—10

*Referred to on p. 250 of the text.

STATEMENT I—(*contd.*)

NET CAPITAL FORMATION IN INDIA IN THE PUBLIC AND THE PRIVATE SECTORS 1951-1958

(*in crores of rupees*)

	1951	*1952*	*1953*	*1954*	*1955*	*1956*	*1957*	*1958*
OF PRIVATE SECTOR :								
(i) Corporate Sector	*123*	*7*	17	*80*	*143*	*279*	266	96
(a) Fixed Assets	14	40	42	62	99	144	190	106
(b) Inventories	109	—33	—25	18	44	135	76	—10
(ii) Non-Corporate Sector ..	*56*	*4*	*8*	*36*	*64*	*124*	116	*48*
(a) Fixed Assets ..	8	20	20	28	44	64	84	52
(b) Inventories	48	—16	—12	8	20	60	32	—4
(iii) Small Enterprises	*60*	*56*	*48*	*42*	*47*	*48*	*51*	*52*
(a) Fixed Assets	52	52	46	46	45	46	47	48
(b) Inventories	8	4	2	—4	2	2	4	4
(iv) Private Transport, etc. ..	3	9	9	13	20	30	39	39
(v) Construction	171	175	204	190	195	215	214	233
(vi) Agriculture Fixed Assets ..	89	87	98	100	103	108	115	109

STATEMENT II*

PERSONAL SAVINGS IN INDIA 1951-1958

(in crores of rupees)

	1951	*1952*	*1953*	*1954*	*1955*	*1956*	*1957*	*1958*
Total Personal Savings (excluding agricultural inventories)	347	480	571	728	798	890	859	874
A. Deposits	—49	9	28	87	115	181	96	110
1. Personal	—10	19	15	35	43	67	28	76
2. Unincorporated Business ..	—39	—10	13	52	72	114	68	34
B. Currency with Public and with Unincorporated Sector	—116	—17	28	80	193	53	52	119
C. Small Savings	34	39	40	56	68	62	71	70
D. Insurance	15	24	28	30	29	26	31	38

*Referred to on p. 253 of the text.

STATEMENT II—(*contd.*)

PERSONAL SAVINGS IN INDIA 1951-1958

(*in crores of rupees*)

	1951	*1952*	*1953*	*1954*	*1955*	*1956*	*1957*	*1958*
E. Subscription to Corporate Sectors' Capital	69	33	27	43	8	43	29	32
F. Subscription to Government Loans	2	12	47	51	50	7	—15	—30
G. Provident Funds : Private Sector ..	4	8	10	13	16	20	25	26
H. Provident Funds : Public Sector ..	13	12	19	24	24	27	29	22
I.1 Direct Investment	403	291	467	189	461	725	499	649
I.2 Inventories in Agriculture ..	24	—40	100	—192	32	200	—36	168
I.3 Direct Investment *minus* Inventories in Agriculture	379	331	367	381	429	525	535	481
I.4 Bank Credit to Non-corporate Sector	4	—29	23	37	134	54	—6	—6
I.5 Net Direct Investment (I.3—I.4) ..	375	360	344	344	295	471	541	487

STATEMENT III

SOURCES OF FINANCE : PUBLIC SECTOR

(in crores of rupees)

	1951	*1952*	*1953*	*1954*	*1955*	*1956*	*1957*	*1958*
A. TOTAL RESOURCES	160	142	222	462	443	558	743	770
B. GOVERNMENT SAVINGS ..	82	—52	64	155	39	46	—25	—22
1. Revenue Surplus	76	—46	—91	56	—63	19	5	—94
2. Surpluses of Public Enterprises	46	41	50	57	59	67	78	73
3. Miscellaneous Funds	—40	—47	105	42	43	—40	—108	—1
C. MARKET BORROWINGS FROM: ..	—23	16	2	120	89	146	78	228
1. Commercial Banks	—25	9	18	28	21	—12	81	174
2. Insurance Organisation ..	12	9	10	10	9	56	32	29

STATEMENT III (*Contd.*)

SOURCES OF FINANCE : PUBLIC SECTOR

(*in crores of rupees*)

	1951	*1952*	*1953*	*1954*	*1955*	*1956*	*1957*	*1958*
3. Finance Corporations and Local Authorities	—1	..	2	1	6	7	..	..
4. Private Sector Provident Funds	4	7	9	12	14	18	23	23
5. Non-Institutional Public ..	—2	—12	—47	51	50	7	15	—30
6. Estimated Support by the R.B.I.	—15	—21	—84	18	—11	—70	43	—32
D. SMALL SAVINGS	34	39	40	56	68	62	71	70
E. PUBLIC SECTOR PROVIDENT FUNDS ..	13	12	19	24	24	27	29	22
F. EXTERNAL CAPITAL	65	46	19	16	43	38	95	325
G. DEFICIT FINANCING	—11	81	78	91	180	239	495	147

Appendix

NOTES ON STATISTICAL SOURCES

Statement I

Figures regarding the *public sector* obtained from Government of India Economic Survey, 1958-59.

Figures regarding the *corporate sector* obtained on the basis of the Reserve Bank of India Bulletin (RBI Bulletin) articles on 'Company Finances.' The RBI data covers 750 public limited companies during 1950-55. Since 1955-56, it has covered 1,001 public limited companies. These comprise about 75 per cent of public limited companies. Data regarding the private limited companies is available from 1956 onwards. The data of 750 companies for 1950-55 has been readjusted for 1,001 companies on the basis of data for both sets of companies appearing in 1955. For earlier years, the growth of the private limited companies is estimated at ⅛th of that of public limited companies. The assumption here is that private limited companies in earlier years have grown at the same rate as during 1956-57; their relative position is assumed to have remained unchanged vis-a-vis public limited companies.

The *non-corporate sector* is estimated to be about four times the size of the private limited companies.

Data regarding *small enterprises* has been extrapolated on the basis of the information given in the paper, 'Capital Formation in Indian Economy, 1948-54' by the Central Statistical Organization (CSO) (Government of India), in "Papers relating to the formulation of the Second Plan" (Government of India, 1956). Adjustment for inventories has been made on the assumption that inventories form about 20 per cent of net output, the ratio holding true in the case of private limited companies.

Figures in respect of *private transport* and *construction* have been extrapolated on the basis of the data in the CSO paper.

In respect of *agriculture*, the CSO data contained in the paper mentioned earlier, has been used upto 1953-54. Thereafter, fixed investment estimates have been worked out on the basis of indices of irrigated acreage. Figures regarding investment in agricultural implements have been obtained on the basis of the Census of Live-stock which gives figures relating to agricultural implements. The data in this respect is available for 1951-56. Investment in implements is supposed to continue at the same rate as during 1950-56. So far, no estimates in respect of investment in inventories in agriculture have been made in any of the calculations on investment. This appears to have been an important item inasmuch as agricultural output over the period has increased by about 25 per cent and constitutes between 45 to 50 per cent of the total output of the economy.

Statement II

No data is available on the pattern of income distribution in India. The data of the income-tax authorities excludes low-income groups and agricultural incomes. We have tried to bring together the data pertaining to different categories of individuals' savings, government savings and corporate savings. One of the difficulties in arriving at an estimate of savings pertains to double counting of various items. Care has been taken in our estimates to avoid duplication of items.

The annual reports on 'Trend and Progress of Banking,' published by the Reserve Bank of India, contain data in respect of ownership of *deposits in scheduled banks;* data for the non-scheduled banks is obtained on the basis of a sample survey. These data are available under three headings: (*a*) demand deposits, (*b*) time deposits, and (*c*) savings deposits. In our estimate we have excluded the deposits held by financial institutions and government and quasi-government bodies. We have also excluded the deposits held at the State Bank of India by the U.S. Treasury under P.L. 480. The size of P.L. 480 funds has been estimated by an examination of the annual balance sheets of the State Bank of India. Increase in time deposits at the State Bank during 1957 and 1958, over and above what the Bank would have obtained on the basis of the normal rate of expansion of deposit resources, has been assumed to be due to the P.L. 480 account.

In *personal deposits,* we have included deposits held by individuals and others in co-operative societies. Information in this respect is available in the annual reports of the Reserve Bank of India on the Cooperative Movement. Data on Company Finances published in the Reserve Bank of India Bulletins give information regarding the holdings of cash and bank balances of the companies. Using this as the basis, we have estimated the total deposit and cash holdings of the entire corporate sector. Similar adjustments for currency held with the public and unincorporated enterprises have been made.

Information in respect of *small savings* is available from the Central Government budget papers and the Annual Reports on Currency and Finance published by the Reserve Bank of India.

Data in respect of *life insurance funds* for earlier years is obtained from the Insurance Year Books published by the Controller of Insurance; for later years, the annual reports of the Life Insurance Corporation have been used. Our figures refer to the growth of the life insurance funds.

In item E dealing with *subscription to corporate sector's capital,* we have excluded subscription to debentures, as debentures would be largely subscribed to by financial institutions as well as units of the corporate sector. Data in this respect has been obtained from the reports of the Registrar of Joint-Stock Companies.

In item F dealing with *subscription to government loans,* we have excluded investment in government securities by (*a*) commercial banks, (*b*) life insurance organization, (*c*) provident fund authorities, (*d*) local authorities, and (*e*) estimated changes of ownership of marketable rupee loans by the

Reserve Bank as part of its policy of open market operations. Figures regarding (*f*) for all the years have not been made public, though figures regarding a number of years have been made available intermittently.

Figures regarding item G, dealing with *provident fund of the private sector,* are compiled from the report of the Employees' State Insurance Organization. We have taken into account only the net increment in resources. Adjustments have also been made for the increment in resources held in the Coal Mines Provident Fund. The custom of holding provident fund is common in the organised sector. The Provident Fund Act does not cover all concerns. Part of the resources might be re-invested in the concerns and part may be utilised for payment of insurance premia, investment in small savings, etc. The annual accruals through various provident funds in the private sector for the economy may be slightly more than double the amount indicated in our figures.

Item H, regarding *provident fund of the public sector,* gives figures of the growth of 'unfunded debt' in the accounts of the Central and the State Governments. Annual increments in the size of the debt are included in our figures.

Item I includes investment in the *non-corporate sector,* small enterprises, private transport, construction and in fixed assets in agriculture. We have given estimates also of changes in inventory holdings in agriculture.

Statement III

Data processed from Government budgets.

Table 2

Vide Notes on U.S. P.L. 480 Funds given in Statement II.

Table 4

Data for 1951 to 1956 obtained from 'Estimates of National Income in the Indian Union, 1948-49 to 1957-58' (CSO, Government of India).

Table 8

Data from Government budgets and the Annual Reports of the Reserve Bank of India; data regarding outlay on the Plans from 'Plan Resources and Appraisal' (Planning Commission, Government of India).

Table 10

Data processed from Annual Reports of the Reserve Bank of India.

Table 11

Data processed from the Reserve Bank of India Bulletin articles on 'Company Finances'.

Table 13

Data from the Annual Reports of the Reserve Bank of India.

Part IV

SOME ALLIED ASPECTS OF DEVELOPMENT

1. The Economic Basis of the Communal Tension in India

   Lecture delivered under the auspices of the Elphinstone College, Bombay with Mr. M. A. Jinnah in the Chair (December 1930).

2. The Unity of the Social Sciences

   Paper submitted to the Seminar on Social Sciences convened by UNESCO at Delhi in January 1955.

3. Business Leadership in Underdeveloped Countries

   Paper submitted to the Panel on Management convened by the United Nations at New York in September 1957; later published in revised form in "Industrialisation and Productivity", Bulletin 2, United Nations, March 1959.

4. Social Implications of Technological Change at the Level of the Community

   Paper submitted to the Round Table Conference on the subject held at Paris, 19-25 March 1959 under the sponsorship of the International Social Science Council with the support of UNESCO. Published by the Council in a Volume under the same title, Paris, 1962.

5. The Role of the Labour Economist

   Address as President of the Sixth Indian Labour Economics Conference, held at Ahmedabad, under the auspices of the University of Gujarat on 26 December 1962.

The Economic Basis of the Communal Tension in India*

Introduction

ONE of the most prominent, yet unfortunate questions which is before the public at present is the communal tension between the two great communities of this country. The tension is gradually assuming such proportions that the life of the country may be dominated by this issue to the sacrifice of more vital things.

This unfortunate problem has been given a religious aspect; each community is supposed to look at it from the point of view of the religion it professes. It is also given a political colour of great importance in view of the impending constitutional changes. The deeper causes of the trouble are however economic, which are forgotten due to religious fanaticism on the one hand and political excitement on the other.

The Problem

The outward form which the tension has taken is that of cow killing and music before mosques. If these questions were of a fundamental nature, why were they not raised all these years? I come from a village in which the population is almost equally divided half Hindus, half Mohammedans. But they have lived peacefully all these years and respected the feelings of one another. The Hindus invariably stop music if they are going in a procession accompanied by music as soon as they come near a mosque; the Mohommedans have not thought of killing a cow in a Hindu locality or of passing through a Hindu locality with a killed cow.

To a complete stranger not familiar with Indian conditions, it would be an inexplicable mystery if he were told that people fly at one another's throat on the questions of asserting their so called

*Lecture by the author, at Elphinstone College, Bombay, with Mr. M. A Jinnah in the Chair, December, 1930.

rights regarding cow killing or music before mosques. To me it appears that the real causes of the present tension are deeper and of a different nature; that these causes are responsible for a certain amount of heart burning among these two communities; cow killing or music before mosques have become the excuses for manifesting this heart-burning; and when once let loose, the excuse has become a dangerous weapon in the hands of fanatics.

If we think over the problem calmly and dispassionately the real reason is not far to seek; and if this reason is appreciated or is brought home to people, the remedy is also within our reach.

I submit that the real reason of this unrest is economic. It is due to the general poverty and the low standard of life not only of the masses, but also of the increasing number of the educated middle class, which must be the backbone of any society, and which find nothing but disappointment in its efforts to have a better standard of life and comfort.

The Indian Graduate

In every country some of the best youths look forward with ambition to a career of public service either as high administrative officers or as ministers of state. Such careers are sought not only because of the pecuniary value attached to them, but also because of the public esteem in which they are held, and above all because of the patronage which they bring to the successful few, patronage which they usually bestow upon their circle of friends and sympathisers or admirers. The tactful distribution of this patronage enables them in turn to continue or rise in power and position and therefore in public esteem.

In countries like England or America, the rising generation has splendid opportunities in trade and industry including agriculture. In spite of the great avenues open to the young men of such countries in such other walks of life, the attraction for public service of the kind mentioned above has not diminished.

Now let us consider the position of India in 1914, or during the period immediately preceding the War. The Indian Universities were fast turning out a large and increasing number of graduates every year. But the ambitious designs of most young graduates could not be realised; to their utter disappointment they found that their market value was very low after graduation. They considered themselves above, in fact, their education made them unfit for the greatest industry of the country, namely, agriculture. The trade and industry of the country could offer a few small openings to only some of them. There are several reasons for this. In the first place the trade and industry of the country have not yet developed to such an extent as to be able to absorb such large numbers of men, who could only do general work of a clerical nature, and were unfit for technical work, for which foreigners had to be imported. Besides, some of our biggest concerns are in the hands of non-Indians, who prefer men of their own nationality for important work. In the case of those concerns which are in the hands of Indians, the opportunities have also been curtailed because of two reasons. First, the Indian capitalist is expected to and usually does find employment for young relatives, who left on their own would fare much worse. Second, a good deal of our business is in the hands of uneducated people, who are not able to appreciate the value of educated men in their concerns, except in a very subordinate position. On account of the combination of these causes the Indian graduate found that he had very limited opportunities for a career in trade and industry.

In many cases he therefore turned to the only other career, namely, Government service. Here too the highest ranks were shut against him; he was expected to begin at the lowest stage, in many cases with a clerkship of Rs. 40/- per month, and his maximum rise was upto the position of a subordinate officer, of the rank of say a Mamlatdar. Only a fortunate few could penetrate the bureaucratic preserve by passing at great sacrifice the I.C.S. examination, then held in England.

In brief, we had a steady stream of educated young men coming out of the Universities, who learnt in their college days modern ways of life, and were taught among other things that the low standard of life in India was a curse, and felt in them the ambition and power to raise their own standard of life with the help of their education. Whether this utilitarian view of education is correct or not is another question; that it has been in existence is a fact that cannot be denied.

On the other hand as we have seen above, the openings for these young men were comparatively few, and therefore disappointment was naturally in store for most of them. A growing discontent with things around them was the inevitable consequence; and a conscious desire to get out of this predicament somehow was bound to be created. Unlike the masses of our people, who are not vocal, these increasing number of educated men could understand and voice their difficulties with growing intensity. But with the existing political and economic organisation of the country, they found that their aspirations were controlled and even chained on all hands.

Indianisation

There was however one ray of hope. It was this very state of affairs which had made the demand for Indianisation of the public services louder and louder, and the authorities were slowly preceiving the necessity of yielding to it, lest it may lead to undesirable consequences. And the same demand for Indianisation of private services in trade and industry was also being increasingly felt.

It was at such a time that the appointment of an eminent Indian like Lord Sinha (then Sir P. P. Sinha) to the high post of the Viceroy's Council was hailed with joy by educated India. For in such an appointment, irrespective of the man's community, both Hindus and Mohammedans, had a common feeling that here was a beginning of a process by which positions both high and small would be available to them in increasing numbers. And by this time the successful working of the highest industrial venture in the country, namely, the Tata Steel Works, also led to similar hopes of an early day when Indian industrial and commercial magnates would be able to provide increasing opportunities to the young educated men of the country.

War Period

Like many other things, the effective realisation of these hopes had to be postponed during the War period. But the War itself provided an opportunity hitherto not available to Indians. Both in private and public work of importance, which had grown on account of the War, large numbers of educated men were wanted to fill the places of Europeans who had been called away to serve in the War, or who could not be imported because of the same reason.

The Reforms

But what was an inevitable experiment during the War period had to be made a matter of policy in the immediate future, with the introduction of the Reforms in 1921. Indianisation in the various services to a certain extent was definitely laid down, and Indian ministers and elected legislatures came into existence to see that these pledges were carried out. The long delayed hopes of educated India were at last to be realised, if not wholly, at least partially. And the same effect is found in trade and industry. For, with the Reforms has come the policy of Discriminating Protection, by which an industry receiving protection is bound to carry out Indianisation of its services as far as possible. And the effect of this in unprotected industries or in business in general is bound to be felt.

But the prizes thus thrown open to Indians by a partial policy of Indianisation are yet comparatively speaking few. For to the already patiently waiting numbers of disappointed educated Indians the Universities were adding large number of graduates every year. Besides, the number of Universities was also increasing, and they, with some honourable exceptions, continued to commit the mistake of providing only general education to the neglect of scientific and technical or vocational education, which may enable young men to take to other fields of work.

This naturally resulted in a struggle among the educated classes to capture the few prizes thus available in Government or private service. But this struggle was now on a large scale than ever, because the prizes available were also larger in number and greater in value, though compared with the numbers of the educated they were still few.

Communal Preference

In the midst of this struggle, was introduced another element pregnant with dangerous issues. The only real test of the success of any piece of work, Government or private, is efficiency. On the grounds of efficiency only those who were by their education or experience qualified for these new careers were likely to obtain them. If this had taken place, the great majority of these careers would have gone to Hindus among whom were to be found men in large numbers with superior qualifications.

The Mohammedans had not taken sufficient advantage of the educational facilities available to all alike in the different Universities. And as a community they found themselves unprepared to capture with success that share of these new careers which they thought was due to them in proportion to their population. And this feeling was accentuated by the fact of communal representation in the Reformed Legislatures. It is not suggested that those eminent Mohammedans who now sit in the Indian Legislatures would not have been there in the absence of communal representation. They would indeed have been there in the same strength, but they would then have felt their responsibilities as Indians first, and Mohammedans next. But when once this communal feeling was developed in members belonging to one community, it was natural that the same should be the case with others. Instead of developing a truly national spirit, the fact of their being in the legislatures as representing their community makes the legislators think more in terms of the community than in terms of the nation as a whole.

This being the case, the Mohammedan legislators felt it their duty to find a way out of their difficulty mentioned above, namely, the possibilities or otherwise of obtaining a suitable number of the new careers for members of their own community. And in this effort they found useful allies in the so-called Depressed classes of the Hindus, in some provinces known as non-Brahmins. All this has led to the distinction between the so-called "advanced" and "backward" classes for the purposes of Government appointments —high or low. A certain number of such appointments came to be reserved for members of the "backward" classes, among whom were put Mohammedans and the "Depressed classes". The distinction was applied not in small appointments only; it was carried in the hitherto most highly prized service, namely, the I.C.S. A certain number of candidates who have not been successful at the competitive examination are nevertheless taken in the I.C.S. on the ground of making up for communal inequalities, as can be seen from the Government communiques issued every year in connection with the I.C.S. Examination.

The Efficiency Test

Lest we may be led away by personal bias, let us look at the question from a detached point of view. When we were asking for the Indianisation of the services, even as we do now, our demand amounted to and amounts to this: that so long as an Indian of the necessary qualification is available, an Englishman should not be appointed.

We do not say, we dare not say, that an unqualified Indian shall be appointed to a post simply because he is an Indian. We may say with justice that if qualified Indians are not available for particular kinds of work, steps should be taken by a system of foreign scholarships or practical apprenticeship to train Indians. We all know that though Indianisation has been accepted in principle, in certain cases Indians are not yet appointed on the ground that an Indian of the requisite qualification is not available. In short, the progress of Indianisation is limited by the qualifications of the Indian candidates available. In other words efficiency is the test in putting the principle in practice.

But within the limits of Indianised Services, the test of efficiency has been given up in preference to the pressure of communal claims. Within these limits an Indian of the backward classes may be appointed, and is certainly appointed even though he may be inferior in qualifications to other candidates who are brushed aside because they belong to the advanced classes, who find that out of the new careers created by the Reforms, a very great percentage is reserved for the backward classes.

Super Castes

The advanced classes or the more educated classes are doubly hit; they have equipped themselves at a great sacrifice with certain qualifications; their claims have been hitherto denied because Indianisation did not exist. When Indianisation does come their claims are restricted by being told that they are advanced. The fact of their being advanced is now put at a discount, and they are made to scratch their heads to find a solution out of the dilemma. "Down with the caste-system" is the slogan of our Social Reformers and of our English rulers. We are taught to do so many things in a broad catholic spirit "irrespective of caste, colour or creed". And here is a policy of the Government which leads to the creation of two hostile castes or super-castes of backward and advanced classes, based on the fact of their education, and sustained by the distribution of Government favours on grounds other than those of efficiency.

The Root Cause

I submit that this policy has created and is creating a deep seated feeling of discontent and resentment among the educated classes, and the smouldering smokes of this feeling are really responsible for the communal tension.

Let me put the matter in the form of an illustration. Suppose that the head of a family, has a son or brother, or another dependent for whom he wishes to get some suitable employment. The party has obtained certain qualifications, say a good University education. He applies for an appointment which is quite within his abilities. He is told that he belongs to the advanced class, and therefore has no chance; that a member of the backward class, even though of inferior qualifications has been appointed, and that this is done under the orders of the Government. As a human being, both the candidate, and the head of the family anxious for his welfare, are bound to have a burning feeling at this undeserved rebuff, a feeling of injustice and wrong done by the state as a matter of policy. In the circle of their friends and sympathisers this episode with all its communal significance will filter down, and a conviction will be created that the Government is unduly favouring the Mahammedans or the non-Brahmins as the case may be against the advanced classes or the educated Hindus.

Its Effects

A feeling of hatred between the communities is the inevitable consequence when such events take place in large numbers, in cases small or big. The "backward" community tries to be aggressive and therefore offensive at each step of its forward march; if there is any delay in its progress it kicks up a row and looks upon the other community with jealousy and anger; the "advanced" community feels the losing ground at each stage and finds itself in a terrible dilemma at an order of things which it explains by the belief that the Government has adopted the policy of Divide and Rule between the different communities of this country. We are sometimes told that behind the communal riots which occur now and then in the country, there is some intelligence; if there is any truth in this, the reason why intelligence should be so misused is obvious; it is the natural consequence of creating two opposite camps of educated classes, each of which looks on the other from the point of view of bread and butter.

While this is the obvious effect, there are others, which may lead to a continuation of the tension, and retard the national progress of the country. They may be briefly stated as (a) demoralisation of the public services, and (b) of political life in the country.

When the test of efficiency is suspended in appointments to public services, high and low, we are bound to have in them people who instead of proving the capacity of Indians for administration and organisation, may give illustrations of weakness and inefficiency to the enemies of Indian progress. At a time when we require the best available men to join the higher services and prove the administrative capacity of Indians in comparison with the most efficient European in any department, we have a situation by which quite the opposite results may ensue.

The political life of the country is demoralised because the minority and so called backward communities are thus taught to believe that the existing foreign Government is their real benefactor, and the advanced Hindu Community is their great enemy. Legislators and ministers who happen to be Mahommedans or members of the backward classes find that they can get Government appointments for members of their community, if they keep well with the Executive Government; and the Executive Government finds on the other hand that in exchange for the distribution of Government patronage in this way, they can rely on the votes of the legislators belonging to these communities; the result is that the officials in each legislature—provincial or central—who are in a minority, and who represent no section of the people, plus the members of the minority communities, form a majority as against the representatives of the majority community in the country. We have therefore a situation by which the English Government can pass an important piece of legislation or other measure, which is against the wishes of the majority of the elected members, because of this unholy alliance. The actions of the legislatures may not therefore be national in spirit and outlook; and the limited measure of self-government that we have got under the present system is nullified.

The same demoralisation of political life is likely to affect the future as is evident from the attitude of different political parties and groups towards the Simon Commission and its work.

I do not hold a brief for the advanced classes. I have every sympathy with the aspirations of the backward classes. I am trying to analyse and understand the effects of the situation created by this policy. I do not attribute motives in the adoption of it either. But granting that this has been done with the best of intentions, the consequences as briefly outlined above, cannot be denied. I would not have cared to pen this picture of the communal tension, unless I was convinced that this apparently religious and political struggle is really due to economic causes, briefly mentioned by me and therefore, the real solution is also of an economic nature. We have drifted along wrong lines; we must cry halt and put the progress of the country on sound lines, based on sound economic foundations. No amount of Unity Conferences and Unity resolutions or anti-Goonda legislation will be of any avail so long as these fundamental causes are in operation. The real unifying force among the communities must be economic—a consciousness that there is enough in this country to occupy the energies of the members of all communities, educated or not,—a consciousness followed by an early practical realisation that the work available to all is fruitful and is worthy of the ambition created by modern education.

Remedy

If this analysis of the situation is correct, the remedy is obvious. What we want is rapid economic development of an all round character which will provide wider and greater opportunities to all classes of people—advanced or backward; high or low; Hindus or Mahommedans. In other words it is a question of finding suitable employment for the unemployed, or the under-employed or the ill-employed of different classes.

Unemployment

We have heard of unemployment in England and other countries after the war and the steps taken in that connection. These countries have been wiser; their statesmen realised in time the evil effects on Society of large numbers of the unemployed. Unemployment in a general sense is much greater in our country than in Europe.

The difference is that European countries have statistics of the unemployed which speak; they take definite measures to remove the evil and these are reported. The unemployment in our country is so chronic, that it has become natural or normal, and is therefore not noticed; and it is so great and frightening in volume that our leaders, Government or national, even when they realise it are afraid of referring to it. But the unemployment of the agriculturists for several months in the year to which I refer, did not create that restlessness which has arisen by the unemployment of large numbers of educated young men in the country.

And let me here pay a tribute to that much misunderstood, but universally respected person, Mahatma Gandhi. He has above all others appreciated the fact of this chronic unemployment of the people of this country, and his economic weapon, the charkha, however feeble and insignificant against modern machinery, is a standing reminder of this great unemployment, and is under our present conditions, the only possible first step towards the removal of the great unemployment which we witness in this country.

But the Charkha does not appeal to the educated Indian in his disappointment. His dreams have gone much further. Just as an Englishman may legitimately aspire to be the Prime Minister or an American to be the President of the Republic, the educated Indian delights in the splendid dream of being a Minister under the Reformed Government. But when in his efforts to advance in life, he finds himself kicked off the ground on communal considerations, he wants something more powerful, something more active than the Charkha. Unless the restless energies of such disappointed people find congenial work, the danger of their being led to acts of violence or leading others to them must remain.

The Need for Prompt Action and Comprehensive Organisation

When I say that we want rapid economic development of an all round character what I mean is something like what Mussolini does at present for Italy. The difference between the work of Mussolini and that done in India is that whereas the former acts, we are still in the inquiry stage. We have had in recent years various committees and commissions of enquiry of an economic nature. They are all good in their own way. But it is indeed unfortunate that when other countries like Japan could seize the opportunities created by the War, we were still busy with such enquiries instead of prompt action. By now we have had plenty of such inquiries, and we may add to our information in a similar way in future, whenever necessary. But what we want more urgently is the will and the machinery to take consistent and systematic action to bring about the development of the country in all directions as rapidly as possible. What we lack is an efficient organisation which will take stock of the position from time to time and coordinate the activities of an economic nature, either Government or private, on the one hand, and initiate new activities under a comprehensive plan on the other. If England has a Minister of Unemployment to-day, we need ministers of unemployment in every province.

If by such comprehensive organisation we are able to create careers for our educated young men, and work for the masses, in which men of different capacities will find ample scope and opportunities of a varied character, the need for such dangerous palliatives like communal representation or communal preference in the struggle for jobs will no longer remain. If this is realised by the leaders of both the communities and by the Government, that the problem is essentially economic and that by an active and comprehensive organisation the restless energies now in existence and likely to be created in the near future, can be diverted to useful channels —then instead of finding excuses for communal riots, people will settle down to useful work. We have such an enormous amount of work at our very doors, that if we are all properly employed in carrying it out, we shall be doing good to ourselves individually and advancing the country as a whole—and incidentally there will neither be time nor leisure of that mischievous character which finds expression in communal riots.

If out of the present chaos, we are to take steps that will lead us on to this very desirable state of affairs, we should all be in earnest, and actively cooperate in devising and working out a comprehensive organisation, which alone can help us to realise the goal. And though private efforts must also be organised and brought in line with public efforts, the initiative must lie with the Government in view of the magnitude of the problem. It is comparatively more easy to work out such a scheme than to work out temporary pacts to patch up the communal tension. It would be a more fruitful, more effective and permanent remedy than the occasional compromises which are flung at us from different quarters. I am not attempting to give such a scheme here, because that would be beyond my scope; my purpose has been to establish the real causes of the communal tension and to indicate that the remedy must also be economic. The general nature of the remedy I have explained; details may be left to experts.

The European Community

But let me give one warning. In any systematic effort of a comprehensive character to remove unemployment in this country, and to provide adequate work for all classes of people, we shall be faced with a communal problem of another character. The vested interests of the European community in India, in trade and industry, as well as in Government service, will have to be overcome before we can hope to achieve the goal. That more than ourselves, the European community is alive to this possible conflict is seen in their demand before the Simon Commission that though a definite advance towards self-government in India be made, the future legislatures of India should not have the power to legislate in economic matters, which may endanger their position in any way.

The Unity of the Social Sciences*

The Scope

THE SCOPE of the paper may be described in brief. It starts with a reference to the common object of study of social sciences, namely, man. The differences in methodology in different social sciences and the tendency to specialisation in each are pointed out. The need for widening the frontiers of each social science is emphasised and in this connection the desirability of cooperation between different social sciences is brought out. For this purpose, the problem of inter-communication between different social sciences is raised and the need for broader training and outlook for each social science is discussed. The fact that the unity of social sciences is also of practical importance in view of their influence on policy in different countries is pointed out. For this purpose, the need for an even growth of all social sciences is emphasised. While doing so, the prevailing neglect of social sciences in underdeveloped countries generally is referred to with due reference to conditions in India. In this connection, the threats to social sciences from Mathematics or Statistics on the one hand and from Technology on the other, are mentioned. Finally, the hope is expressed that the prevailing confusion of ideas on the subject will be removed as a result of this Conference and that social scientists will have opportunities to demonstrate the unity of their diverse disciplines, as also their practical utility in the progress of nations, if viewed in the light of this unity in the formation of policy.

Common Object of Study

The different social sciences have a common object of study in a broad sense of the term. They deal with the different facets of the activities of man in relation to the diverse aspects of his environment. Though each of the social sciences has limited the scope and range of its study by concentrating upon some special aspect

*Paper Submitted to the Seminar on Social Sciences by the UNESCO at Delhi in January 1955.

of this relationship, it has not been possible, nor is it necessary to define rigidly the borders of each social science. Because of the underlying unity imposed by the common object of study, the conclusions arrived at in each science bear a close relationship with those arrived at in others. Each exists as a separate science only as a matter of convenience as this facilitates specialisation; it is seldom possible to classify problems arising out of man's relationship with other men and groups in society as being the exclusive preserve of any particular specialised field of study; often they concern two or more fields simultaneously. Different sets of motives and influences play upon human beings and determine the type, pattern and intensity of their reactions to the varied changes in their environment. We have to take into account at least to an approximate extent the relative degrees of influences exerted by the different sets of motives. It is in this connection that the underlying unity between the different social sciences becomes most clearly manifest. At the same time, the absence of proper understanding and of cooperation between them not merely leads to delay in the acquisition and extension of knowledge, but also contributes to inadequate and incorrect conclusions.

Methodology and Specialisation

Though there is unity in regard to the subject matter of study in the broad sense of the term, the methodology and the perspective adopted by each of the sciences differ from one another. This has resulted in a considerable diversity of techniques and of the analytical apparatus adopted by these sciences. The richness and the diversity of techniques are no doubt a strong asset of social sciences considered as a body. But the difficulty is that the different social sciences might be adopting techniques which are of different degrees of exactitude. How each science solves the problem of relative emphasis to be placed on empirical investigation and on deductive logic is a matter of concern not merely to that particular science but also to all the social sciences in general. This is so because no final statement about human behaviour and relationships can be made unless we draw upon the conclusions arrived at in different social sciences and integrate the results. In the early stage of development of these sciences, it was possible for the leading lights to be masters in several fields of knowledge. This cannot be attributed to sheer brilliance. We do not think there is any reason to believe that the number of experts in the different social sciences is less at present as compared to their number in the latter half of the 19th century. The amount of knowledge available in different social sciences has increased to a phenomenal extent. By pursuing the path of specialisation it has been possible to explore the intricate details of several aspects of social phenomena. Further, with the increasing popularity of the empirical method, a vast amount of information on the different problems has been collected. It becomes however more and more difficult to arrive at integrated conclusions, which tend to place on appropriate emphasis on the knowledge of human behaviour and relationships derived from each of the social sciences. The vision of several social scientists in the last century that it would be possible to evolve a common, integrated social science which embodied within itself the conclusions arrived at in different fields, has not been fulfilled. On the other hand, the trend has been in other directions. The problem is no longer merely one of deficiency of total knowledge. It is also one of co-ordination and integration of the given body of knowledge. This becomes more and more difficult because the trend towards further research has been in the direction of a more intensive cultivation of specialised fields, with the result that the problem of co-ordination is increasing in importance day by day. This is partly due to the desire of the scientists to carve out a special place for their subject-matter in the vast ocean of knowledge, and partly also due to the trend towards specialisation. What has happened is that each of the scientists finds that after a particular depth of study of any given problem, the frontiers of his science are reached. Any further extension of these frontiers would depend upon collaboration with experts in other social sciences.

Need for Widening the Frontiers of Each Social Science

Each of the social sciences might profit by extension of its frontiers with the aid of knowledge and the techniques of other social sciences. Though the need for such extension is felt in all quarters, it does not follow that corresponding efforts are being made to bring together the accumulated knowledge of different sciences. This depends as much upon the individual attitudes of the scientists themselves, as upon the opportunities available for those who undertake such co-operative efforts. Whatever may be the ideal to be pursued by each social scientist, there are several difficulties to be overcome before one can make a reasonable approximation towards its attainment. Firstly, there is the limitation of the human material. Art (or rather science) is long and time is fleeting; even *within* a given social science, it is difficult for individual scientists to keep abreast of the latest trends of thought in the several aspects of the same subject. Within each given science there is the problem of inter-communication. Much more is it so when we come across problems of inter-relation *between* different social sciences themselves. There may be a significant gain if the economist, for example, devotes adequate time for equipping himself with the trends of thought in Sociology or in Political Science. But with the persistent trend of specialisation in his own subject, the greater the time that he devotes for straying away from his special field, the greater will be the prospect of his falling behind in the race. Unfortunately nobody can deny that there is a considerable amount of competition —not necessarily of the healthy type even in regard to matters like pursuit of knowledge. This makes it clear that unless there is a strongly felt general desire among the different scientists within a given subject to make themselves acquainted with what is happening in a sister science, individual students might find it difficult to break away from the well established traditions. When any given scientist equips himself with the knowledge of the technique adopted and conclusions arrived at in related sciences, he may be in a position to view his own subject matter in a better light. For example, knowledge of sociology would certainly make economists good sociologists, but it might make them better economists as well. The same holds true in the case of workers in other social sciences. Apart from the light-giving aspect of such knowledge, there is a great possibility that such studies might lead to fruitful results. Part of the difficulty in achieving actual co-operation and collaboration arises therefore mainly from the fact that increasing importance is attached to specialisation. Specialisation in any given field, no doubt, leads to more productive results, but is there not some gain to be had if further efforts are made towards widening the areas of knowledge tackled by each science?

Co-operation between Different Social Sciences

Both when embarking on a detailed study of social phenomena and when making a final assessment of the exact nature of the inter-relationships it is appropriate that the social scientist should see that he has equipped himself with a larger set of tools and a greater stock of knowledge than what his specialised field alone can supply. The need for co-operation should not therefore be looked at from the point of view of the extension of a given stock of know-ledge available for any particular social science. In many cases, a greater intensive cultivation of those aspects of study, which are *exclusive* to any particular social science, itself depends upon a change in perspective or in methodology. It may be that there may be hidden areas of knowledge which are not accessible, if one pur-sues only one's own sphere of study. It may be that such knowledge can only be had on the basis of a study of what has been done in other sciences. Apart from filling up the deficiencies in the stock of knowledge necessary for the further advance in any given social science, it may be possible that the entire methodology of a given science may be revolutionised, if there is constant co-operation between different social sciences.[1] Such studies would tend to make individual research workers better scientists in their own field, let alone adding to their knowledge of related phenomena belonging to other social sciences.

Difficulties of Inter-Communication between Social Sciences

A common difficulty for those who want to undertake such work is that pertaining to difficulties of communication. There may be any number of books in Sociology or Economics, for example, deal-ing with the subject for the layman. But there may be hardly few

[1] What a large scope for cooperative and coordinated effort lies in fields like the analysis of effects of population growth and attitude of different types of people towards the problem of population restraint, the organisation of socio-economic enquiries in the various regions and areas which are at present subject to the high pressure policies or influences of industrialisation or community development schemes, the conducting of detailed enquiries regarding the relative impact exerted by different types of social, economic and political influences, the formulation of study pro-grammes which seek to unravel the complex reasons and conditions which enable some regions and groups to out-distance others in the race for pro-gress and so on?

dealing with sociology for economists and economics for sociologists. A keen student of a specialised branch of a social science might not find the necessary time and patience to go through books which are meant generally for the beginner; or if he can afford the time, he may not find such a course profitable. He would, for example, be anxious to know how best the techniques and conclusions of a sister social science can be utilised to solve some of *his* problems; for this he could not be expected to go through the entire literature in the related sciences in order to find it out. There is a tendency among social scientists to pursue a particular problem upto a particular length (or depth), and then to leave it at that by a statement to the effect that they have reached the border lands or frontier of that particular science or of the particular specialised branch of knowledge. It may be that economists, for example, study a given problem and point out that any further analysis or solution of the problem has to be studied by the sociologist or the political scientist. Very often, there may be none else to carry on the torch with the result that in several aspects connected with their subject matter, problems await further study or solution depending upon a chance possibility of the emergence of some worker who can carry on the study or the problem further. It is obvious that such a trend is not healthy from the point of view of rapid development of knowledge.

Need for Broader Training and Outlook

If the present trend which is biased too much in favour of specialisation has to be altered, then each research worker in any particular field of study has to reconcile himself to a period of broader training and outlook. He should no longer merely think in terms of concentrating his attention on exploring new phenomena or of delving deeper into hitherto slightly known fields of study. For a considerable period of time, he may have to become a student rather than an explorer. This naturally requires some sacrifice on the part of the social scientist. Is there not a need for each individual knowing more about what has already been known in related fields than that he should at a very early stage in his career, concentrate on the task of *adding* to the stock of knowledge in his special field? It is unfortunate that the craze for specialisation has gone so far that individual scientists have no time to pause and ponder over what has been already done in sister sciences. It is possible that learned works on related topics might be produced in which there is very little realisation of the relationship existing between different categories of phenomena studied independently by different social scientists. It is necessary, therefore, that the social scientist should devote some time and trouble for studying the extent of knowledge that is available in related sciences regarding the particular field in which he is interested. As pointed out earlier, the problem is not merely one of communication, but also that which vitally affects the *growth* of each of the social sciences. The evolution of appropriate methods of inter-communication between economics and sociology is a matter of as much concern for the economist as for the sociologist. Otherwise, the frontiers would continue to be frontiers; very often there emerge problems which partake of the character of no scientist's land. Unless the workers in each of the subjects pursue studies further, on the basis of the knowledge that is available in other sciences, the exploration of the frontiers and borderlands might be left to those who might work on amateurish hypothesis or premises. It may be that the economist, for example, may be perfectly certain that the particular hypothesis or fundamental or intermediate premise which he borrows from other sciences is the best suited for a particular occasion. It may be that on a further examination, the sociologist might disavow the responsibility for the sanctity of such a premise or assumption. Here is a field where it is quite possible that the economist who is working on the basis of his particular intuition might be having a better sociological insight than the sociologist himself. It may be that if he has the necessary time and resources, he may point out why the particular assumption was the best suited under the circumstances. On the other hand, it is quite possible that on the basis of further study, if the sociologist can devote time to testing the economist's premises, he may be in a better position to throw light about the economist's difficulties. In matters concerning the development of knowledge, it is difficult to be dogmatic. The importance of co-operation can hardly be over-emphasised in the case of a study of the so-called borderline problems. A preliminary difficulty is that *most* of the problems, after a particular range of study, tend to become borderline problems. Further work depends, as stated earlier, on the intensity of co-operation among the different social scientists and the co-ordination of the work done so far in such field. This is not merely a task for a *new* co-ordinator but is, to a considerable extent the work of individual social scientists pursuing specialised fields of study. It is not enough of an inducement for an economist to work in co-operation with a sociologist, if he feels that he has little to learn from others or that there is very little that he can contribute to a given problem which involves certain inter-relationships between different sciences. Both these attitudes are not conducive to greater co-operation. The social scientist in his own special field must be convinced that the time devoted to an acquisition of some knowledge of other social sciences is of great benefit to his own field of study.

Influence on Policy

The need for the acceptance of the underlying unity of different social sciences is not to be viewed mainly from its academic possibilities. It must be borne in mind that the views, findings and opinions of social scientists have a considerable influence on the way different policies are formulated in different countries. More often than not, these policies affect the lives and welfare of human beings in a vital manner. The problem that arises here is whether these policies have been formulated after a careful consideration of the importance to be attached to the different aspects of a given situation. No expert in any single science can present an all sided point of view. It is necessary to realise that unless policies are conceived of and planned in such manner that due emphasis on different aspects pointed out by different social sciences is accorded, they may lead to considerable frustration or even failure. Because of this the question of the need for an even rate of growth of different social sciences in each country becomes of considerable practical significance. It would be incorrect to assume that conditions are automatically created in every country, such that different social sciences grow up at an even pace in relation to each other and that the experts in each social science have the same extent of influence over the shaping of different policies. The problem is not merely one of collaboration between scientists belonging to different social sciences which tend to be ignored or neglected. It might happen that if any one of the sciences say for example, economics, is developed in a country at a greater pace to the neglect of other sciences, the policies might tend to have a greater economic bias which, after all, may not be warranted. Such a trend of development has a snow ball effect. It becomes more and more difficult for related sciences to develop rapidly in the face of the dominance of any single science.

Even Growth of All Social Sciences

The solution is not to put down the rate of development of the former, but to encourage a quick development of the latter. Such a course would gradually tend to bring about a greater sense of mutual respect among the different workers in different social sciences. Very often Government, as policy framers, have to go by whatever stock of knowledge that is or can be made available. Any deficiency in any field which may be vital for the success of the policy may be just ignored or not even noted. This is more so in the case of a country like India where we are witnessing a large-scale effort at diverse reforms being imposed through state legislation on a community, which has several sections and groups each having its own socio-economic growth. The heterogeneity of the different sections of the community in certain essential fields imposes the need for a careful and perhaps a particularistic approach in matters of policy. The policy framers, on the other hand, may not have the patience nor the knowledge necessary to formulate the optimum approach in matters of legislation. What might happen is that a community with a variegated cultural pattern may be either reduced to a dull uniformity or that the policy may manifest a lesser extent of success or a greater extent of failure, which sometimes may lead to significant frustration. Different men react to the same incentives sometimes in a radically different manner. In order to get the maximum extent of response towards several social needs, it may be necessary to evolve different types or patterns of incentives. Sometimes some sections want to go fast, while some others want to go slow. Not always can all these impulses be described as manifestations of radicalism or conservatism. Often these desires and impluses are the result of the accumulated social, cultural and economic influences of the past. To ride rough shod over the variegated structure of human impulses might lead to all types of reactions. It may be that there may be considerable hidden sources of strength in several of the influences shaping the activities of human beings in different parts of the country. It may be that the policy formulators themselves might plead for the strengthening of such influences, but in actual practice they may not be in a position to accord the required emphasis in legislation on these aspects. This as pointed out earlier, may often be due to deficiency of knowledge or deficiency of appropriate attention by different social sciences to the required extent. This is a problem of great urgency not merely in the case of India, but also affects vitally all the so-called underdeveloped countries. That is why the recognition of the unity of different social sciences is not merely an academic problem, but also one which is of immediate concern in regard to the welfare of the millions in these countries.

In the case of several underdeveloped countries, the need for mutual cooperation and coordination is obvious because of the above noted dominance of the accent on policy. As pointed out above, these countries contain groups of people or regions which are heterogenous in character. We cannot solely depend upon any one particular social science to give us precise and acceptable conclusions. What we know about the laws of growth even in the developed countries, which have a creditable history of scientific study behind them, is itself considered to be inadequate compared to the requirements. How much more difficult is the problem facing social scientists in countries like ours? We have little to go by; yet we have to go very far. The difficulty is all the greater because it is so easy to arrive at hasty conclusions and generalisations, which may be based upon superficial or one-sided observations. The uneven rate at which different social sciences have grown in these countries makes it exceedingly difficult to organise cooperative research. In some of these countries, there may be hardly anyone who has pursued an intensive study of some of the branches of social sciences which have been recently developed in western countries. The opportunities available to specialists are not the same as in developed countries. Before individual scientists can be induced to put themselves on a level with those in other countries, appropriate employment and research opportunities should be first created. Even that extent of specialisation that has been attained in some of the 'older' social sciences in the advanced countries has not been approached in these underdeveloped areas. There is no doubt a great need for coordination and integration; but before the latter objective can be attained, we must first have in existence the needed stock of knowledge. There is, however, one incidental advantage for these countries. They can emphasise at an early stage upon the research workers the unity of social sciences and it is possible that further research would be on a broader basis than was the case in other countries. Hence, the problem of coordination in these countries may tend to be less difficult than it has been elsewhere.

Neglect of Social Sciences

All this, of course, assumes, that the State and other interested parties would pay adequate importance to the development of social sciences. Considering the experience of a country like India, this may be too optimistic an assumption. Whatever development has taken place in any of the social sciences in India is mostly due to the limited efforts of Universities with meagre resources. The State has been only too eager to assist in the development of the physical and natural sciences, in which the results are perhaps more spectacular. Private donors have also shown willingness to help in the advancement of technological knowledge. Social sciences continue to be neglected by the State. Industrialists are also not willing to help in the development of humanities. In consequence, the overall development of social sciences has been limited as compared to the growing need for more adequate knowledge on different aspects of social phenomena. In view of the continued neglect which the social sciences have suffered at the hands of the State and other parties, one might justifiably be pessimistic regarding their future. There is however a ray of hope. The efforts at planned economic development have slowly brought awareness in the minds of those in power that social sciences have their place in the ordered development of the country. There is a half-hearted acknowledgement of this consciousness in the Report of the Planning Commission, and some partial efforts of a limited character are being made to develop research in economic and social sciences. It is however not realised that successful research cannot be done unless the staffs of the Universities are considerably strengthened and adequate facilities given to them.

Besides, there are two threats to the healthy development of the social sciences in countries like India. On the one hand, there is the ever increasing dominance of mathematics and statistics in the methodology and technical apparatus of the social sciences. On the other, there is the expanding power and influence exerted by technologists in the determination of State policy regarding subsidisation of research and knowledge-increasing agencies. We need only draw attention here to the simple but not always well understood fact that there are limits to which the quantitative method can be made applicable in the analysis of diverse types of social phenomena. In the immediate stages of its application the results are bound to be somewhat significant and may even be spectacular. But as human behaviour itself is subject to considerable uncertainty and as the amount of qualitative knowledge we have about the nature of the inter-relationships between different aspects of man's social activities is itself limited and to a great extent uncoordinated, there may be a serious danger that such applications may involve a value judgment in favour of the easily measurable phenomena. We might have precision and exactitude in the form of the results; though the researches might be deficient in breadth and depth. Moreover, there may be none to countercheck the premises or hypothesis underlying the quantitative results which have a fascinating appeal to the lay politicians in power. The danger is all the greater in underdeveloped countries because the amount of available qualitative knowledge in the various social sciences is itself negligible. The inter-relationships involved are too many and we cannot be certain that any one motive dominates given activities. Generalisation is therefore more difficult. We also witness some anomalies, such as the tendency to treat statistics as something bigger than or equal to a social science, ignoring the fact that it is a mere tool of social as well as other sciences. The threat from technology is however of greater potency. As stated earlier there is already a strong bias for diversion of resources to it to the neglect of social sciences. Just as there is a great danger in the uneven development of different social sciences in relation to one another, the danger from an unbalanced rate of growth between physical and natural sciences and technology on the one hand, and social sciences on the other is still greater. An example may be cited. The teaching of Industrial Administration, which may involve several social and economic problems, is being entrusted to technologists as if it is a branch of technology. These illustrations are given to show the narrow role that social sciences are assigned in the minds of those who decide policy. It is to be hoped that this confusion of ideas will disappear soon and that the work of this Conference will help in removing it; it is also to be hoped that in the meanwhile this confusion will not lead to any serious disaster; and that social scientists will have opportunities to demonstrate the unity of their diverse disciplines, as also their practical utility in the progress of nations, if viewed in the light of this unity in the formation of policy.

Business Leadership in Under-Developed Countries*

Sociological and Institutional Aspects

THE OBJECT of this paper is to draw attention to certain sociological and institutional factors which tend to affect the supply and composition of entrepreneurial and managerial personnel in under-developed countries. This is a broad field of inquiry and many questions arise within its context: Is the prevailing social and institutional atmosphere conducive to providing the economy with the required quantity and quality of business leadership? Does business leadership in under-developed countries differ substantially from that in the developed countries, as regards structure and performance? To what extent is performance—both individual and group—dependent on factors beyond the control of management? In other words, to what extent is it constrained by pressures, frictions and rigidities arising on account of institutional and social factors? Is poor performance a reflection or a cause of backwardness? To what extent can the situation be remedied through action by business leaders, the State or public or private agencies? To provide an answer to these questions, much research in hitherto little-explored fields is necessary. This article is confined to a preliminary investigation of some of the factors having an inhibiting effect on business leadership, with special reference to conditions in India.

Business Leadership

In discussions concerned business leadership, the three terms—manager, entrepreneur and innovator—are sometimes used synonymously. By and large, the same conditions influence the supply of entrepreneurial and managerial personnel and therefore that

* Paper submitted to the Panel on Management convened by the United Nations at New York in September 1957; later published in a revised form in *Industrialisation and Productivity,* Bulletin 2, United Nations, March 1959.

of innovational talent. However, innovation as such should be clearly distinguished from the performance of managerial and of entrepreneurial functions. Professor Schumpeter conceived of innovations as including the introduction in the economy of new factors, new products, new methods of production, new sources of supply, and the creation of new sources of demand. Essentially, innovations represent the introduction of new production functions by new business leaders or entrepreneurs. Older established firms are as a rule less inclined to innovate; they are accustomed to routine and are reluctant to take the risks involved in large changes. In the Schumpeter system, the process of economic development is characterised by the rise and fall of firms and of business leaders; the entire complex of the phenomena of development and business cycles is linked with innovation, and the innovator is the hero—albeit a tragic one—of the drama of economic dynamics.

Many economists recognize that Schumpeter's picture of development contains certain essential and relevant factors but consider that less emphasis should be given to the role of the innovator. They point out that various types of business leaders and firms participate in the process of development; that established as well as new firms play a role therein; that all developmental changes need not be big and spectacular, nor far-reaching in character and impact. In this different light, the distinction between a successful manager or entrepreneur and an innovator becomes one of degree rather than of kind.

Requisites of Efficient Management

It is not easy to define efficient business leadership.[1] Some qualities associated with it lend themselves better to empirical than to analytical definition. Among them is the maintenance of a high level of performance. A business leader having this quality—which can be appreciated only by comparison with prevailing standards of performance—is able to keep a footing of equality with competing firms. Another quality is the capacity to adapt the firm's operations continuously and successfully in the face of changing

[1] See C. N. Vakil and P. R. Brahmananda, "Technical Knowledge and Managerial Capacity as Limiting Factors on Industrial Expansion in Underdeveloped Countries", in *Economic Progress*, edited by Leon H. Dupriez, Institute de Recherches economiques et sociales (Louvain, 1955).

internal and external conditions. This requires a sense of perception and a strong degree of resilience and points to the dynamic character of business leadership requirements. Then there is a capacity to take what might be termed "calculated risks", a quality of pioneering and innovation, involving a willingness and a capability tempered by caution to venture along unfamiliar paths. A firm may have to contend with opposition from other firms, with obstacles raised by social interferences of various sorts—in particular, prejudices and biases which might hinder its expansion and block its markets—and sometimes with hostile attitudes from the government itself. The behaviour and mode of action of a pioneer are frequently such that they tend to upset the atmosphere of complacency and stagnation, not merely within his own firm but also with the wider economic environment with which he comes in contact. Not only does he meet obstacles when attempting to translate his ideas into action, but he may expose himself to latent and even open hostile reactions. It is perhaps this quality of pioneering which is particularly scarce among business leaders in under-developed countries.

Effective leadership is not merely a matter of contributing to the economic and financial fortunes of the leader's own firm. The task of business leadership has increasingly to be performed in the context of a socio-political atmosphere permeated with a high degree of social consciousness. Business practices and methods are increasingly subject to scrutiny by the government and the public, not only from a strictly legalistic standpoint but also from the point of view of ethics and social values. The standards of evaluation of business leadership largely rest on the contribution which it makes to the social needs of the community.

It is a gross over simplification and a hardly acceptable general proposition to say that under-development is caused by lack of business leadership of an appropriate type, although, within limits, effective business leadership might raise the rate of economic growth and might help overcome certain obstacles to economic development; it is far, however, from being a panacea. Nor is it correct to contend that business leadership in under-developed countries is intrinsically of "inferior" quality: it has taken the developed countries a long time to evolve suitable business standards and related social viewpoints. Also, it is hardly proper to assert that a low level of business performance is due to some deficiencies in the personalities of the business leaders: such a view tends to confuse symptoms with causes and surface phenomena with deep-rooted motivating factors. While it is not proper to consider deficiency in business leadership as a central limiting factor, neither is it appropriate to ignore or minimize a certain number of institutional and sociological deficiencies inherent in the structure of the under-developed countries. In a concerted programme of economic development designed for a simultaneous attack on various inhibiting factors, a specific remedy must be found for each major deficiency. These ideas must be kept in mind if an answer is to be given to such questions as: What forms of business leadership would be the most appropriate for a given country? What measures might be adopted for improving business leadership? How could knowledge of these techniques be disseminated? What social values should be kept in mind in attempting to improve business leadership?

Structure and Composition of Managerial Personnel in India

To generalize about the problem of business leadership is hazardous under any circumstances, all the more so in the case of management in under-developed countries. More may be gained by discussing business leadership in a narrower context; in what follows, a few indications will be given concerning the structure and composition of entrepreneurial and managerial personnel in India.

In India, entrepreneurial as well as managerial personnel are drawn mostly from certain castes. Thus, the dominant groups in Indian industry and business are the Marwaris of Rajasthan, the Gujaratis of Gujarat, the Chettiars of Madras, the Sindhis of the former Hindu community of Sind, which is now part of Pakistan, and the Parsis.

The key positions in business and industry are generally obtained on the basis of family status rather than by recruitment from outside sources or by promotion of personnel who are not members of the families in control. These leading families have wide interlocking interest. Besides caste and family connections, marriage is a means of entry into leadership groups, but it is restricted by widely prevalent traditions and customs which rule out infusion of fresh blood. Leading business and industrial firms in different regions are linked by family relationships, and competition between enterprises is frequently based on rivalry between different families owning or controlling firms or groups of firms.

The most important source of finance for the growth of business is internal accumulation. Not only are credit institutions still few and little-developed, but it is next to impossible for outsiders, whether individuals or firms, however enterprising they may be, to obtain from these institutions large credits for long periods. The concentration of financial resources within particular closed groups thus creates additional obstacles to the inflow of newcomers into industry and trade.

In spite of these obstacles, breaches have been made in recent years in the entrenched position of family concerns and their tightly knit management structure. This change is mainly due to the accelerated rate of industrialization which calls for diversified abilities and, above all, for trained talent. Population growth is another factor, inasmuch as it exerts a pressure for greater inter-occupational and inter-regional mobility. Fewer employment opportunities and lower earnings in traditionally "superior" caste occupations cause the more ambitious members of these castes to shift to new occupations. Limited as they may be, the facilities for credit provided by newly established credit institutions also make possible the establishment of some new ventures by "outsiders".

The characteristic form of organization of the entrepreneurial personnel in India is the joint family management. In large firms, it takes the form of the managing agency system. A managing agency firm consists as a rule of a group of relatives. Its continuity is ensured by succession to partnership of sons or sons-in-law of the original members, who often become partners during the lifetime of the latter. The managing agent combines the functions of promotor, financier, and controller of the joint stock company of which he is in charge. He controls the policy of the company, as he nominates the board of directors—formally elected by the shareholders—and he also conducts the company's day-to-day administration. He controls the shareholders' meetings, where he and his associates hold the voting power. He usually provides the necessary capital investment and working capital. His dominant position is secure.

The following two examples illustrate the types of organization prevailing in Indian managing agency firms. In one leading firm, a parent company controls another large concern and a holding company. The former is itself managing agent of a number of other companies. Each of the directors of the concern is in charge of one or several of the controlled companies and is expected to act as an adviser in his special field for other companies as well. Among the companies controlled are iron and steel works, mechanical industries, cotton mills, oil mills and chemical plants. Directors are paid on a salary basis, but some of them are given a fractional share of the commission accruing to the managing agency firm; the managed companies themselves do not bear the cost of this top managerial staff. Each top director is assisted by executives employed by the managing agency, as well as by the managerial personnel who are on the payroll of the controlled company. There is a second-line management structure consisting of executives with well-defined functional restructure consisting of executives with well-defined functional responsibilities.

Production is taken care of by a manager, office administration by a secretary and accountant, marketing usually by a superintendent of marketing, and purchasing by another officer; all are directly responsible to the director-in-charge. In the case of big companies controlled by the firm, there is usually also a technical adviser. On the whole, there is considerable delegation of responsibility in this firm, and the day-to-day administration and decision-making is carried out at the second executive level without interference from the top. Appointment to all posts is made by special committees with the assistance of executives representing the companies concerned; directors do not sit on such committees. Higher executives are appointed by directors, preference being generally given to promotion of persons from lower categories. The organization of personnel and the management structure are in this case rigidly defined and there is little room for personal interference.

In another leading industrial group, a private company controls a managing agency firm; these exercise jointly the financial control of a great number of other industrial concerns. There is considerably diversification of investment in this group, which controls such industries as jute, rayon, paper, soda ash, calcium carbide, and air-conditioning equipment. The group is family controlled, and the directorate includes hardly any outsiders. The over-all control of each managed firm is entrusted to one or more members of the large family—several brothers, and sons and sons-in-law of each. The top executives of each firm or group of firms managed by them are appointed by the directors. While operational duties are in the hands of managers, secretaries and similar officials, responsibility in this group is largely concentrated in the hands of the directors and top executives. The personnel organization is fluid and the personal element is present to a high degree in staff management.

Most large Indian firms under the managing agency system present features similar to those described above. A few local groups, however have somewhat different set-ups. For instance, one family-controlled managing agency, which today has a large stake in Indian cotton mills as well as in the manufacturing of starch, dye-stuffs and pharmaceuticals, started out by obtaining a substantial proportion of its capital in the form of "deposits" from shroffs (indigenous bankers). The cotton mills were primarily financed with these resources and their paid-up share capital remained very small. Some of the depositors eventually received shares in the managing agency concern, which thus includes a number of sleeping partners not belonging to the family.

With a few exceptions, one of which was described above, decision-making is highly centralized in managing agency firms, and the senior partners usually maintain a close watch over day-to-day affairs. This method, which is sometimes called the *pedhi* (small firm) way of controlling business, is generally possible only when the agents restrict the scope of their business to a few lines. Delegation of responsibility is usually associated with higher diversification.

A different managerial set-up exists also in certain industries subject to government controls, for instance, in the cement industry, where prices are government-controlled and trading is a State monopoly, or in steamship companies, which have to depend to a large extent on government loans and subsidies. A recent trend in these industries has been to employ former Indian Civil Service officers as top executives, in order to take advantage of their experience in government administration.

The system of family management, though not unique to underdeveloped countries, has a special significance when it is a dominant feature of a stagnant or slowly growing economic system which allows little scope to enterprises of a corporate type. As a rule, the family management system does not provide a sufficient number of suitable positions for all members of the family; on the other hand, the remaining members are discouraged from seeking employment outside the family firms. This tends to increase the ratio of dependents to earners in the family. Even where employment is given to members of the family, often it is either unproductive, or could be filled by better outside candidates. Excessive dependency reduces the saving capacity of the family as a group, while overstaffing and incompetence lead to inefficiency. The parental authority basis of the system makes it difficult for the younger men to develop qualities of leadership; the atmosphere of security breeds complacency and unwillingness to exercise initiative. A feeling tends to develop that any problem can be solved through assistance provided by the family.

While the managing agency system has done its part in establishing modern industry in India under British rule, its weaknesses have long been apparent. In recent years, some steps—for instance, the Company Law Amendment Act and the Company Administration Law—were taken by the Government to regulate and curb the activities of the managing agent. Many of the managers concerned fear that the future will bring further and greater restrictions on their freedom of action to the point where the system is bound to disappear.

In the early days, when firms were relatively small and the relationships between them were few and simple, the system could perpetuate itself without exerting a too debilitating effect on management efficiency. This is, to some extent, still true today for many small-scale enterprises. However, for large-scale firms which have to steer their way through the increasingly complex net-work of industrial relationships involving their sources of supply of raw materials, factors of production, credit, and outlets for their products, and have to maintain their position in wider and increasingly competitive markets, the situation is quite different. It is the increasing complexity of the managerial functions required today, and the spur of competition, perhaps more than the measures of restriction taken by the Government, that doom the system of joint family management, at least as regards large establishments.

As a result, aside from government action, some correctives have been taken by the firms themselves. Several business families are discouraging the dependence upon family for recruitment of the management staff. Various types of training on the basis of caste or even sub-caste have been devised, and business leaders are gradually realizing the importance of education as well as of intensified training within the firm. But, by and large, there is still room for adequately recognizing the need to infuse fresh blood and talent into business. One difficulty is that, as mentioned earlier, in India, even today, the methods of granting credit as well as the terms under which it is offered are not conducive to the development of an enterpreneurial class which would be independent of family or caste. The main obstacle, however, arises from the fact that caste and religion are still major factors which make for strong cohesive forces within the family and prevent entry of "outsiders".

The Hold of Caste, Religion and Custom

There is no doubt that caste and religion still play a major role in shaping the occupational structure in India. Although urbanization, spread of education, growing contact with the institutions and ideas of the West, and new developments in the legal, political, and constitutional fields are slowly undermining these barriers, considerable time will pass before the influence of the caste and religious system is reduced.

It is well known that the caste system creates a powerful obstacle to moving from one occupation to another and, to some extent, from one region to another. Under this system, birth rather than education or talent determines eligibility for particular occupations. This results in large and lasting inequalities of income, which tend to grow in the course of time. Along with the caste system there developed certain social attitudes influenced by religious beliefs which gave rise to occupational taboos. Some professions came to be thought of as "superior", some less "high", and some "inferior". Business occupations were not considered to belong to the "superior" category. It was adjudged below the dignity of the highest castes—whose role was essentially to spread knowledge—

to enter industry or trade. Thus, a chasm developed between educational competence and occupational skill. This was not a serious drawback as long as effective performance in trade and industry did not demand an extensive background of general and technical knowledge; with the more complex requirements of the industry of today, the acute shortage of trained talent has become a problem of national importance.

Another obstacle of a social nature is raised by the inheritance system, the most prevalent form of which, in India, leads to fragmentation of ancestral property. This dampens the initiative and enterprise of members of the family and is unfavourable to their financial capacity. In the case of agriculture, the economic effects of the inheritance system are nearly catastrophic.

Among other inhibiting factors might be mentioned the social and religious prejudices against interest, which retard the growth of capital accumulation. Religious restrictions on sea travel, or attachment to particular locations or areas, tend to impede mobility and reduce the opportunity for enterprise. Finally, the subordinate social status assigned to women is a serious limiting factor upon the supply of latent talent.

* * *

To summarize the foregoing, while there is need in India, as in other countries, for making available the best talent to carry out entrepreneurial and managerial functions in a way conducive to economic growth, there are considerable difficulties in achieving this because of certain structural characteristics of the society. Prior to India's independence, these difficulties were compounded by an institutional set-up imposed by the ruling country, which concentrated the major economic functions in the hands of its own nationals; at that time, the best talent available in India devoted itself largely to the struggle for independence rather than to economic endeavours. Despite considerable handicaps, indigenous enterprise still succeeded in developing various industries even in that period. In the decade which has elapsed since India became an independent country, great strides towards expanding and diversifying industry have taken place; these point to the changes to be achieved in the future.

It will take a long time to break up basic attitudes, traditions and conventions. In the short run, the problem is one of providing those in family enterprises who possess the financial means with the other resources which they usually lack, namely, education, training and experience. The younger men in industry—and also in banking and finance—should get sufficient general education and some specialized technical knowledge in their fields of activity. Education should be supplemented with experience gained by training periods in various occupations within the firm. This should be carried out in such a way that no preferential treatment is given to trainees with family connections; any such practice would vitiate the object of the training. On the other hand, taking young men away from the sheltered atmosphere of the family firm and training them outside the narrow managerial circle would ease the break with traditional practices. These preliminary steps will facilitate the next task of recruiting managerial talent from outside the family.

In the long run, action should be directed at removing the rigidities which contribute to maintain managerial and entrepreneurial performance at a low level. It is not enough, in order to improve performance to the degree and on the scale required, that educational and training facilities be increased and that a few large enterprises provide executive employment to competent "outsiders". Adjustments are called for on the part of the various caste groups participating, in managerial, technical or financial functions, in the productive process. Such adjustments as allowing intermarriage between members of different castes and providing employment opportunities in executive positions regardless of caste would constitute a major breach in the caste system. Above all, these adjustments call for profound changes in attitudes. While economic progress will in due course build up pressure for such changes, further legislative measures of the type already introduced by the Government would accelerate the transition.

Social Implications of Technological Change at the Level of the Community*

With Special Reference To India

Historical Background

BEFORE the Industrial Revolution (towards the end of the 18th century), the level of economic development in India, from what evidence is available about modes of production, systems of economic organization, and nature and volume of foreign trade, was not likely to have been very different from that prevailing in other countries. The population had not out-run the land-resources, and though industrial production was essentially for internal consumption, and occasionally even for self-consumption, simple hand-technology was sufficiently well-developed in quality and size to enable exports of manufactured articles, like cotton textiles, to be made.

Urban centres existed around princely courts, or arose in places of pilgrimage, or were based on commerce; cities formed around princely courts had industries satisfying a luxury demand; in places of pilgrimage, brassware and other metalware industries, catering to the special demands of pilgrims, grew up; commercial towns lay

* Paper submitted to the Round Table Conference on the subject held at Paris, 19-25 March 1959, under the auspices of the International Social Science Council with the support of UNESCO. Published by the Council in a Volume entitled "Social Implications of Technological Change" in 1962. The word *community* in India refers to the religious differentiation among its peoples, for example, Hindus, Muslims, Sikhs Parsis and so on. This meaning of community is not relevant to the subject of this paper. Consequently, throughout this paper, generally, the word "community" is to be interpreted as referring to the Indian society which comprises the religious groupings; in certain cases, where distinctions are introduced according to State, religion, caste or other groupings, these are specifically made clear.

on major trade routes and helped in the carrying on of internal and external trade. Many trades and crafts were organized on guild lines, and a system of journeyman was not unknown. The village satisfied its own needs, sending out or bringing in few goods; the poor state of communications was both a cause and a result of village insolation.

Family loyalties were governed by tradition and religion, and the village society, with occupations and mutual relations based on tradition and cast considerations, had managed to immunise itself from political changes going on around it. Central political control varied inversely with its distance from the village and political changes hardly affected the even tenor of life in the village. The Indian society was essentially non-competitive in organization, status and occupations being hereditary. The custom was assured, the market was personal, and the incentive to innovate little. There were no internal forces existing in the society, which could bring about changes in it from within.

The advent of British rule increased political stability in the country and simultaneously central political control over villages. At the same time, imports of factory-produced cotton textiles tended to disintegrate the economic organization of the villages.

Introduction of Modern Technology

The decade 1850-60 marked an important turning point in India's history: firstly, it saw the formal transfer of power from the East Indian Company's hands to the British crown; the fact of foreign political domination was established both *de facto* and *de jure*; secondly, it saw the construction of the first railway; village isolation making for village autonomy could no longer hope to continue for long; and thirdly, it saw the first beginnings of industrialization; imports of cotton textiles were sufficiently large then to induce some local magnates to start cotton textile mills in Bombay on factory lines; the success of the jute textile industry in Dundee led to its imitation in Calcutta on factory lines about the same time; and plantations, started in Assam, introduced the principle of large-scale organization in agriculture; except for the cotton textile industry, the other industries were started by foreigners, mostly, the

British (the Scotch pioneered the jute textiles, entrepreneurs from Lancashire and Manchester took to the cotton textile industry).

The Broad Consequences of Changing Technology

The impact of technological change on different societies varies, according to the extent of the change involved and the ability of the societies to assimilate it in their social structure. In the case of a static society, the impact of technological change may be large, and its capacity to assimilate limited. This last was the case in India.

Essentially, the impact of changing technology on Indian society was negative. It broke up a well-ordered society without replacing it by a new social order. The Industrial Revolution broke up the village economy of contentment; it disorganized the balance between agriculture and manufacture existing in the village. The self-sufficient village society disintegrated, and became dependent upon outside impersonal sources for supplies and markets.

Economic Consequences

The essential impact of technological change consisted in introducing an impersonal element in economic relations. Where commodities were exchanged between persons on the basis of traditional and hereditary relations, cheap factory-produced goods introduced an element of competition and of impersonal relationship in exchange of goods. Traditional manufacture had not the ability to adapt itself to the changing trends in economic relations. Moreover, the nature of demand changed from that of luxury goods required by princely courts to cheap goods required by the new intelligentsia. Against the changing requirements of the new society, traditional industry was unable to carry out the necessary adaptation, with the result that it decayed.

Social Consequences

Family relations, caste hierarchy and mode of livelihood were interrelated in Indian society; any disturbance in any one of these would have repercussions on the other relations also. With the loss of balance in the village economy also came social disintegration. The handicraftsmen who were displaced from their jobs went first to the untilled land, then to fill the ranks of the disguised unemployed to which agriculture lends itself so easily, and ultimately to man the factories whose victims they had been.

The pace of technological progress was uneven in different branches; there was greater growth in sanitation and medicine which increased population-growth potentiality than in industry to absorb the displaced, and even the increasing, labour force. The village began to come across the limit to livelihood inherent in the village economy, and it often became necessary for a male member or two to seek livelihood outside the village, often in cities and their factories. Against the impact of economic forces, family adhesion gave way, and separation, relieved only by occasional visits, began to be accepted as an economic necessity.

The greatest impact of the change in livelihood patterns due to change in technology was on caste relations which were finely related to the original livelihood patterns. The caste system laid down the various functions of persons belonging to different castes; the social organization of the village made for payment for these functions according to fixed rules. The economic and social interrelations built up in a village helped to maintain the caste system. When these were broken up by the introduction of factory-produced goods, the caste system itself bcame subject to economic pressure. It was no longer possible to follow the caste profession or be paid for the services rendered in the traditional way. Every census operation reveals a decrease in the number of persons following their caste-occupation.

The cities were the melting-pot of castes and cultures. Very often, caste-occupations had no counterparts in city factory life: even where such counterparts existed, it was not possible to maintain many caste restrictions (social contact with other castes) in a city-factory atmosphere. Changes in economic opportunities afforded by city-factory life also tended to break down caste barriers; the lower castes had, for the first time, the opportunity offered by the city-factory life to take up higher occupations and to raise their social status. Caste disintegration necessarily took place more in the cities than in the villages.

Influence of New Technology

The level of social advancement, for example, literacy, reached in villages was not high. The only outside influences acting on the villages were those brought by the migrants (who had gone to the factory) who came back to villages with new experiences and by the transport system which made possible contacts between cities and villages.

Industrialization was confined to city-centres and its influence outside the city-limits was limited. This influence was indirect, felt mainly through the labour and commodity transactions—absorption of raw materials and labour from villages and supply to them of finished goods—between cities and villages.

The extent of urbanization was limited and the link provided by railways small. Apart from metropolitan cities, the other urban centres were overgrown towns with some factories. Urban influences were felt most fully in the vicinity of cities and of railway stations. Away from these centres, the urban influence declined, and traditional villages untouched by urban influences, except some trade, continued to live on. Still more distant, there were tribal areas which reflected more primitive forms of society. The penetration of industrial ideologies in villages was small, thus creating sharp differentiation between urban and rural areas.

The New Class Structure

Besides creating new forms of production, the new technology had other effects on persons participating in the process. In the earlier self-sufficient form of society, competition between peoples of different castes or States was lacking; each State had its own quota of providers of service from its own people. In the impersonal markets created by the introduction of the factory system in India, the cushion provided by the village system to inefficient providers of service was removed. Industry tended to be concentrated in the hands of particular communities which displaced others from the industrial field. Thus, the industrial system created opportunities which were more suitable to, and, therefore, more readily grasped by, some sections of the Indian society than others. The scope for vertical division of society increased, and the basis of such division changed from family status to industrial genius.

Industrialization on modern lines made slow progress in the country. The reasons for this were many. The political stability, established by British rule, should have tended to liberate enterprise by the security it offered to property. However, the economic risks of enterprise, owing to free competition from abroad and fear of political discrimination, were great. Entrepreneurship, with which the country was well-endowed, till then consisted in having trading acumen and desire for quick and high returns on short-term investment; entrepreneurial habits consistent with the new forms of production remained to be acquired and developed. A new form of economic organization, the managing agency system, was evolved by foreign entrepreneurs operating in India, and later adopted by Indian entrepreneurs. This system enabled the Indian entrepreneurs' inability to raise finance from the open market and their desire for family control of enterprise to be reconciled with the need for adopting the corporate form of business organisation necessary under the new industrial system.

The construction of railways and the setting up of factories created a demand for unattached labour (casual labourers), which was not known then and, hence, not immediately satisfied. The initial impact of the new construction was, therefore, to loosen the village bonds of labour, in the process, forcing up wage-levels in the villages. For many (small landholders and artisans, for instance), besides the usual shift from a non-industrial to an industrial occupation, the master-servant relationship might have appeared disconcerting.

An industrial proletariat was slow to emerge, particularly so long as agriculture could provide some livelihood; local scarcities of free labour were not uncommon. However, with the development of the railways, migration became easier and cheaper. It is the first wave of migration, the pioneering migration, which creates difficulty; later waves of migrants can always hope to derive help from the pioneer migrants. At an early stage in the development of industries on modern lines in India, it was noticed that workers came from all parts of the country. Moreover, the artisans who migrated had industrial skills, and though this was of not much use in the factory, they tended to select, if they could, work according to their skills, spinners and handloom weavers going into the spinning and weaving departments of cotton textile mills, *luhars* (blacksmiths) into foundries, *chamars* (caste doing work on leather) into tanneries, and so on.

Labour also tended to keep its village link, and its commitment to industry was not full. The defence-mechanism against the inequities of the industrial system grew slowly because the work-force was small and isolated from village society. The first steps towards labour unionism were taken only in the 1880s; the main influence favouring workers' rights came from foreign sources, Lancashire millowners, who feared competition from goods made by cheap Indian labour.

In many other respects, the components of Indian society, differentiated by language, food, dress and other habits, withstood the uniformalising influence of the industrial society. Even in urban centres, a uniform culture failed to arise, people in different States and cities continuing to follow their own food and dress habits. When migrating, people carried their cultural characteristics to the new places. The change in work-habits failed to have a great influence on personal habits, constituting the culture of the different culture-groups in India. However, outside the home, contacts among peoples increased, and they acquired common interests dictated by the industrial system.

Summing up

The initial impact of industrial technology on the Indian society as it existed in the 1850s may be described as under:

The essential influences of technical change were, in the first instance, destructive. The balance in the village between agriculture and industry was disorganised; in the city, with the disappearance of princely courts, the luxury industries, hangers on a feudal order, decayed. With the limited capacity of indigenous industry to meet the changed situation, there was decay without re-creation. The gap in the supply of goods was filled by imports and only slowly by indigenous enterprise. Artisans hung on to ancient crafts but were no match against cheap factory-produced goods; being unable to innovate, sooner or later, they were forced out of their crafts, increased the pressure on land-resources, and later formed part of the emerging industrial proletariat.

It was clear that the initial impact would be overshadowed by the ultimate consequences. Railway and other communications helped to bring about stability in prices of commodities all over the country, helping to integrate the country in an economic sense. At the same time, they laid open the economy to external forces—the competition of cheap foreign-made factory goods, the introduction of money crops (the rise in cotton prices during the American Civil War and the equally catastrophic fall after it was over was one example), and the setting up of industries (jute, textiles, plantations) to cater to a foreign demand. Except in the case of the cotton textile industry, the new industries were owned and controlled by foreigners; mainly the British Economic domination penetrated side by side with political domination.

The changing impact was not so much of the British rule as of the Industrial Revolution; into a society well-established to the extent of being static, it introduced the first social revolution. Destruction, the first step of new construction, was completed before the end of the nineteenth century; with a free press, a new basis of land rights, new educational facilities and increased communications, the beginnings of a new social order emerged.

Present Trends

The industrial development in India till 1950 only skimmed the problem of economic development. If the pace of industrialization increased after 1920, so also did the rate of population-growth. Consequently, the impact of urbanization and industrialization was felt more in the social sphere than in economic betterment.

Since 1950, owing to planned effort, the rate of economic growth has more firmly tended to out-pace the rate of population growth. It would, however, not be proper to speak here of the consequences of only changing technology; in a deliberate process of social reconstruction, many changes, particularly in villages, are not technological, though they involve a break in the mode of earning one's livelihood. It is necessary to take into account such changes (as, for example, replanning land-use) also because they may make possible the adoption of technological changes.

Catalytic Agents

Moreover, economic change is no longer the only original or catalytic force influencing social change, as in the past. Alongside technological change, social changes, for example, improvement of educational facilities and wider spread of knowledge through mass communication media, are also being carried out. Thus, those who come in contact with technological change are better able to adapt themselves to the changing requirements of the industrial society, and even those who do not so come in contact are able to understand and acquire the attitudes appropriate to the industrial society. The dualistic society—dividing society between the modern and the primitive or the tribal—which was prevalent in the past is not likely to be maintained in the present.

The State itself tries to break down, by direct legislation, social systems and social customs characteristic of the earlier modes of living, as being contrary to the new circumstances. In India, the attack on the caste system and untouchability reflects these attempts. But for some protection afforded to backward castes, caste distinctions are being officially played down in granting jobs and in census operations. The practice of untouchability has been made illegal. Moreover, feudal practices, like the levy of compulsory labour prevalent under the zamindari system, are disappearing along with the economic institutions which gave rise to them.

The State itself plays a greater role in bringing about technological change and adaptation to it. The pace of industrialization is hastened by the State providing ancillary services, like transport and communications, and by its direct entry into the industrial field. State provision of education is not only an ancillary service but also facilitates adaptation to technical change in the case of those taking it. Finally, the State whose measures earlier tended to bring down the death-rate seeks to-day to influence the birth-rate in a similar direction by propaganda and grant of facilities for family planning.

Influence of Technology on the Village

The technological influences acting on the village itself to-day are multifarious. A new social adhesion is sought to be imparted to the village in the areas in which the community development projects have been operating. The adhesion, however, is different from that prevailing in earlier times. It is no longer intended to maintain the traditional social structure but to bring about economic change. Activity is carried on not on the basis of traditional hierarchy but on a basis of equality, functions (including that of leadership) being divided according to ability rather than social status. However, the schemes are often outside-originated and authority-imposed, though attempts are made to revive, foster and harness local initiative.

Technological changes are taking place in carrying on agriculture; artificial fertilisers, farm implements and diesel power are being used to increase productivity in agriculture. These changes help to acquaint villagers with machine technology and new work-methods. The large irrigation projects not only bring the benefits of science to the farmer's work; the concurrent supply of electricity from multipurpose projects also affects his mode of living. The availability of electricity made possible by multipurpose projects, a policy of decentralization of industry and an attempt to revive village crafts on modern lines have tended to bring villagers in direct contact with industry in a rural environment.

Finally, the ubiquitous bus has brought about greater contact between nearby villages, which railways were unable to provide; stories and peoples travel faster and cheaper now; and as a villager tends to learn more from those near him and following his own profession and tends to be impressed more by happenings around him, the proselytising influence of a developed village becomes greater.

Technology in the Cities

One other consequence of planned development to-day has been to broaden the industrial process instead of concentrating it in one or two cities as was the case till recently. Town planning and industrial legislation have tried to disperse industry and prevent its concentration in a few metropolitan cities. Consequently, more urban influence tends to be more evenly spread over the country. The nucleus around which the urban centres arise are sources of power as in the case of multipurpose projects, referred to above, or some particular factory or industry, as in the case of the steel towns (existing and those coming up), or the general-purpose towns where various industries, industrial and professional services and commerce grow up simultaneously. Thus, there slowly arises a hierarchy of towns from small townships having one or two small factories, to big towns built round some industry, to metropolitan towns which have many industries and provide services ancillary to them.

These tendencies have further reduced disparities between villages and cities, and, therefore, the extent of adjustment required of migrants from villages. Because of a policy of decentralization of industry, a migrant may be able to find work in a small town adjacent to his village, and may, in any case, have not to go outside the State. Moreover, a villager has acquired some acquaintance with machines in the village and is conscious of regularity in timings, thanks to the bus or the railway passing through his village. He thus has a smaller adjustment to make, and he is better prepared for it, than his forerunners in the 1850s.

Influence of Technology on Economic Organization

The influence of technology on industrial organisation, referred to in brief earlier, needs to be analysed further. The managing agency form of organization enabled various enterprises to be managed by managing agents who initially were individuals or partners and are now also organized as limited companies.

The managing agency system lent itself easily to the creation of industrial empires. It concentrated in the same hands powers of finance and management, and made for horizontal and vertical expansion of business. It made possible economy in managerial costs, though not all these economies were always passed on to the shareholders. A successful managing agent could use, besides his name, the resources of companies managed by him to start new ones in diverse fields. Thus, industrial empires connected with various families (Tatas, Birlas, Dalmias), covering such diverse enterprises as cement companies, banking, (before nationalization of life insurance), insurance and newspapers, grew up. Each group tried to satisfy as many of its needs from internal supplies as it could. This reduced the scope for new parties to come up as providers of ancillary services, and prevented the industrial process from becoming widespread.

The Government have tended to rid the managing agency system of some of its abuses. In the process, it has, through the Companies Act, imposed various restrictions on companies, with the result that the entry of new parties, particularly on a small scale, has become difficult, owing to the heavy overhead costs of floating companies and the need to have contacts with the Government. On the other hand, the Government have made various attempts to help small industries, have granted various exemptions to industries, and, through their planning effort, have created a guaranteed market for goods. This has helped to broad-base the industrial process.

Management, Labour and Technology

Certain communities were able to come up rapidly in the industrial field owing to their talents. Parsis are the most westernized community in India, and they took to modern industry in its early stages in India. Gujaratis were traders, and to them, taking up industry only meant a vertical expansion of business. Marwaris came naturally from the moneylending to the speculative field, and from the speculative to the industrial they are in the ascendant in industry to-day. Other communities (peoples belonging to other religions or States) remained behind in the industrial field. The influence of caste, communal, State and other groupings is still visible in management practices; some chambers of commerce are formed on these lines.

The rural areas still remain the main source of labour for industry. The city still does not provide a sufficiently attractive life to induce migrants to come in because of its attraction; villagers are still pushed out by the economic need. An unattached and committed labour-force is slowly coming up. Its links with the village are diminishing, many having been in industry for three generations. Its organization in trade unions is easier to-day—though cultural differences still tend to make it difficult—and the rivalry among the various national associations of trade unions makes unionization rapid, though not necessarily healthy. The trade union movement itself remains weak owing to these divisions, but the political leverage it exercises through its link with political parties has helped it to cover up this weakness. It has won important rights through legislation and State intervention.

The broader impact of technological change to-day helps to minimize the extent of adaptation required from those who become part of the industrial system. Moreover, a greater realization by the State of its social responsibilities has tended to reduce through legislation (Factory Acts, laws providing for compensation in case of lay-off or retrenchment, and so on) its harmful consequences. The incursion of the State into industry has made it more subject to the control of public opinion. Greater social consciousness among people has tended to avoid many of the harmful social effects of industrialization noticed in the nineteenth century, though only by increasing the overhead cost of industrialization. Trade Unionism is widespread, but its influence is small owing to political divisions within the movement; on the other hand, its political strength is shown by the legislation (referred to above) passed at its instance. The progress of industrialization has brought new communities, for example, Marwaris, to the fore; communal antagonisms created by such a process are expressed in political demands, such as linguistic States. The starting of industries by the State has brought the nonentrepreneurial communities into control and management of industries, thus broadening the enterpreneurial class.

Conclusion

The importance of urbanization increases owing to the limits to livelihood available in villages, despite attempts to regenerate the village-economy. At the same time, the transition from the village to the city life is not so severe as before, as the disparity between villages and cities has narrowed, and urban centres rise with gradations from small townships to metropolitan cities. Moreover, once the initial shock of technological change is absorbed, its further impact requires imitative adaptation of social life, for which, besides necessity, example exists; workers, forced out of their villages, stay with relatives or persons belonging to their own State, who help them to adjust to the new environment. A nuclear family, equality in social relations, a wider community of interest and change in economic status are more readily accepted in social life to-day; regular hours, discipline in work and change in work-habits are also more readily accepted in industrial life to-day.

The Role of the Labour Economist*

Introduction

THE Indian Society of Labour Economics has completed its infant stage and is naturally making efforts to grow. It was suggested to me that it would be appropriate to take this opportunity to review the work of the Society and determine the role of the Labour Economist in the rapidly changing affairs of the country. This may help the Society to develop its work in such manner that it may be more effective in the ordered development of the country. I found the suggestion welcome because it happens to be consistent with outlook adopted by me on similar occasions in the past. About a generation ago, presiding over the Indian Economic Conference at Patna in 1934, I had occasion to discuss the problem of "the Formation of Economic Opinion in India". The voice of the Economist was not yet heard because of the many difficulties which were in existence at the time. The role of the Economist in the Formation of Economic Opinion was discussed and the way in which the Indian Economic Association, as the only organization of academic economists in the country could play a more useful part was pointed out. Looking back to the history of the past generation, I am happy to note the changes that have occurred in the position of the Economist in the affairs of the country. Though there is considerable room for improvement, it must be admitted that the role of the Economist is being increasingly, though slowly, recognised in the affairs of the country. In this effort the Indian Society of Agricultural Economics has contributed its share by emphasizing the special position of Agricultural Economics in a country like ours. Exactly ten years ago presiding over the Agricultural Economics Conference at Trivandrum in 1952, I had occasion to discuss the work and functions of the Agricultural Economics Society, and the way in which the Agricultural Econo-

* Address delivered by the author as President of the Sixth All-India Labour Economics Conference held at Ahmedabad under the auspices of the University of Gujarat on 26 December 1962.

mist could play a more useful role. It is satisfactory to note that in recent years the development of Agricultural Economics in different Universities has been in the right direction and the Governments of the country have also realised the importance of giving due weight to the work of the Agricultural Economist.

I am grateful to the Society for giving me an opportunity to attempt a similar piece of work in the cause of Labour Economics by electing me as President of the Labour Economics Conference this year. My young friends, Prof. Pillai and Mr. Tarlok Singh, holding charge of the Senior Organizations, have given you learned and lengthy discourses. Coming as I do at the end of the series of talks today when you have had enough intellectual food to digest, I shall not commit the indiscretion of inflicting a long speech on you. It would be more appropriate for this infant organisation to excite your interest in its growth by a briefer statement of its ambitions, so that with your help and blessings, it may grow into a well developed institution, playing its appropriate role in the affairs of the country.

The Indian Society of Labour Economics

With the policy of rapid industrialization that we have adopted, the subject of Labour Economics was bound to attract greater attention. It was in the fitness of things therefore that such a devoted worker, in the field of Labour Economics like Mr. Giri, should have thought of initiating and organizing a Labour Economics Society six years ago, when he was Governor of the U.P. It is unusual for the Governor of a State in our country to take such an active interest in the development of a learned society, and Economists in general must be grateful to Mr. Giri for the sustained interest that he has maintained in the cause. He has shown that even the comfortable position of a Governor of a State has not succeeded in preventing him from giving due attention to his first love, 'Labour'. The Society has passed through its teething troubles and has by now established its position alongside the two senior organizations in the field of Economics. Its objective of a scientific study of problems of Labour Economics, the development of specialists in this branch in view of the growing complexity of the subject, and the effort to draw attention of all concerned to a detached examination of labour problems in order to find a solution out of the conflicting claims of interested parties—these are worthy aims towards which some success has been achieved. Besides holding its Annual Conference under the auspices of different Universities, meeting as far as possible along with the senior organizations, and the publication of a Quarterly Journal, the Society more recently has organized Seminars on special topics. During 1961, a Seminar on the Methodology of Research in Labour Economics was organized at Poona; during this year a Seminar on the Bonus Question was organized at Lucknow. The former was intended to stimulate interest in Research on Labour Problems and the latter was intended to contribute to the solution of an acute current problem of great importance to workers and management.

The problems in which the study of Labour Economics can help are many. The usual problem of relations between Labour and Capital are viewed as those between two interested groups. They have a wider significance under the rapidly changing economic structure of the country. They affect the life of society in general at several points, because anything that disturbs industrial peace is bound to have its repercussions on the life of the people. In view of this, problems of better labour-management co-operation and of healthy development of trade unions as well as of the evolution of a sound labour policy by the Government, require careful and detailed study by persons who are not participants in the struggle, but have a detached outlook in the interests of the country. It is easy to see, therefore, that the importance of Labour Economics as a branch of study is great and should be recognized as such. It has naturally become a special branch of study requiring more time and attention than has been hitherto given to the problems of labour in the study of Economics. A few illustrations may be given in support of this view.

Social Implications of Industrialization

We are passing through very exciting times in the history of the world. The achievement of Independence in India was rapidly followed by Independence to countries in South East Asia as well as in Africa. It brought about the death of colonialism. Political independence of several backward countries was naturally accompanied by an urge for economic development. Whereas in the history of Western countries the Economic and Industrial Revolution preceded political changes, in countries like ours the political change has come first; the economic revolution has to be brought about subsequently. The problem is more complicated and more difficult than the one that was faced by the leading industrial countries of the West. The Industrial Revolution in the Western countries was spread over a century or more. Our circumstances compel us to bring about a revolution, perhaps, in a generation. Modern technology grew as it were in the soil from slow beginnings to the highest stage in Western countries. We are importing modern technology in its developed form, without having passed through the earlier stages. We have the contrast of the bullock-cart and the jet engine working simultaneously in the country. In Western countries, over a long period, an industrial society was developed with the industrial worker as an important element in it, devoted solely to industrial work. We are still in the transition period so far as the development of an industrial society is concerned and the industrial worker in the country has still his attachment to the land.

The worker in our country usually drawn from rural areas is accustomed to a traditional way of life, living more in the open, working on the field in a leisurely way, deciding his own time of working as far as possible, not affected by the strains of a city life. Such a worker when he joins a factory has to adjust himself to certain regular working hours. He has to work with machines as well as along with others of his own type. He has to work under the orders of superiors. His work is under the factory shed surrounded by noisy machines, often with dust and other impurities, where breathing of fresh air may not be possible. His living conditions are, as a rule, far from satisfactory. In consequence he often lives by himself, keeping the family in the village, as he does not have enough accommodation for the family. If he succeeds in due course in getting his family to the town, his ties with the joint family to which he is accustomed in the village become loose. He no longer finds amongst his co-workers among whom he lives, people of the same caste and of the same type. He gradually makes friends with persons of different types unlike what he does in rural areas. The strain of factory work compels him to seek some recreation. The recreation available to him in cities is different from the one to which he is accustomed in rural areas. Perhaps, he wanders aimlessly in the streets of the city, envying the lot of others whom he observes, and feels lonely among many, or he is attracted to a cinema house of a low type. He is also exposed to other evils peculiar to the city. His health may not be as robust as in the village due to the congestion of the city on the one hand and the tensions of the new environment on the other. Though there are agencies connected with certain factories as well as private organizations trying to help the industrial worker to adjust to the new environment, it must be admitted that the problem is not easy of solution. We have referred to the effect of urban life on the rural worker. Rural areas are also affected partly by the occasional visits that the industrial worker is bound to pay to his village. Besides, the village is getting nearer to the city because of modern communications and the impact of urban life thus caused has its inevitable effect on rural areas. These random illustrations of the social implications of industrialization point to an almost unlimited scope for research on social change, that is bound to come in the wake of economic change which we are bringing about by Planning. Unless the Planners take due note of the social change and try to remove the undesirable effects in time, we may leave for the next generations more goods to enjoy, but also more social evils to suffer from. The scope for examination of these problems and of finding appropriate remedies in time by the social scientist is unlimited. The Labour Economist has a wide field of work in this connection.

While these features by themselves present vast problems for scientific examination, the situation is complicated by extraneous factors such as the existence of two powerful Blocs in the world. With our policy of non-alignment, we do not wish to be identified with either the Capitalist or the Communist Bloc. We are trying to develop our own indigenous system of growth in a pragmatic way adopting whichever method is useful in the capitalist or the communist system. In consequence, we are wedded neither to a system of complete Free Enterprise nor to a system of complete Centralized Planning. We are evolving our own process of planning by the democratic method which by its very nature is relatively slow, though we are anxious to bring about rapid development. Due to a combination of these forces and our desire to bring about economic progress in all spheres as rapidly as possible, we have probably created many more problems which await solution. No wonder that the Western observer finds a human laboratory in this country, with the consequence that a large number of Western observers who wish to study our economic and social problems are attracted to the country.

Training of Labour

In this grand effort as embodied in the Five Year Plans, it is easy to see that the objectives can be realized only with the active and willing co-operation of labour. Whereas the Plan recognizes that the worker is the principal instrument in the fulfilment of the targets of the Plan and in the achievement of economic progress in general, we have also to see that the worker is in a position to play his role in an effective manner. We have the difficult problem of training the worker to be conscious both of his rights and responsibilities in the development of the country. The Socialistic Pattern of Society assumes better distribution which includes not only a better reward to labour, but also includes a sense of discipline and awareness of responsibility on the part of those who benefit by such better distribution. It should be realized that greater production and more equitable distribution have to go hand in hand.

Though several steps have been taken by Government to see that training is given to labour at different levels, and though industry is co-operating in this effort in its own interest, the fact remains that we have still to do a good deal in improving the efficiency and productivity of Labour. In order to assess the effect of the existing efforts in this connection and to find out ways and means for further improvement, systematic research has to be organized in different industries, which is the task of the Labour Economist. Some beginning has been made in this direction in the form of stray research in the Universities and encouragement of a few studies by the Research Programmes Committee of the Planning Commission. But this is obviously not enough. To give only one illustration, in the difficult task of Export Promotion, unless the unit cost of our goods is reduced by increased productivity, an increase in exports may not be possible.

Labour has also to be trained to take more conscious and continuous interest in the Trade Union Movement instead of depending wholly on outside leaders, however well-intentioned they may be. If the Trade Union Movement is to be rid of political influences and made an effective instrument of collective bargaining by Labour for Labour, it is essential that the movement should have among its office-bearers suitable persons from the workers themselves.

Labour Legislation

The amount of Labour Legislation enacted in the country both by the Centre and the States in recent years is enormous. This is creating the need for specialists to deal with the problem. We have the emergence of a few Labour lawyers practising in the different Courts dealing with Labour disputes. Industrial Houses are engaging legal advisers to help them in matters connected with Labour problems. At the same time a good deal of case law has arisen based on the decisions of High Courts in important cases dealing with Labour matters. In all this effort, the Economist is at a discount. Some years ago, I acted as an assessor with the Bombay Industrial Tribunal in an important matter. I was amused at the ignorance of eminent lawyers about the basic economic issues and the facts of the matter. I was still more amused at the way in which elementary text books, which students of Economics read, were quoted as the high authorities on which the lawyers based their arguments. This situation has not yet improved. Perhaps, it has become worse because the case law which has grown, is often confusing. It is not difficult to find contrary decisions of two High Courts on the same type of dispute, each having viewed it from a different legal angle. A careful examination of important judicial decisions will show that in several cases the principle of collective bargaining on which the legislation is based is defeated, because of the legalistic attitude of some learned judges, otherwise innocent of Labour Economics and the intentions of the Legislature.

I think I am right in suggesting that it is high time that the Labour Economist is actively associated at all stages, namely while enacting labour legislation, and also while interpreting the same in a judicial way. If some Labour Economists practise before Industrial Tribunals, they would, I am sure, have a successful career. In any case it is essential that a detailed examination of the various laws on Labour should be undertaken in the light of decisions already made by the Courts. Such a study by itself would be an eye-opener to all concerned and will establish the need for important changes in the existing laws. It would be in the fitness of things for the Ministry of Labour to encourage such an effort. It would also be desirable to make a continuous study of our Labour Legislation and decisions arising from the same in comparison with similar laws in other countries. The large amount of literature which the International Labour Office publishes can be utilised with advantage for this purpose. Here is a task of great importance in which the joint efforts of a Labour Economist and a Labour Lawyer would be required.

Inter-Disciplinary Approach

Though the phrase 'Labour Economics' implies that the subject is a branch of Economics, it should be borne in mind that it has a wider connotation. Unlike other branches of Economics, this involves the study of human relations i.e., relations between employers and workers and between workers as among themselves as well as the position of workers in the new Industrial Society. A study of Labour Economics therefore is not merely an economic study, but involves an examination of both social and psychological factors. The adjustment of the worker to the new environment to which he is exposed and the way in which he behaves are matters of psychology; whereas the way in which his living conditions are affected as well as his relations to others, are social matters not strictly economic. For a fuller understanding of the various problems which affect Labour, it is necessary to have a joint approach in which the Sociologist and the Psychologist may have to play an important part in co-operation with the Economist. Most of the problems which emerge in connection with Labour in Industrial towns are of this type and any effort at a one-sided study of the same would not be appropriate. It is, therefore, that in some Western Universities the subject is designated as Industrial Relations or Human Relations in order to bring out the inter-disciplinary approach involved in the same. Though the phrase 'Labour Economics' is used by us, it should be realised that it is a subject in which the help of the other disciplines must be utilised. Universities and Research Institutions should introduce appropriate changes in their courses, so that persons who wish to specialize in Labour Economics may receive instruction and guidance not only from the Economist but also from the Sociologist and the Psychologist. For the purposes of research in the subject it is obvious that an adequate background of Statistics is essential.

International Labour Organization

As a member of the ILO we are in touch with the industrial conditions and movements in other countries. Though some of the members of the delegations who go to the ILO meetings may be aware of those movements, it is not possible to say that the Labour Economist has made any intensive comparative study of the growing ILO literature. We have plenty to learn from the situation in other countries and the way in which they have solved their problems. We cannot, of course, apply foreign solutions to our conditions, but it should be possible for us to determine the applicability of foreign experience to our conditions with suitable modifications. The way in which foreign experience in this field can be utilised to solve the growing problems of our rapidly increasing industrial class is a matter for research and investigation by the Labour Economist. This is obviously an unexplored field which it is hoped will be covered by Labour Economists in the country without delay.

Tripartite Labour Machinery

In one respect we have borrowed a model from the ILO. The ILO has accepted three principal parties for what is called the Tripartite Labour Machinery in its Governing Body, the General Conference and the Industrial Advisory Committee. In all these bodies, they have representatives of Governments, Employers and Workers. The principle of the representation of these three parties in connection with Labour problems was endorsed by the Royal Commission of Labour in India (1929-31), which recommended the creation of an Industrial Council consisting of representatives of the three parties.

This was brought home, when the 1935 Act made 'Labour' as a concurrent subject, thereby emphasizing the need to establish some central machinery for coordination of policy. The first Indian Labour Conference, on the tripartite principle, was convened in 1942 with the following main aims and objects:

(*i*) the promotion of uniformity in labour legislation;

(*ii*) the laying down of a procedure for the settlement of industrial disputes; and

(*iii*) the discussion of all matters of all-India importance as between employers and employees.

The machinery which was officially designated as Indian Labour Conference and Standing Labour Committee came into existence in November 1945. Since then, the Conference is being held annually and has proved useful for the evolution of Labour Policy in India. The tripartite principle has also been extended in respect of a number of bodies such as the committees on workers' education, workers' participation in management, discipline in industry, implementations of the ILO. Conventions and evolution and implementation of the code of discipline. Even in the field of administration this principle has been followed, e.g., tripartite bodies suggested in different labour laws like the Minimum Wages Act, the Employees' State Insurance Act and the Employees' Provident Fund Act. The various State Governments have also set-up tripartite bodies on the all-India model. The Tripartite Labour Machinery has proved useful for processing of various legislative and administrative proposals, giving a positive orientation to the labour policy and implementing the decisions taken by the machinery itself.

The question, however, is whether in applying the Tripartite principle to our conditions we have overlooked an important consideration. This principle is obviously suited to the ILO. Besides, it is possible that in industrially advanced countries where labour is well organized and capital is more enlightened, the Government while reconciling the interests of labour and capital would be able to see that the interests of the consumer and of the country as a whole are not sacrificed. In a developing country like ours where the labourer is not yet fully attached to industrial work, where labour organizations are dominated by political parties, where capital is trying to grow gradually by committing mistakes and improving on the same, where the Government is the biggest employer, it is possible that in the efforts at reconciling the conflicting claims of capital and labour, the interests of consumers are not always safeguarded by the Government, because the Government itself is liable to political considerations of having an eye to the electorate under conditions of adult suffrage. At a time when we are still in the transition stage, the application of a method suited to advanced countries without regard to our situation may not be wise. For example, it would be a useful piece of research to ascertain whether in the various steps taken by or on behalf of Government to settle industrial disputes in the country, political considerations have not influenced the decisions and whether in the process the interests of the consumer have not been sacrificed. It would also be of interest to ascertain the extent to which the high cost-structure of our manufactured goods making exports difficult is not due to some extent to such forces. In other words, in the working of the Tripartite machinery in our country, we have an important lacuna in as much there is no one in this machinery to take an objective view of the national interest or of the consumer's point of view. It is suggested, therefore, that instead of three parties in the Labour machinery, we should have four, and utilise the Labour Economist as the most appropriate person to work as its fourth partner, so that he may provide the balance which is now lacking.

The Labour Economist

In other countries the Labour Economist who is an expert in industrial relations has a more important part to play. His advice is sought by all parties and he is utilized effectively in the settlement of industrial disputes. Though we have in India a few persons who have devoted themselves to the study of Labour Economics, it is not possible to say that this subject has received due attention from the Indian Universities. Labour Economics has a subordinate position in the curriculum of Economics. Often it is studied in a casual manner. In a few cases in connection with research theses some intensive work has been done by students in some Universities. Similarly a few research projects have been encouraged by the RPC. Though this has resulted in a few Indian publications on Labour Economics, we have yet to refer to the work of foreign scholars who have studied our labour conditions. It is high time that Labour Economics is considered as a special subject of study even as we have Agricultural Economics or Monetary Economics. In fact, it should be an independent subject not necessarily attached to Economics, but drawing also on other allied Social Sciences or working in co-operation with Sociology, Psychology and Law. If for this purpose, the phrase 'Industrial and Human Relations' is used, it would perhaps be better.

Central Institute of Labour Research

The Government of India have realized the importance of Labour Economics, particularly of the need for systematic research in this subject. The Ministry of Labour convened a Conference for this purpose in September 1960. As a result of the deliberations of this Conference, it has been decided to set up a Central Institute of Labour Research at Bombay with the following objectives:

(*a*) To undertake, aid and promote research in the field of labour particularly in problems having a bearing on (*i*) development of harmonious relations between employers and employees, (*ii*) creation of atmosphere for improvement in productivity, (*iii*) promotion of better working and living conditions for labour and (*iv*) evolution of rational wage and benefit policies.

(*b*) To identify and define labour problems that call for research with a view to discovering possible lines of solution to these problems.

(*c*) To undertake objective research studies in these problems and to arrange for some specific research projects to be carried out by other competent existing agencies.

(*d*) To undertake training programmes for the benefit of research workers in fields related to the objects of the Institute, and for those who may be expected to carry on research outside the institute.

Along with the work of Productivity Councils on the one hand and the work of the New Institute of Man Power Research on the other, the proposed Institute of Labour Research will fulfil a great need in the country. While this is a step in the right direction, it is in the fitness of things for this Society to draw attention to the fact that intensive research of the type proposed to be done at the new Institute of Labour Research presupposes the existence of a suitable number of research workers in Labour Economics. It is true that it is one of the objects of the new Institute to undertake training programmes for the benefit of research workers. It should be desirable however, to give an impetus to the study of Labour Economics in the University Courses so that it may be possible for those interested to acquire basic knowledge of the subject at the University stage. Such an arrangement would provide suitable recruits for training in research which is one of the objects of the new Institute. Though the Central Institute of Labour Research may be able to do some pioneer work, it would be necessary to have suitable units of research at different industrial centres in the country either connected with Universities or independently of them in view of the large size of the country. It would not be possible to create the necessary research personnel in Labour Economics unless simultaneously with the creation of such an Institute, the subject of Labour Economics is given an appropriate place at earlier stages in University courses, as already suggested.

War Effort

The mobilization of resources of the country for defence under the present emergency gives a new dimension to problems of Labour and incidentally of Labour Economics. Industry, private or public, is expected to have a truce as far as industrial disputes are concerned, and to work harmoniously for greater production for the war effort. The intention is to encourage more work and to discourage strikes. In other words, the demand for a rise in wages may have to stop unless the Government by its own initiative arranges for the same in case of an increase in prices. In fact, the Government is anxious to see that essentials of life do not rise in prices, removing thereby the most important justification for a demand for increase in wages. A greater discipline and higher efficiency in industrial production are thus expected. Some of the weaknesses in our industrial structure may give way to a better state of affairs under the stress of War. Labour may have an opportunity to prove that it is capable of achieving greater production by harder work and greater efficiency, on account of the incentives provided by the War effort. Such an achievement could then be repeated under peace-time conditions. The incentives of War may have to be replaced by suitable incentives of peace-time.

In the same manner, at a time when rapid movement of men and material for the purposes of the War is required, the workers in the Transport industry will be expected to show a similar performance. The proverbial delays of our transport system can no longer be tolerated, and all concerned in the transport system will be expected to co-operate in the war effort by seeing that the right type of goods reach appropriate places at the right time. The efficiency which the workers in the Transport system will learn in this manner should be retained under peace-time conditions. It would be necessary to give suitable peace-time incentives to the transport workers in order to maintain the efficiency thus acquired.

Similarly labour of different types will be required to support the soldier in the field. Besides the supplies of war materials, the rapid construction of roads, bridges, temporary camps and hospitals and other ancilliary work will require efficient workers in large numbers. It would thus give an opportunity to labour of various types not only to find employment, but also to show that they can rise to the occasion in the cause of national effort by greater efficiency and harder work.

It would be a fascinating study for the Labour Economist to examine the behaviour of labour in these diverse fields under war conditions, compared with the efficiency of labour in peace-time in different industries. At the same time, it would be possible for the research worker making such comparative studies to determine the method by which such efficiency can be maintained in peacetime. In other words, we should see that the lessons of War learned in a hard way are not forgotten in peace time, but are translated effectively in the cause of development.

This rapid survey of some of the problems in which the Labour Economist is interested is not exhaustive. Other illustrations could be given. It will be seen, however, from our discussion that the Labour Economist has a vast field in which he can do useful work. If we are asking for a better status for the Labour Economist and recognition for his work, it should be possible for us to see that the Labour Economist does everything in his power to deserve such recognition and status. It is for this purpose that a more appropriate place is suggested for Labour Economics in University courses, so that research of the type contemplated in the

Central Research Institute can have qualified recruits and can fructify in the interests of the country. In this effort, it should not be merely the Government that should give the necessary encouragement; industry would do well in providing the necessary facilities and impetus to research workers devoted to this subject. As far as the Indian Society of Labour Economics is concerned, it has led the way for the recognition of this subject during the few years of its existence, thanks to the efforts of Mr. Giri and others who have co-operated with him. But there is plenty to be done in this direction in which the Society can contribute. It should be possible, for example, to make suitable arrangements for active co-operation between the Society and the Central Institute of Labour Research. The Governing Body of the Institute should consist of persons who have either done some work in this field or associated themselves actively with the same. The proposed method of representation to several organizations may bring to the Governing Body busy persons more concerned with other things, but not conversant with Labour Economics. A method suited to an organization where vested interests have to be satisfied is not necessarily suited to an institution where scientific work has to be done independent of any bias from any quarter, from employers or workers, and even from Government. If the Director and the staff of the Institute are to be encouraged to work in an atmosphere of freedom in the interests of truth, they should be free from having to respect the vested interests now proposed to be represented in the Governing Body. The Government of India should be bold enough in such cases to give up its traditional outlook, and trust a small compact team of persons who can really encourage the workers of the Institute with sympathy and understanding. In any case, such persons should be able to give time to the work of the Institute. There are instances of persons having been selected to certain positions because of their prestige, but as such persons have not been able to do the work assigned to them, their prestige often becomes a hindrance than a source of strength. In the effort to create a competent body to look after the Institute, the Indian Society of Labour Economics with Mr. Giri at the head, is in a position to render valuable help though it has been so far neglected in the deliberations regarding the Institute. In the actual conduct of research, it should be possible for the Institute to arrange for the co-operation of workers in the field in different parts of the country. The Society is gradually increasing its activities; it may hold more seminars and also improve their quality in the light of experience; it may also undertake research projects in co-operation with the Institute. Let us hope that along with rapid industrialization for which the country is working, the Society will be able to see that independent study of Labour Economics grows in the country, making it possible for a better understanding between Labour and Capital, providing useful and constructive criticism of the Labour Policy of the Government, and safeguarding the Consumer's interests in the process, thus contributing its share to the balanced development of the country.

BIBLIOGRAPHY

I. PUBLICATIONS OF PROFESSOR C. N. VAKIL

1.	1923	Our Fiscal Policy	
2.	1924	Financial Developments in Modern India 1860-1924.	
3.	1926	Currency and Prices in India	*Jointly with* S. K. Muranjan.
4.	1931	Growth of Trade and Industry in Modern India.	*Jointly with* S. C. Bose *and* P. V. Deolalkar.
5.	1932	The Ottawa Agreement between India and U.K.	*Jointly with* M. C. Munshi.
6.	1934	Economic Outlook in Federal India	*Sir Kikabhai Premchand Readership Lectures, University of Delhi.*
7.	1934	Formation of Economic Opinion in India.	*Speech as President of the Eighteenth Indian Economic Conference at Patna 1934.*
8.	1936	The Working of the Policy of Discriminating Protection.	*Madon Memorial Lectures.*
9.	1943	Price Control and Food Supply with Special Reference to Bombay City	*Jointly with* J. J. Anjaria *and* D. T. Lakdawala.
10.	1943	The Financial Burden of the War on India.	
11.	1943	The Falling Rupee	
12.	1945	The Future of the Rupee	*Jointly with* J. J. Anjaria.
13.	1948	Economic Crisis—Rising Prices and Falling Production	
14.	1948	Our Sterling Balances	
15.	1950	Economic Consequences of Divided India.	
16.	1952	Economics of Electricity Planning with reference to Electricity Cut in Bombay.	*Jointly with* P. R. Brahmananda.
17.	1952	Planning for a Shortage Economy	—Do— —do—
18.	1952	Role of Agricultural Economies in Indian Society.	*Speech as President of the Thirteenth Indian Agricultural Economics Conference, Trivandrum 1952.*
19.	1953	Investment of Foreign Capital in India.	
20.	1953	The Economic Survey of Saurashtra	*For the Government of Saurashtra.*
21.	1956	Planning for an Expanding Economy	*Jointly with* P. R. Brahmananda.

22.	1956	Government and the Displaced persons.	*Jointly with* Dr. Miss P. H. Cabinetmaker.
23.	1956	Government and the Governed—A Study in Social Tensions.	*Jointly with* Dr. Miss Usha Mehta.
24.	1961	The Industrial Revolution in India	*Walchand Memorial Lecture.*
25.	1961	Stages of Economic Growth with Special Reference to India.	*Visvesvarayya Lectures: Indian Institute of Economics, Hyderabad.*
26.	1961	The Human Factor in Economic Development.	*Laski Memorial Lecture, Laski Institute, Ahmedabad.*
27.	1962	Role of the Labour Economist	*Speech as President of the Sixth Indian Labour Economics Conference, Ahmedabad 1962.*

II. PUBLICATIONS BASED ON RESEARCH WORK DONE UNDER THE GUIDANCE OF AND IN MOST CASES EDITED BY PROFESSOR C. N. VAKIL

1.	1930	B. T. Ranadive	Population Problems of India with special reference to Food Supply.
2.	1930	G. C. Mukhtyar	Life and Labour in a South Gujarat Village.
3.	1931	V. K. R. V. Rao	Taxation of Income in India.
4.	1934	M. C. Munshi	Industrial Policy of India with special reference to Customs Tariff.
5.	1937	D. R. Samant & M. A. Mulky	Organisation & Finance of Industries in India.
6.	1937	J. B. Shukla	Life and Labour in a Gujarat Taluka.
7.	1937	R. D. Tiwari	Railway Rates in Relation to Trade and Industry in India.
8.	1937	M. L. Dantwala	Marketing of Raw Cotton in India.
9.	1937	D. N. Maluste	Commercial Relations between India & Japan.
10.	1940	M. H. Patel	Finance under Provincial Autonomy.
11.	1941	R. P. Cholia	Dock Labourers in Bombay.
12.	1942	H. L. Dholakia	Futures Trading and Futures Markets in Cotton with Special Reference to India.
13.	1943	P. J. J. Pinto	System of Financial Administration in India.
14.	1946	D. T. Lakdawala	Justice in Taxation in India with special reference to British Gujarat.
15.	1948	M. B. Desai	The Rural Economy of Gujarat.
16.	1948	S. D. Punekar	Trade Unionism in India.

17. 1949 B. V. KRISHNA — Pricing in Planned Economy.
18. 1950 S. D. PUNEKAR — Social Insurance for Industrial workers in India.
19. 1953 S. D. MEHTA — Indian Cotton Textile Industry—An Economic Analysis.
20. 1954 K. A. ZACHARIAH — Industrial Relations and Personnel Problems.
21. 1956 V. R. CIRVANTE — The Indian Capital Market.
22. 1960 MISS K. C. SHAH — Pattern of Corporate Savings and Investment.

III. UNPUBLISHED RESEARCH THESIS DONE UNDER THE GUIDANCE OF PROF. C. N. VAKIL, AVAILABLE IN THE LIBRARY OF THE UNIVERSITY OF BOMBAY

A. *Thesis Approved for the Ph.D. Degree.*

1. 1940 R. M. RAY — History and Development of Life Insurance in India, 1940.
2. 1940 R. D. TIWARI — The Technique of Modern Commercial Policy, with Special reference to Commercial Treaties.
3. 1941 S. G. PATWARDHAN — Local Passenger Transport in Bombay.
4. 1944 S. T. MERANI — Wages and Conditions of Work of Factory Labour in Karachi.
5. 1944 M. GANJU — Textile Industries of Kashmir.
6. 1946 S. P. CHABLANI — Economic Conditions in Sind.
7. 1946 A. B. TRIVEDI — Wealth of Gujarat.
8. 1947 V. V. SAYANA — Land System of Madras Province.
9. 1948 N. A. SARMA — Taxation of Income.
10. 1949 S. A. PANDIT — Regional Distribution of Industries.
11. 1950 R. M. HONAVAR — A Critical Review of the Theory of Employment.
12. 1950 MISS S. NEHALCHAND — Economic Case for Socialism in India, 1950.
13. 1950 R. C. COOPER — Corporation Finance and Management in India.
14. 1950 D. S. DUGGAL — Industrial Punjab—A Study in Partition Problems.
15. 1951 J. J. PARDIWALA — Exchange Banks in India
16. 1951 T. M. DESAI — The Finance of Bombay Govt., 1935-36 to 1950-51.
17. 1951 K. M. BHOURASKAR — Municipal Finance in Certain Leading Indian States.
18. 1951 R. G. KAMAT — Problems of Indian Shipping.

19.	1953	K. S. RAO	Measurement of Structural Changes in an Economy, with special reference to India (1919-49)
20.	1953	J. P. CONTRACTOR	Insurance and the State.
21.	1954	P. B. MEDHORA	Investment Pattern in Developing Economy.
22.	1954	MISS K. S. NAYAMPALLI	Economic Effects of British impact in India during 1857-1950.
23.	1954	P. V. GUNISHASTRI	Effects of Protection on the Industrial Development of India.
24.	1955	B. K. ABADIAN	A Study in General Selective Credit Control (with special reference to India).
25.	1955	G. RAGHAVRAO	Economic Development of Kenya.
26.	1956	B. C. DESAI	Recent Trends in the Industrial Economy of India.
27.	1956	H. M. EZEKIEL	Social Accounting and National Income Calculations with special reference to under-developed countries.
28.	1956	K. R. PAYMASTER	State Control of Industries in India.
29.	1957	R. K. HAZARI	The Nature of Underdevelopment; an essay on Economic Growth.

B. *Thesis Approved for the M. A. Degree.*

1.	1922	V. G. DESHPANDE	Income-tax in India.
2.	1924	V. G. RANADE	Economic and Social Survey of a Konkan Village.
3.	1924	MISS S. V. PANDIT	The position of Women Workers in Bombay Cotton Mills.
4.	1928	P. FURTADO	The Entrepreneur in Modern Economic Society with special reference to Indian conditions.
5.	1929	G. S. KARBHARI	Public Debt in India.
6.	1929	P. M. JOSHI	Some non-textile Industries in India.
7.	1930	C. A. MEHTA	A historical and analytical study of British Land Revenue Policy in Deccan and Gujarat.
8.	1930	J. D. KHARAS	Indian Customs Tariff with special reference to Trade and Industry, 1913-29.
9.	1930	D. N. MARSHALL	The Indian Transport System.
10.	1931	V. G. MOHILE	Subdivision and Fragmentation of Agricultural holdings in India.
11.	1931	A. H. SYED	Methods and Machinery of Investments in India.

12.	1932	K. C. Badheka	Transport facilities in Kathiawar.
13.	1935	S. CHAWLA	Fallacy of the Gold Standard.
14.	1935	B. M. KALE	Economics of Primary Education in Bombay City.
15.	1935	D. J. JOSHI	Finance of the Bombay Municipality.
16.	1936	M. M. A. BHAIJI	The Mussalmans of Bombay—An Economic Survey
17.	1936	R. M. DESAI	Economic Conditions of Baroda State.
18.	1938	D. R. MAHADESHWAR	Income-tax in India.
19.	1939	J. J. PARDIWALA	Banks in relation to Industry in India.
20.	1941	C. K. MEHTA	Stock Exchanges—A Comparative Study.
21.	1942	S. THOTAPALLI	Crop Forecasting.
22.	1942	V. V. KARKHANIS	Investment of Insurance Funds in India with special reference to Industrial Finance.
23.	1943	S. M. MASANI	Possibilities of the Development of Banking in India.
24.	1945	MISS S. G. GOKHALE	Bidi Workers in the City of Bombay.
25.	1947	C. B. Kapasi	The Economic Development of Baroda State.
26.	1952	M. S. NADKARNI	Banking Legislation in India.

IV. OTHER PUBLICATIONS EDITED BY PROF. C. N. VAKIL

1.	1944	VARIOUS AUTHORS	India Speaking—The Annals of the American Academy of Social and Political Science (jointly with Sir M. B. Nanavati).
2.	1947	S. B. RANGNEKAR	Imperfect Competition in International Trade.
3.	1948	D. G. KARVE	Indian Population.
4.	1949	M. L. DANTWALA	Indian Agriculture.
5.	1952	S. D. PUNEKAR	Industrial Peace in India.
6.	1951	VARIOUS AUTHORS	Group Prejudices in India—A symposium (jointly with Sir M. B. Nanavati).
7.	1953	J. C. KUMARAPPA	Gandhian Economic Thought.
8.	1953	K. N. NAIK	The Co-operative Movement in the Bombay State.
9.	1954	OSCAR A. ORNATI	Jobs and Workers in India (Introduction).
10.	1958	VARIOUS AUTHORS	Regional Seminar on Techniques of Social Research (UNESCO Publication).

11. 1961 VARIOUS AUTHORS Social and Cultural Factors affecting productivity of Industrial Workers in India (UNESCO Publication).

12. 1962 VARIOUS AUTHORS Social Aspects of Small Industries in India (UNESCO Publication).

NOTE : *It has not been possible to include a list of various articles and papers written by Prof. Vakil from time to time in this Bibliography; nor has it been possible to include his contributions to several Government, U. N. and other Committees of which he was a member.*

INDEX

(The letter n *denotes footnote)*

Academic Economist, 57

Agricultural Economics :—
Finance for research in, 154; Indian Society of, 158 ; Neglect of, 147 ; Role of, 142
Agricultural Workers, inquiry regarding, 155
All India Spinners' Association, 33
All India Village Industries' Association, 53
Anti-depression phychology, 119
Ashby, Professor, 148
Association, International Economics, 165, 167n, 214, 246n

Barbour, Sir David, 9

Bhatt V. V., 249n
Bowle, Dr., 64
Brahmananda, P. R., 165, 167, 176, 190n, 214n, 246n
British and Empire Economic Policy, 47, 49

Capital, attitude of, 111

Capital resources, 31
Capitalists, foreign, 29
Capitalism, reform of, 113
Capital Supply and Growth-Source of Savings, 165, 246
Clash of Ideals and methods, 91
Cobden, 47
College, Elphinstone, 281, 283n
Community Projects, evolution of, 157
Communal Tension, economic basis of, 281, 283
Conference : 18th Indian Economic, 45, 333 ; Agricultural Economics, 333 ; Labour Economics, 281, 333n
Congress Ideals of Service, 89; Ideology and Efforts, 100
Curzon, Lord, 9

Dadabhoy Naoroji, 9

Dalal, Sir Ardeshir, 117, 143
Development, some allied aspects of, 281

Economic Analysis, and the Plan, 150 ; need for independent, 152
Economic basis of the movement, 87
Economic measures, recent, by the people, 53
Economic opinion, formation of, 45, 54, 55
Economic unrest, 105
Electricity Planning, economics of, 178n
Empire Economic Plan, 48, 49
Empire interests, subordination of national to, 50
Employment, a positive policy for, 197, 208

Financial difficulties, under the New Regime, 89

Flexibility, measures for built-in, 197, 204

Gandhiji, 4, 5, 6, 7, 21, 40, 198
Giri, V. V., 334, 347
Gregory, Sir Theodore, 143
Gregg, 42
Gold standard, 47

Indian Economic Association, 65, 66, 67
Indian Economic Enquiry Committee-1925, 63

Industries, nationalisation of, 30
International Labour Organisation, 341
Investment and source of savings, 247

Jinnah, M. A., 281, 283n

Karve, Prof. D. G., 157
Kyklos, 165, 234n

Labour Economist, role of, 281, 333, 343
Labour Power, measures to utilise idle or under-utilised, 196, 202
Labour Welfare, policy towards, 198, 212
Labour Research, Central Institute of, 344
Laissez faire policy, 18, 47

Management, panel of, 281, 309
Marketable surplus, problem of increasing the rate of procurement of, 195, 199
Marshall Aid, 97
Medhora, Dr. P. B., 246n
Mukherjee, M., 249n
Murdeshwar, A. P., 246n

Nanavati, Sir Manilal, 142, 159, 160
National Sample Survey, 156
Nations, size of, and dynamic adjustment, 214
Net Capital Formation, 247, 248
Nurkse, Professor, 234, 235, 237, 238

Osmania University, 69
Ottawa Trade Agreement, 50

Pakistan, relations with, 98
Plan, Bombay, 117 ; Institutional implications of a bolder, 190 ; Second Five Year, investment pattern in, 176
Planning and Development, technical papers on, 165
Planning, defective mechanism of, 135
Planning, U. N. meeting of, experts on problems of, 117n
Plans, execution of, 124 ; Summary of, 120-121
Planning Commission, 138-39
Planning Commission, Panel of Economists, 165, 176n, 190n
Planning for an expanding economy, 234n
Planning for a shortage economy, 176
Partition, effects of, 108
Pillai, Professor, 334
Price stabilisation, implications of, 241
Price stabilisation *vs.* Fiscal stabilisation, 165, 234
Price stabilisation, Fiscal stabilisation and Aggregate welfare, 242
Private Enterprise, role of, 137
Protection, Discriminating, 28
Poverty, causes and remedies, 15 ; Internal causes, 15 ; external causes, 17, Remedies of, 23 ; tests of, 7

Railway Rates, G.I.P., 60n
Ranadive, B. T., 12
Research, Social and Economic, 105
Revolution, Economic and Social, 99, 104
Robertson, Sir Denis, 64, 64n
Rural Credit Survey, 157

Salter, Sir Arthur, 63
Santa Margharata, 165, 167
Sardar Patel, 96
Sastry, N. S. R., 249n
Savings, small, categories of, 256
Savings, personal, 252
Schunu Peter, Professor, 310
Schuster, Sir George, 64

Sectors, division between public and private, 257
Shirras, Findlay, 9
Size of nations, 165
Small Scale Industries, Development of, positive policy for, 187
Social changes, 36
Social Science, International Councial of, 281, 320n
Social Sciences; even growth of, 304; neglect of, 306; unity of, 281, 296
State, absence of one State in India, 72
State, and Agriculture, 76 ; and Currency and Banking, 80 ; and Industries, 78 ; and Economic Life, 45 ; and Finance Policy, 77; and Railways, 79 ; and Want of Equilibrium, 81
State, Bureaucratic, 73
State, Change in outlook of process of education regarding, 83
State, Civil Disobedience Movement, 87
State Conception prior to 1921 ; gradual change since 1921, 76
State in modern times, 70-71 ; in relation to economic progress in India, 69; in the nineteenth century, 69-70
State, new ideas in practice, 85 ; recent economic measures by, 50-52 ; slow change in outlook, 82 struggles of the period 1921-37 ; theoretical change in the conception of, 85 ; unlimited powers with a limited outlook, 82
States, the Indian, 92
Swadeshi, 53

Tar lok Singh, 334

Tax Policy, towards an optimal, 194n
Technological change, social implications of, 281, 320
Technical knowledge and Managerial capacity, 167
Theory of Paramountcy, 96
Thoothi, Dr. N. A., 38
Transition, from world peace, from dependence to independence, from feudalism to democracy, 99
Taxation, relief in, 112

Universities, the role of, 153

Underdeveloped countries, business leadership in, 281, 309

Visveswaraya, Sir M, 9, 117

Vakil, C. N., 9, 21, 22, 40
Vakil and Brahmananda, 176, 178n, 234n, 310n
Vinoba Bhave, 198

Young India. 7

www.ingramcontent.com/pod-product-compliance
Ingram Content Group UK Ltd.
Pitfield, Milton Keynes, MK11 3LW, UK
UKHW020221290926
15470UKWH00001B/319

9 780837 173207